Speechifying

Speechifying

THE WORDS AND LEGACY OF
JOHNNETTA BETSCH COLE

. . . .

Johnnetta Betsch Cole

Celeste Watkins-Hayes and
Erica Lorraine Williams, editors

Duke University Press   *Durham and London*   2023

Project Editor: Lisa Lawley
Designed by Courtney Leigh Richardson
Typeset in Untitled Serif by Westchester Publishing Services

Library of Congress Cataloging-in-Publication Data
Names: Cole, Johnnetta B., author. | Watkins-Hayes, Celeste, editor, writer
of supplementary textual content. | Williams, Erica Lorraine, editor, writer of
supplementary textual content.
Title: Speechifying : the words and legacy of Johnnetta Betsch Cole /
Johnnetta Betsch Cole, Celeste Watkins-Hayes, Erica L. Williams.
Other titles: The words and legacy of Johnnetta Betsch Cole
Description: Durham : Duke University Press, 2023. | Includes bibliographical
references and index.
Identifiers: LCCN 2022056031 (print)
LCCN 2022056032 (ebook)
ISBN 9781478024897 (paperback)
ISBN 9781478020233 (hardcover)
ISBN 9781478027188 (ebook)
Subjects: LCSH: Cole, Johnnetta B.—Oratory. | Spelman College—Presidents. |
Speeches, addresses, etc., American—African American authors. | African
American college presidents. | African American anthropologists. | College
presidents—United States. | Racism in higher education—United States. |
Educational equalization—United States. | BISAC: EDUCATION / Schools /
Levels / Higher | SOCIAL SCIENCE / Ethnic Studies / American / African
American & Black Studies
Classification: LCC PS3553.047294 A5 2023 (print) | LCC PS3553.047294 (ebook)
| DDC 815/.54—dc23/eng/20230503
LC record available at https://lccn.loc.gov/2022056031
LC ebook record available at https://lccn.loc.gov/2022056032

Cover art: Johnnetta Betsch Cole, Wheaton College commencement,
Norton, Massachusetts, 2014. © Keith Nordstrom/Wheaton
College (Massachusetts).

speechifying \ˈspē-chə-ˌfī-ing \

· · · · · · ·

verb: *the African and Black diasporic oral tradition and art of delivering speeches rooted in justice to galvanize and inspire change.*

Note: While dictionary definitions of this word often have derogatory connotations (i.e., to harangue or pontificate using tedious or self-important language), we offer a definition of speechifying as an African and Black diasporic oral tradition that embraces the power of language to establish intimacy with, and inspire action among, a broad range of audiences.

Dr. Johnnetta Betsch Cole's speechifying draws upon personal narratives, Black historical legacies, and storytelling to impart important lessons to her listeners.

CONTENTS

The Speeches

• • • • • • •

EDITORS' PREFACE

CELESTE WATKINS-HAYES AND ERICA LORRAINE WILLIAMS

Speeches are artifacts that capture a particular moment in time. As such, they are an important part of the archive. When Williams visited the Johnnetta B. Cole Collection at the Spelman College Archives, she found speeches written on notecards and others typed up with handwritten notes in the margins. One notable find from the archives was a 1957 article from the *Oberlin Review* about Johnnetta Betsch winning the first-place prize of $54 at the Civic League Oratorical Contest at Western Reserve University. She was then a senior in college and the first college student to place in this contest since 1950. Her speech was called "Ghana, The Goal of Africa." She also won the Class of 1915 Public Speaking Contest and Debate Contest. Thus, we see the early emergence of Cole's prowess as a public speaker.

Archives offer an opportunity to witness one's development, ideas, and shifts in thinking over time. Archives capture the little moments, mementos, and artifacts that reveal the different steps and experiences that have helped a person construct their life. The selected speeches showcase Cole's intellect, wisdom, activism, creativity, and trailblazing roles as a college president, scholar, and museum director.

Thinking of speeches as an artifact has guided many of our editorial decisions. We thought it important to preserve each speech—to some extent—in its original form, rather than revise and update it with language that has evolved politically. While we chose to edit speeches for clarity, grammatical flow, and formatting to enhance readability, we did not revise them from our contemporary lens to account for evolutions in language. For instance, we did not change "My Sisters and Brothers All" to "My Siblings" or change "transgendered" to "transgender," even though today Cole would opt for more inclusive language. We did not change "Latino" or "Latina" to "Latinx" because it would have felt odd and inauthentic to do so for the time period in which the speech was given. The one exception to this guiding principle was that we created speech titles for some untitled speeches to better help the reader navigate the book.

Thinking of speeches as capturing particular moments in time also helps us remember that what we know about events and people are framed within that moment. For instance, there are certain things, people, or events mentioned in speeches that have not "aged well." One notable example includes references to Bill Cosby. While Cosby's large financial gift to Spelman was one of the great accomplishments of Cole's presidency, the fact that he would later face allegations of rape, drug-facilitated sexual assault, sexual battery, and other sexual misconduct from over sixty women has arguably cast a negative shadow on this part of her legacy.[1] However, we chose not to remove mentions of Cosby's name from the speeches or interviews because it is a part of the archive.

There may be references in a speech that made sense in 1996 but would be anachronistic and out of touch in 2023. Nonetheless, regardless of the time or the place, what we know for sure is that Johnnetta Betsch Cole has sought to place the best interests of Black women and humankind at the heart of her efforts. A deep love of people, fairness, equity, and justice is the continuous thread that travels throughout her body of work. Even her use of the language, "My Sisters and Brothers All," was fundamentally about unification. It was about truly *seeing* people. As language and politics have changed over time, these core principles have persisted.

Speechifying is an integral part of oral traditions that have been vital to African diasporic and Black communities around the world for centuries, from the African *griot*[2] to *krik krak* storytelling in Haiti (Danticat 1995). While dictionary definitions of the word "speechifying" often have derogatory connotations (i.e., to harangue with tedious or self-important information), we offer a definition of speechifying as an oral tradition that embraces the power of language to establish intimacy with and inspire action among a broad range of audiences. This is all the more significant when we consider the struggles for literacy that have plagued African diaspora populations who have been denied educational opportunities for generations. We think of Black orality as a tool for accessibility. Whether one is extremely learned or illiterate, one can connect to *speechifying*. That is probably part of the appeal of institutions like the Black church.

Speechifying enables Cole to speak to very diverse audiences, not just in terms of racial diversity but also class diversity within Black communities. While the written word may only reach a certain segment of the population, speechifying is more widely accessible to a larger audience.

Dr. Johnnetta Betsch Cole's speechifying draws upon personal narratives, Black historical legacies, and storytelling to impart important lessons to her listeners. As you read these speeches, you may notice the range of audiences that Cole has addressed over time. This is a testament to the accessibility of her speechifying. How many anthropologists or sociologists have been invited to give a speech at the Duke Ellington School of the Arts, Goldman Sachs, and the Congressional Black Caucus? Through speechifying, Cole has reached corporate, philanthropic, academic, government, and museum audiences. This reveals that Cole can be legible to so many different groups in so many different ways, while at the same time being 100 percent herself. That legibility allows her to move with ease and grace from the highest echelons of corporate America to small community-based organizations with a shoestring budgets. She uses anthropology, the discipline in which she earned her doctorate degree, to offer lessons that are accessible to those who may or may not be familiar with the field in order to enhance diversity, equity, and inclusion in the service of forging deeper connections across humanity.

We encourage readers to engage these speeches with a lens of retrospection. We highlight the dates of speeches in the chapter framings and the speech titles, so readers can always situate themselves in that particular period. This book can serve as an important resource or tool for educators, who can engage students around its lessons, as well as the politics of language and legacy.

Now, for a roadmap to help you navigate your way through this book: before getting to the speeches, we have a few documents to help situate Cole, her accomplishments and legacy, and the art of speechifying. There is a brief introductory letter from Johnnetta Betsch Cole herself, followed by a career timeline. After that, there are two interviews with Cole that offer more details about her career trajectory. The first was conducted by Williams at Spelman College in June 2018 and later published in *Feminist Anthropology* (2020). The second, conducted by Watkins-Hayes in July 2018, focuses on the art of speechifying. Following that, we move into the speeches.

NOTES

1. Cosby was convicted by a jury of three counts of aggravated indecent assault in 2018. The Pennsylvania Supreme Court overturned his conviction on the grounds that he had an agreement with a previous prosecutor that should have prevented him from being charged, and he was released in 2021 (see Savage 2021).

2. In West African cultures, griots are historians and storytellers who preserve the history, genealogies, and oral traditions of their people (see Gates 1989).

ACKNOWLEDGMENTS

This project began when Allecia Alexander Harley, a Spelman College alumna, contacted Watkins-Hayes and asked, "Where is the book of Dr. Cole's speeches?" They soon realized that it didn't exist! Watkins-Hayes then reached out to Cole, who sent several boxes of her speeches. Graduate student research assistants at Northwestern University, where Watkins-Hayes was on the faculty at the time, went through the process of reading, scanning, and thematically organizing the speeches. When Williams heard Watkins-Hayes mention this book project while speaking at Spelman, she expressed her interest in collaborating, since she had explored Cole's personal papers in the Spelman College Archives. Watkins-Hayes's mentee and colleague Dr. Dominique Adams-Santos joined the project to help coordinate and support our efforts, and we then had the right team in place to carry out this momentous project. As we met with Cole over video calls, categorizing the speeches and ranking them in terms of priority for inclusion in the book, we deepened our understanding of how these texts have served as a critical medium to map a life of enormous service.

We therefore owe a debt of gratitude to Ms. Harley because her question sparked this book project. We would also like to thank Spelman College archivist Holly Smith for her excellent and meticulous work helping us identify photos for this manuscript, which beautifully capture decades of Cole's work. Holly welcomed the original versions of Dr. Cole's speeches for inclusion into the Spelman Archives, and we are thrilled that they now have a permanent home in the historical record at Spelman.

We also want to express our deep appreciation to the journals *Feminist Anthropology* and *Sage: A Scholarly Journal on Black Women* for allowing us to reprint the interviews conducted by Erica L. Williams and Paula Giddings, respectively. We thank author and Spelman alumna Tayari Jones for her helpful insights on the manuscript as well as Julian Glover, who worked on the project as a graduate student at Northwestern University. A special thanks to freelance editor Rose Ernst for her extremely helpful insights on the manuscript. We want to thank Dr. E. Patrick Johnson for his strong support of the book as we sought a publisher and the team at Duke University Press for their extraordinary work, support, and encouragement. Editor extraordinaire Courtney Berger understood the vision of the project from the start and has been tireless in her support of this book. We also thank Lisa Lawley at Duke University Press, John Donohue and Sally Quinn at Westchester Publishing Services, and our anonymous reviewers for their insightful comments, critiques, and suggestions.

We also owe a very special thanks to Dr. Adams-Santos. She began working on this project as a graduate research assistant and then became the project's chief coordinator: diligently calling us together for meetings, facilitating our discussions about speech selection, and providing brilliant editorial advice on the book. The completion and quality of this book is due in no small part to her efforts, and we are eternally grateful.

Lastly, we want to thank our families, who provided steadfast support as we completed this project. Mr. James "JD" Staton, Dr. Cole's husband, graciously helped Dr. Cole assemble and organize her speeches and mailed them by the boxful to Watkins-Hayes. We also want to offer our appreciation to Dr. Cole's son, Mr. Aaron Cole, who provided editorial support through his very thoughtful comments on the manuscript.

TIMELINE OF DR. JOHNNETTA BETSCH COLE'S LIFE AND CAREER

1936	Born October 19, 1936, in Jacksonville, Florida
1952	Enrolled at Fisk University's Basic College at the age of fifteen
1953	Transferred to Oberlin College
1957	Completed BA in sociology at Oberlin College
1959	Completed MA in anthropology at Northwestern University
1960–1962	Conducted dissertation field research in Liberia, West Africa
1962–1970	Served as assistant professor of anthropology at Washington State University
1967	Earned PhD in Anthropology from Northwestern University
1969–1970	Served as founding director of the Black Studies program at Washington State
1970–1983	Served as professor at the University of Massachusetts at Amherst W. E. B Du Bois Department of Afro-American Studies, Anthropology, and Women's Studies
1980	Elected president of the Association of Black Anthropologists

1981–1983	Served as provost for undergraduate education at UMass Amherst
1982	Published *Anthropology for the Eighties: Introductory Readings*
1983–1987	Served as Russell Sage Professor in Anthropology at Hunter College and as Director of Women's Studies and Director of Latin American and Caribbean Studies at the City University of New York
1986	Appointed visiting professor of Women's Studies at Oberlin College
1986	Published *All American Women: Lines That Divide, Ties That Bind*
1987–1997	Served as the first Black woman president of Spelman College
1988	Published *Anthropology for the Nineties*
1988	Received the Candace Award from the National Coalition for 100 Black Women
1990	Appointed a founding member of President George H. W. Bush's Thousand Points of Light Foundation Board
1991	Received the Achievement Award from the American Association of University Women
1991	Named Outstanding Citizen of the State of Georgia
1991	Received the Northwestern University Alumni Merit Award
1991	Received *Glamour* magazine Woman of the Year Award
1992–1993	Appointed to President Bill Clinton's transition team as Cluster Coordinator for Education, Labor, Arts, and Humanities
1992–1996	Worked on the Atlanta Project, an initiative launched by President Jimmy Carter and the Carter Center to create a coordinated effort to assist disadvantaged families in the Atlanta area
1993	Received the American Anthropological Association Distinguished Service Award

1993	Published *Conversations: Straight Talk with America's Sister President*
1995	Received the NAACP Pathway to Excellence Award
1996	Received the Mayor's Proclamation designating May 17 as Dr. Johnnetta B. Cole Day in the City of Atlanta
1996	Received honorary membership in Phi Beta Kappa from Yale University
1997	Published *Dream the Boldest Dreams and Other Lessons of Life*
1997	Retired as president emerita of Spelman College
1998	Received the Dorothy I. Height Dream Maker Award from the National Council of Negro Women
1998	Inducted into the American Academy of Arts and Sciences
1998	Received the Eleanor Roosevelt Foundation Education Achievement Award from the Women's National Democratic Club
1998	Received the TransAfrica Forum Global Public Service Award
1998–1999	Appointed to President Bill Clinton's Commission on the Celebration of Women in American History
1998–2001	Appointed Presidential Distinguished Professor of Anthropology, Women's Studies, and African American Studies at Emory University
1999	Appointed to Georgia governor Roy Barnes's Commission on Education Reform
1999	Received the Big Brothers Big Sisters of Metro Atlanta Legacy Award
1999	Received the Eleanor Roosevelt Val-Kill Medal
1999	Received the Radcliffe College Medal from the Alumnae Association
1999	Received the President's Medal from Hunter College
2001	Received the Alexis de Tocqueville Award for Community Service from United Way of America

2002	Received the Women of Courage and Strength Award from *American Legacy* magazine
2002	Received the Women Who Make a Difference Award from the National Council for Research on Women
2002–2007	Served as president of Bennett College for Women
2003	Published *Gender Talk: The Struggle for Women's Equality in African American Communities* (with Beverly Guy-Sheftall)
2004	Appointed chair of the Johnnetta B. Cole Global Diversity and Inclusion Institute at Bennett College
2004	Received the Joseph Prize for Human Rights from the Anti-Defamation League
2004–2006	Served as chair of the Board of Trustees of United Way of America; first African American chair of the board
2006	Received the Lenore and George W. Romney Citizen Volunteer Award from the Points of Light Foundation
2006	Building at Spelman College is named the Johnnetta B. Cole Living and Learning Center
2006–2008	Appointed to Secretary of State Condoleezza Rice's Committee on Transformational Diplomacy
2007	Retired from presidency of Bennett College for Women and appointed president emerita
2008	Invited to deliver the 2008 Distinguished Lecture for the American Anthropological Association
2009	Received the Human Rights Campaign National Ally of Equality Award
2009	Published *I Am Your Sister: Published and Unpublished Writings of Audre Lorde* (with Rudolph Byrd and Beverly Guy-Sheftall)
2009–2017	Served as director of the Smithsonian Institution for the National Museum of African Art

2013	Received the Alston-Jones International Civil and Human Rights Award from the International Civil Rights Center and Museum
2015	Received the BET Honors Award for Education
2017	Received the Asa G. Hilliard Model of Excellence Award
2017	Received the Award for Distinguished Service to Museums from the American Alliance of Museums

Prologue

Dear Reader,

I am grateful that you have an interest in this book, as it has a title that might easily discourage you from wanting to read it. After all, speechifying is a noun that is defined as "the making of speeches in a tedious or pompous way." Let me be clear. Being tedious or pompous is not on the list of ways that I want my speeches to be described.

Speechifying is used in the title of this book in the way that in African American colloquial speech, words are sometimes used to stress that the speaker wants to lift up an antonym. For example, "bad" is sometimes used to mean that something or somebody is truly "good." Colloquial Black English also uses words to create an image that is the antithesis of what is meant. For example, saying that something is "the bomb" is not to say that something is destructive. And many words in English have meanings now that are quite different from when they were first used. For example, in the 1300s, "awful" meant something that was awe inspiring, worthy of admiration and respect.

One of my sons started using the word "speechifying" in a positive way to refer to how I give speeches. I liked the sound of the word and began using it with a commitment to myself to do everything possible to make my speeches the opposite of being tedious and pompous.

The first speech that I remember giving was in the 1940s at Mt. Olive AME Church, where everyone in my family worshiped. My father and grandfather were deacons of that church. My mother was the organist, pianist, and director of all of the choirs. And A. L. Lewis, my great grandfather who was known as Jacksonville's most prominent Black citizen, was the superintendent of the Sunday school.

Along with all of the other children in that Sunday school, I was given a speech to memorize in preparation for a children's program on Easter Sunday. For that special day, my sister and I were dressed in matching yellow dresses, our hair in Shirley Temple curls, and we each had a big yellow bow in our hair.

I remember being nervous about giving my speech, but I was also excited to have the spotlight on me. When my turn came to say what I had memorized and practiced for two weeks, I carefully pinched each side of my dress and did a curtsy the way I and all of the Sunday school girls had been taught to do. Seeing that all eyes of the grown-ups were on me, I took a deep breath and then I said: "Whatcha looking at me so hard for? I didn't come to stay; I just came to tell you that today is Easter day." And then I did another curtsy to bookend my performance. The loud applause of the adults mixed with laughter let me know that my speech was well received. In our car on the way home from church, my parents assured me that I did an excellent job in reciting my speech, and they assured my sister that her piano performance was also excellent.

On an occasion when I shared this story with Dr. Maya Angelou, the well-known poet whom I was privileged to know, she reminded me that during Jim Crow days, in most Black churches, there was someone we might call "the culture lady." While Black children could not go to plays, concerts, and museums that were "for whites only," the culture lady in Black churches worked with youngsters to create their own cultural events.

I hope that any speech that I give is informative and inspiring, and I always do a critique of every speech after I have given it. The speech that I wish I could change was given many years ago when I was a senior at Oberlin College and a member of the debate team. The year was 1957, and there were celebrations around the world of Ghana's independence from Britain's colonial rule. I was among Oberlin's "star" debaters, and it was my assignment to give the closing speech. I do not recall the exact words that I used, but I can't forget that after I gave an impassioned speech about Ghana's independence, I said that I mourned the fact that I might not live to see the end of apartheid in South Africa. How could I have felt such pessimism about the ability of a movement led by Nelson Mandela to end that profoundly racist system?

Over the years, as I have sought to become more and more effective in the art of speechifying, I have learned to use certain phrases and employ certain techniques. For example, I often begin a speech with words that I hope will quickly connect me with my audience. The words are: "My Sisters and Brothers All." If I am speaking to an African American audience, there is no need to explain why I am using those terms. My audience will be aware that such kinship terms are repeatedly used in Black churches, at political gatherings, and in any situation where the speaker wishes to acknowledge or establish a closeness with an African American individual or group.

On the topic of kinship, many of the speeches in this book were delivered under the name Johnnetta B. Cole. In more recent times, I began referring to myself as Johnnetta Betsch Cole. Let me explain why. When I divorced, I made the conscious decision that I wanted to share a name with the three sons I birthed, so I did not drop "Cole." A number of years later, I made the decision to spell out my maiden name, Betsch, because, in doing so, I am repeatedly connecting to the paternal side of my family, a part of my heritage that was a bit overshadowed by the famous figures on my maternal side. To know ourselves fully, we must connect with our full stories.

Using the name Johnnetta Betsch Cole is one way that I connect with my full story.

I have also learned that beginning a speech by addressing the audience as "My Sisters and Brothers All" is also an effective way to connect with an audience of predominantly white people. In that case, I follow my greeting by saying that I am sure many in the audience are wondering why I am addressing them in kinship terms. And then I indicate that anthropology and common sense have taught me that kinship is not only about relationships based on common ancestry (descent) or marriage (affinity). Kinship is also about shared beliefs and shared values, and I indicate the specific belief or value that is relevant to a particular audience. For example, I will say that I assume that all in the audience value the beauty and power of the visual arts, just as I do. Or I might say that I am sure that everyone in the audience values a liberal arts education as I do. Or I am sure that everyone in the audience believes, as I do, that we all have a role to play in the ongoing struggle for greater justice and equity in our country and our world.

But we must also face an uncomfortable truth: I write this letter in a time of deep political and cultural division and unsettling tension. The assumptions of a common vision for our world that have grounded my utterances of "My Sisters and Brothers All" have been under assault, and at times the phrase has felt more aspirational than actual. However, unlike that Oberlin College debate student who did not believe she would live to see the fall of apartheid, I hold strong hope and unwavering faith that we will continue to move in a direction that reflects the promise of our common humanity.

A few years ago, I was invited to speak at an organization that advocates for the rights of lesbian, gay, bisexual, transgender, queer, and questioning individuals. I began my talk by saying: "Good Morning, My Sisters and Brothers All." When I completed my talk and opened up for questions and comments, one individual very carefully, but definitively, let me know that the language I used in opening my talk excludes gender-fluid individuals. From that day forward, I began my speeches in a more inclusive way by saying, "My Sisters, My Brothers, My Siblings All." While speechifying is about sharing a message, the lessons are bidirectional.

Just as I begin many of my speeches in the same way, I usually end them with a story or the inspiring words of heroes and sheroes from diverse communities. The story that I tell captures the main point or points I have addressed. As you read the speeches in this book, you will find ones that end with my favorite stories: the story about the old lady and the bird, the story of a girl throwing a starfish back into the ocean, and a story about Sojourner Truth.

On several occasions, I have met people in an airport or some other location who thank me for the speech I gave at their commencement. When I ask if the individual can remember anything about my speech, the response is some version of "I remember the story you told at the end of your speech." That works for me because the story at the end of one of my speeches captures the main point or points that I want the audience to remember.

When I am speechifying, I often draw on the words of heroes and sheroes from diverse communities. I am particularly drawn to quoting the words of Dr. Maya Angelou and Dr. Martin Luther King Jr., of Helen Keller[1] and Rabbi Hillel, of Wilma Mankiller[2] and Cesar Chavez,[3] of Joy Harjo[4] and Gautama Buddha. There is an excellent chance that people listening to my speechifying will remember the words of these women and men long after they have forgotten my words.

I use African proverbs in my speeches because they are short and memorable ways to make a point. Among my favorites are these: "When women lead, streams run uphill"; "When spider webs unite, they can tie up a lion"; "In a crisis, the wise build bridges, the foolish build dams"; "If you want to go fast, go alone. If you want to go far, go together."

In my speeches, there is always a call to action. Why else would one engage in speechifying? A call to action, known as a "CTA" in the world of marketing, should clearly indicate what action to take and how to take it. In my speeches, I aim to indicate what should be done about the issue or problem I am addressing, and then I do my best to motivate people in the audience to take action. When I am speechifying, I often draw on my own experiences. In a speech in which I am addressing systemic racism, systemic sexism, and other systems of inequality, I find it helpful to share experiences from my own life as I grew up during the Jim Crow days in Jacksonville, Florida. When I am speechifying about issues and challenges in the world of education, I have found it useful and effective to cite some of my own experiences as a professor and as a college president.

Dear reader, as I bring closure to this message to you, I want to make this last point. Speechifying at its best is a well-told story. And I thank you for listening to my story. As the African proverb tells us, *"Until the lion [and I add lioness] tell their stories, the tale of the hunt will always glorify the hunter."*

Onward!

—Johnnetta Betsch Cole

NOTES

1. Helen Keller (June 27, 1880–June 1, 1968) was an author and disability rights activist.

2. Wilma Mankiller (1945–2010) was an activist and social worker who was the first female principal chief of the Cherokee Nation.

3. Cesar Chavez (1927–1993) was an organizer of migrant American farmworkers and a cofounder with Dolores Huerta of the National Farm Workers Association in 1962.

4. Joy Harjo (1951–) is a member of the Mvskoke/Creek Nation. She was the first Native American to be poet laureate of the United States, to which she was appointed in 2019.

Interview 1

• • • • • • •

THE PRACTICAL ETHICS
OF JOHNNETTA BETSCH COLE

The Life of a Black Feminist Anthropologist

ERICA LORRAINE WILLIAMS

In summer 2018 I was honored to interview legendary Black feminist shero anthropologist extraordinaire Dr. Johnnetta Betsch Cole. Our conversation took place at the annual Democratizing Knowledge Summer Institute, held at Spelman College.[1] The goal of these summer institutes is to bring together scholar-activists from the humanities and social sciences to examine the state of US higher education, engage with community organizations, and work on collaborative strategies for creating a more just academy and building new kinds of publics. Our conversation offers an opportunity for readers to reflect on the insights and wisdom Cole has to offer a new generation of engaged Black feminist anthropologists in a time of increasing neoliberalization and corporatization of the academy.

Johnnetta Betsch Cole is one of the most prominent Black anthropologists of our time. Her illustrious career and remarkable accomplishments capture what it means to be a scholar-activist and public intellectual. In 1967, Cole was one of only eight African American women to have a PhD in anthropology (Bolles 2001). At Northwestern University she studied under Melville Herskovits, a trailblazer in studies of the African diaspora and a gatekeeper who sometimes discouraged Black anthropologists from doing research in Africa.[2] Cole has conducted research in Liberia, Cuba, Haiti, and the United States. She was part of the first all-Black delegation to Cuba, sponsored by the *Black Scholar*, where she studied the impact of the Cuban Revolution on racism (Yelvington 2003). She has taught at many universities, including Washington State University, the University of Massachusetts Amherst, Hunter College, and Emory University. As a junior faculty member at Washington State University, she cofounded one of the first Black studies departments in the country. She served as the director of the Latin American and Caribbean studies program at Hunter College, and as president of Spelman College from 1987 to 1997. Notably, she was the first Black woman, the first scholar, and the first single mother to ever serve in this capacity (Collins 1987; McHenry 1987).[3]

Johnnetta Betsch Cole has had an illustrious career with many notable accomplishments and contributions to the academy, philanthropy, and civil society. She has authored or edited several books, including *All American Women: Lines That Divide, Ties That Bind* (1986); *Anthropology for the Nineties: Introductory Readings* (1988); *Conversations: Straight Talk with America's Sister President* (1994); and *Dream the Boldest Dreams: And Other Lessons of Life* (1997). She coedited *Gender Talk: The Struggle for Women's Equality in African American Communities* with Beverly Guy-Sheftall (2003). In 2001, she retired as Presidential Distinguished Professor of Anthropology, Women's Studies, and African American Studies at Emory University. She went on to serve as president of Bennett College from 2002 to 2007, and then as director of the Smithsonian's National Museum of African Art for eight years. She was integral to raising the museum's profile as the nation's premier museum focusing on the visual arts of Africa through groundbreaking exhibitions and educational programs. Cole has also received sixty-eight honorary degrees and is the recipient of numerous awards, including the 2015 BET Honors Award for Education (Barnes 2018), the TransAfrica Forum Global Public Service Award, the Radcliffe Medal, and the Eleanor Roosevelt Val-Kill Medal, to name a few.[4] She is a fellow of the American Anthropological Association and the American Academy of Arts and Sciences.

The following candid conversation is a testament to Cole's Black feminist praxis—to her commitment to "living a feminist life" (Ahmed 2017). It reveals how her myriad life experiences—her praxis as a scholar, a mentor, a mother, a descendant of notable ancestors, an institution builder, and more—have shaped her practical ethics. Cole's personal and professional journeys show us how to enact and uphold feminist practices in kinship, mentoring, research, relationship building, and institution building. As Sara Ahmed states, "To live a feminist life is to make everything into something that is questionable" (2017, 2). That is certainly what Cole has done from her earliest days.

In this conversation, I serve as both interviewer and curator, weaving together critical commentary, analysis, and contextualization with key excerpts from the interview transcript. Interviews with Cole have appeared in *Voices: A Publication of the Association for Feminist Anthropology* (Heyward-Rotimi 1998) and *Current Anthropology* (Yelvington 2003); and a recent biographical chapter about her by Riché Daniel Barnes (2018) appears in *The Second Generation of African American Pioneers in Anthropology*. However, this conversation also draws on her personal papers, housed in the Spelman College Archives, to help us understand how her perspective as a Black feminist anthropologist shaped her scholarly and public career.

ERICA LORRAINE WILLIAMS: Good evening, everyone. It is an honor to be here tonight and to be in conversation with one of my sheroes—Johnnetta Betsch Cole. Thank you so much, Dr. Cole, for being here and for engaging in this conversation with us.

JOHNNETTA BETSCH COLE: Thank you.

ERICA LORRAINE WILLIAMS: You credit anthropology with being an effective tool against ethnocentrism and describe how you have used the tools of the discipline in your administrative roles, but at the same time you have challenged mainstream anthropology and the visible lack of diversity within the discipline. Can you speak more about how anthropology informs your scholarly identity and your engagement with and critiques of the field?

JOHNNETTA BETSCH COLE: I barely graduated from Oberlin College before I was at Northwestern studying anthropology. But it didn't take me long to figure out that this discipline that defines itself as the broadest of them all—we almost get too full of ourselves about this—we study the human condition, everything about it. But I kept thinking that there were some human conditions that weren't getting the right kind of attention. So, anthropology, as broad as it was, was not sufficient for me. And so, I began first in the field of Black studies. . . . I woke up one day and said, "This is Black studies, but where are the women?" That led to a discovery of women's studies. And it would not surprise you to know that one day I woke up and said, "Where are the women of color?" and so it's been an extraordinary struggle to really find a place in the academy that genuinely studies the human condition, not in the interest of people watching, but in the interest of contributing in some way to the transformation of human conditions. So, I still am an anthropologist. . . . I wear a set of lenses . . . that do represent how an anthropologist looks at the world. . . . I remember Beverly Guy-Sheftall called for the academy to stop being centered in the three Ws, Western, white, and womanless.[5] That's our ongoing struggle in this academy. I guess you could even say that's what democratizing knowledge is all about.

Cole reflects on her journey through various fields and disciplines, in searching for a meaningful "home" that could satisfy her desire to study the human condition and challenge the inequalities and injustice therein. In an undated speech, Cole describes anthropology as a "greedy discipline" that incorporates many others.[6] She draws on the tools of anthropology to contemplate continuity and change in institutions, saying, "I tend to look at problems in ways that I think are very, very much in the anthropological tradition . . . one appreciates the tradition, but second, one also at least raises the possibility that there are different ways of doing the same thing" (McHenry 1987, 99). In the classic essay, "Seeking the Ancestors: Forging a Black Feminist Tradition in Anthropology," A. Lynn Bolles states that Black women who studied anthropology between 1915 and the 1950s saw it as a "tool to locate the sources of inequality, and . . . as a place where one could participate in finding the 'cure'" (2001, 27). To be sure, Cole transitioned between various fields and disciplines to find that place where her commitment to values of social justice could flourish. She teaches us that sometimes one may have to craft and create that space for oneself.

ERICA LORRAINE WILLIAMS: We've had a lot of conversations around social justice and scholar-activism in the Democratizing Knowledge Summer Institute this week. When President Bill Clinton was considering appointing you as secretary of education in the early 1990s, you were a victim of "red baiting," when conservative groups learned of your research and activism in Cuba.[7] Today, scholars who express solidarity with the Palestinian struggle are "blacklisted" and put on websites like Canary Mission.[8] What lessons can you share with scholars about how to deal with the challenges of engaging in social justice–oriented scholar-activism and collaboration in the academy?

JOHNNETTA BETSCH COLE: Almost from the beginning . . . of my life in the academy, I saw the role of education as one to help folk better understand the world. Simple—who couldn't agree with that? But, secondly, to help folk understand their responsibility to help to change the world. So, when you begin there, then activism is what you do. I mean, how else are you gonna change the world? I know it was many, many, many years later, after becoming a young professor, that I had the unusual honor and privilege of really getting to know Audre Lorde.[9] But I think intuitively from my earliest days in the professoriate, I knew that my silence wasn't gonna save me, and it wasn't gonna save anybody else either. So the first position that I ever held in the academy had activism all intimately entangled with it. Here I am at Washington State University in Pullman, Washington, in 1963. I came back from Liberia doing fieldwork in 1962.[10] I'm going to jail with my students. We're marching up and down, demanding more presence of Black students on our campus.

Helping found a Black studies program was simply an extension of the activism. The activism was simply in cahoots with the scholarship. . . . I began as an activist professor. And I never gave that up.

You do ask how the activism that I experienced in helping to start that program or the activism in spending thirteen years at the University of Massachusetts and launching the first teaching program in a women's prison, how that kind of activism—all the stuff we did on UMass campus out of a place called Africa House—how all that differs from today. . . . My period of activism happened within the context of fairly large, coordinated movements. We call [them] the civil rights movement, the women's movement, the peace movement. And while we are clearly in an era of #BlackLivesMatter, of #MeToo, of #NeverAgain, correct me if I'm off base here, that these are not movements of the same size. Secondly, I really believe that when racism, sexism, heterosexism, ableism, all forms of Islamophobia, anti-Semitism, and ageism come around again with a form of state sanction, it creates a very different atmosphere for activism. So those are the two differences I would say. Let me edit myself. I grew up in an era when there were state-sanctioned systems of inequality, but we did go through a period when that did not seem to be publicly the case. We're in a period now when it does seem to be the case.

ERICA LORRAINE WILLIAMS: What kinds of experiences have you had with community-engagement projects in surrounding communities of the institutions at which you have taught?

JOHNNETTA BETSCH COLE: I go back to what I could call my first community-based project being supporting the Black Panthers' free breakfast program. I have to tell you the other day I was at a meeting of the American Alliance of Museums and there was Ericka Huggins.[11] You can imagine the moment we had. Because that's my era. As a young professor, that's what I did on Saturday mornings. As a young mother, I will never forget the day that David Kamal Betsch Cole said to me as I rushed him to get ready—we were needing to go to another march against the Vietnam War—and David, this little bitty tot, said, "Mommy, I got a great idea: Why don't we get a big net and we can catch the war and we don't have to march anymore!" So when I think of community engagement . . . being a consistent participant in those marches and teach-ins and demonstrations was very much a part of my life. I taught at UMass for thirteen years with extraordinary faculty. . . . One of the things I did was to teach both in the maximum-security prison for men . . . and the prison for women in Framingham.

ERICA LORRAINE WILLIAMS: How did you manage to juggle all those roles—being a professor, a mother, and involved in community-engagement projects—how did you maintain self-care and well-being?

JOHNNETTA BETSCH COLE: I remember when I first came to Spelman, Mary Catherine Bateson came the week after I just arrived.[12] She was writing *Composing a Life* and interviewed me for that book. I remember sitting with Catherine and she was posing a question about how women manage to juggle all these balls and nothing seems to fall. And I said, "You know what, Catherine, I think I've got a better metaphor—I think we womenfolk at our best practice improvisation." And it stuck. It's in *Composing a Life*. This I know. It ain't easy.

But now I've gotta tell something on myself. I was at a dinner that followed a board meeting at Bennett College and almost all of the board members who attended that dinner were women. And this man that I was dating was also there by the name of James Staton. We were kvetching about what we called the double shift. We finally get home. We just put in a lot of work. Now get the children to do their homework, put in a load of washing, answer somebody's question—"Have you seen my socks?" as if you have some kind of special honing device for socks—you call the hospital to see how Aunt Bertha is doing, and you know you just say, "Whew!" And one of the board members said, "These men just don't get it." And this man that I eventually married said, "Oh, I get it. That's exactly what I have done as I began to raise my son as a single father." . . . I think it's important to remember that some men . . . understand what

it is to have a second shift. . . . So in partnering relationships of whatever combination of genders and gender identities, if folks don't get that
collaboration is essential, they don't have the right to be in that relationship. Improvising is what one does.

But I think there's something else that's the key: the key is sisterhood.
Being able to call up somebody who may not be a parent, never wanted
to be, but is willing to listen to your story about the challenges of being
a parent. It's—and this is where I think feminism comes in—it's not just
sisterhood. . . . And so, I would say that much of my ability to play all of
these roles is probably a combination of just pure grit, a whole lot of good
sisterly support, and the marvels of feminism.

These excerpts show us that from very early in her career, Cole was already es-
tablishing herself as a model of an engaged, activist anthropologist before this
concept had even taken root in the discipline. She shows us what it looks like
to be a whole person, enmeshed in the activist struggles of our time, raising
children to be immersed in social justice activism as well. Her reflection on "the
marvels of feminism" demonstrates how to live a feminist life (Ahmed 2017).
Before Sara Ahmed pointed out that "feminism needs to be everywhere" and
encouraged us to "build feminist dwellings" (2), Cole was already illustrating
precisely how to do this.

ERICA LORRAINE WILLIAMS: Can you share any insights with us
about how you have had the courage to make various career transitions
both within and beyond the academy?

JOHNNETTA BETSCH COLE: Well, I'd love to tell a story. I was living in
Atlanta, and I had gone to Washington for a meeting of the scholarly advisory committee for the new museum—the National Museum of African
Art. So we had started this process many years ago and I was privileged
to be on this committee that was chaired by John Hope Franklin.[13] With
amazing folks—we were a pretty righteous band of folk, offering comments, criticism, ideas. So I come back to Atlanta from that meeting and
I get a call from the second person in charge of the whole Smithsonian
(Dr. Richard Kurin).[14]

He says to me, "We are looking for a new director of the National
Museum of African Art," and I gave him a few names.

I flippantly said, "Why does it have to be a national museum in Washington? Move it to Atlanta and I'll do it."

So he said, "Ah ha! You figured out why I was calling. We want you to apply."

I started laughing. I said, "this is the funniest thing I've heard all week! . . . I'm an anthropologist. I don't have a PhD in art history! Yeah, over the course of my life I've actually been a cocurator twice, but I'm not really a curator. You must be kidding!"

He said, "No, I'm serious."

So just to get him off the phone I said, "I'm about to go to Mexico with Beverly [Guy-Sheftall] to finish *Gender Talk*, I'll call you when I get back."

I called my husband, James Staton. I said, "JD, sit down, you're gonna have a good laugh. I've been invited to be a candidate to join the Smithsonian as the director of the National Museum of African Art—isn't that a hoot?"

He said, "No, it's not a hoot, it's got your name all over it!" He then reminded me that at a dinner that we hosted at our new place right at the end of the year, I said, "Let's go around the table and say in the next year what are you going to do that will tickle your heart, that will make you feel good? And don't say lose weight because you said that last year and you didn't do it!" He reminded me that I said, "I think I'll go to the High Museum, take a course and become a docent, and maybe I'll go back to school and get a PhD in art history."

So I decided, Why not? I actually put my name in.

And then I panicked. I called up Richard and I said, "Richard, I'm withdrawing from the search."

He said, "What? In two days, we're going to appoint you!"

I said, "Well I'm sorry, I'm withdrawing."

He said, "Would you at least tell me why?"

"I almost feel like a fake. I don't know enough. I'm not an art historian."

He said, "Listen, before you do this, at least have a conversation with the secretary."

Now you'll love this. . . . The head of the Smithsonian—nineteen museums, nine research centers, and the National Zoo—is called the secretary, and they've all been men. So, I called the secretary, Wayne Clough, retired president from Georgia Institute of Technology.[15] I had known Wayne when I was here at Spelman. So I just kept trying to convince this man that I had to withdraw. Finally, I said, "I'm going to repeat it again, Wayne, I cannot continue in this search because I'm not an art historian."

He said, "We don't need another art historian. We're looking for an exceptional leader."

So I did it.

Now I took a long time to tell that story and let me tell you why. Because I think that so often—particularly those of us who are from underrepresented communities—we misjudge our abilities. Let me tell you, a whole lot of straight white men are doing things that they don't know how to do. So I took the job and it was incredible. One thing I remember so strongly about those eight years was finding a way to use African art to be an activist around all the things that I've always cared about. One of the things that was incredibly important was for us to say, "Where are the women artists? Where are the African artists of the LGBTQ communities?"

So, two messages that I hope you pull out of this rambling here. One, don't sell yourself too short. There are things that we can learn to do, especially when we have a fundamental academic grounding, and we have a passion for knowledge and a better world. And two, . . . regardless of what field you're in, what courses you're teaching, what books you're writing, at some point you're going to still come back to questions of inequality, of lack of access, of the absence of diversity, and the fundamental need for social justice.

ERICA LORRAINE WILLIAMS: I saw a clip of an interview with you from the PBS [Public Broadcasting System] documentary series *Makers: Women Who Make America* (Goodman et al. 2013) where you said that you decided not to go to any meetings without bringing a younger woman with you. Can you talk some more about your role as a mentor?

JOHNNETTA BETSCH COLE: First of all, you have no choice. If you ever get anywhere in life, you didn't get there on your own. . . . You got there because other folk helped you get there. So this is first of all responsibility. We call it pay back, pay it forward, I don't care what you call it. You just owe this. It is not just owing it. There's such joy . . . in mentoring. . . . It's really grounding in a fundamental human notion the anthropologists talk about—it's called reciprocity. . . . One of the things that happens now if you are as old as I am and still engaged in many, many mentoring relationships is that your generation, because of technology, just has such a way of looking at the world and moving through the world that it really does instruct—it teaches me. How can one not be a mentor?

ERICA LORRAINE WILLIAMS: If you could change anything about how you managed your career in the academy, what might that be?

JOHNNETTA BETSCH COLE: I think I would be more courageous than I have been. More bodacious. More outspoken.

ERICA LORRAINE WILLIAMS: Of all the things that you've done, what has been the most rewarding and fulfilling for you?

JOHNNETTA BETSCH COLE: Well, how about if I say among the most fulfilling? That's a tough one. I'm gonna say raising feminist sons, having wonderful sisterly relationships, [and] causing trouble.

Johnnetta Betsch Cole's journey to becoming the director of the National Museum of African Art teaches us that even someone as esteemed as Cole can suffer from impostor syndrome. She shows us that having a community of supporters is vital—whether a life partner or close friends—who can reflect your values back to you and remind you of forgotten goals and dreams.

Following our interview, there was a question-and-answer (Q&A) period with the audience. In response to one question, she elaborated on her point about raising feminist sons.

JOHNNETTA BETSCH COLE: I think I should have been a little more modest when I said I raised feminist sons. I probably should have said I did my best. But you know, feminism first of all is not counted on the chromosome. Therefore, it is possible for any human being to be a feminist. It is learned. . . . Raising sons . . . to think through a different set of assumptions, to challenge what seems so obvious in daily life, is more than a notion. . . . I think the easiest way for us to raise feminist sons is to be feminists so that we are exhibiting the behavior that we ask them to embrace.

*

ERICA LORRAINE WILLIAMS: What are you up to now? And what does retirement look like for you?

JOHNNETTA BETSCH COLE: I'm eighty-one. So you'd think by now I would have learned a number of things, including how to retire. But obviously I haven't. I have failed miserably at it at least four times. And I'm not sure that I ever will, if by that one means that you just are without systematic responsibilities that are meaningful. What I do know is that it would be a good idea for me to do less and so . . . I am actually taking a step toward the possibility that will never come through retirement. When I left the National Museum of African Art on March 31, 2017—and I danced my way out of that museum, it was a wonderful celebration! And then I retired for an entire month. My husband and I went on an old-fashioned road trip. We drove to his hometown in North Carolina and my hometown in Florida. And then on May 1, I began working full time again. I joined a consulting firm called Cook Ross, founded in 1989. It is a firm that does work around issues of diversity, equity, accessibility, and inclusion.[16] I work in a place that looks like the world. . . . We often joke that of the forty folks who work in this office we can only find two straight white guys. That's an amazing collection of human beings. For a year I served as a principal consultant working with corporate folk and higher education folk, and I helped start our work in the world of art museums and cultural institutions. This year I reconfigured my work so that now I only work on projects as opposed to full time.

And—this is something I just really like to share because it makes Thomas Wolfe wrong—who said you can't go home again? I am gonna go home again. We're moving to Florida. And not just to Florida, but to the beach that my great-grandfather founded in 1935. His name was Abraham Lincoln . . . Lewis . . . [*laughter*]. Abraham Lincoln Lewis, with six other Black men, founded the first insurance company in the state of Florida, and he went on to become the first Black millionaire in Florida.[17] In 1935, he withdrew money from the pension bureau of the insurance company and bought this pristine stretch of beach on the Atlantic Ocean. Obviously, in 1935, Black people couldn't go to white people's beaches. . . . He said, "We're founding this beach because Black people need recreation without humiliation." So that beach was literally saved by my incredibly eccentric sister, who bore the name of the "Beach Lady" as developers tried to buy up the beach in recent years ("MaVynee 'Beach Lady' Betsch" n.d.).[18] That beach is still predominantly in the hands of Black people.

I'm gonna end by telling a story of that beach and of Abraham Lincoln Lewis. . . . There's been an enormous amount of information written about my family on the maternal side, including by anthropologists and archeologists. . . . And here, very quickly, is a story.

A young Wolof girl somewhere between the ages of thirteen and fifteen by the name of Anta Madjiguène Ndiaye was captured, taken to Goree Island on the coast of West Africa—Senegal.

Anyone been to Gorée Island and stood in the Door of No Return? . . . It will chill your blood.

I stood in that door, knowing that Anta Madjiguène Ndiaye had, in shackles, gone through that door onto a ship.

She's taken off of that ship in Havana, Cuba, and put on the auction block.

And a very strange British slave owner by the name of Zephaniah Kingsley, who had written such things as "slavery is a decent institution but slaves must be treated humanely," saw Anta Madjiguène Ndiaye, fell in love with her, and decided to marry her.

He was a little off.

This was during the period of Spanish possession when one didn't marry an enslaved woman. But Zephaniah Kingsley studied Wolof until he married her by Wolof custom. He brought her back to [his] plantation, which is now under the guardianship of the National Park Service.

Here's a part of the story I'm not proud of. Anta Madjiguène Ndiaye became wealthy and owned a few human beings herself.

We gotta tell all these stories. We can't tell half of the story.

So today the Kingsley Plantation is under the guardianship of the National Park Service. Every year, all of us who are Kingsley descendants—and we look like the rainbow—come back to the plantation.

Here's the genealogy. My great-great-grandfather, Abraham Lincoln Lewis, married the great-granddaughter of Anta Madjiguène Ndiaye Kingsley and Zephaniah Kingsley. Her name was Mary Salas.[19]

Now I have told that story for a reason. I am convinced that in the academy and in American life until we are willing not just to read about but to understand enslavement, we will never deal with racism. We just will not be able to do it. Why is it that we cannot have truly courageous meaningful conversations about race and about gender, and about sexuality and gender identity and all the rest of these attributes that are simply expressions of human diversity?

This moment in the interview is another testament to Cole's commitment to living a feminist life, with all its risks, rewards, and challenges. While she recognizes her privileged background as someone who can trace her ancestry further back than many African Americans and as the descendant of generational wealth- and slave-holding ancestors, she still acknowledges the importance of reckoning with the legacies of enslavement. Moreover, she takes this sentiment a step further and extends it to a reflection on the need to have meaningful conversations about racism, sexism, sexuality, and other "expressions of human diversity." The discussion of her numerous failed attempts at retirement shows how she has crafted a life where she has been able to move through very different spaces and types of work in a strategic way that embraces her autonomy and desire to be engaged in meaningful work where she can set her own terms.

During the Q&A period, one audience member asked about dealing with the violences enacted in the academy, and how she would encourage young scholars to stay in the academy. Cole's response was quite compelling:

> JOHNNETTA BETSCH COLE: My only response has to be, "Where else are you going? Where do you think it will be safer, better, more rewarding in the deepest sense of what a human being can experience?" It is not so often, it is not a pretty place—the academy and the reason it's not. My view is that two things exist: the reality of inequality and the idea that we are above all of that stuff that's out there in the corporate world—that the academy is better. When the very systems of inequality that plague the larger society plague the academy. So, my only answer is: if you leave, I don't know where you're going. And the other response, of course, is since there's no particularly better place to go, you might as well just stay right where you are and see what you can do to make it a little bit better. We have to tell each other this every now and then and keep saying it until we believe it.

Having worked in many different types of institutions herself, Cole teaches us that the grass is not always greener on the other side.

Cole ended the conversation by sharing a few of her favorite African proverbs:

"When women lead, streams run uphill."

"No matter how long and dark the night is, dawn is going to break."

"If you want to go fast, go alone; if you want to go far, go together."

The first proverb is incredibly poignant. It invokes the power of women's activism and social movements throughout the African diaspora. When women lead, they make things happen that seem impossible—like a stream defying gravity to flow uphill. The second proverb reminds me of the popular refrain in African American Christian tradition that "trouble don't last always." It offers a sense of optimism even in the face of difficult and challenging situations. The third proverb emphasizes quality over quantity and collectivity over individuality. The notion of going far with a group suggests longevity and sustainability, which is worth more than mere speed in getting to the destination. Cole also shared that she is in the process of writing a children's book of African proverbs.[20]

Conclusion

According to Irma McClaurin's (2001) canonical text, Black feminist anthropology draws on Black intellectual thought and feminism to create a theory, methodology, and praxis that centers the experiences of Black women around the world. Not only is Black feminist anthropology deeply committed to scholar-activism, public intellectualism, vindicationism, and decolonizing the discipline, it also foregrounds the contributions of Black women anthropologists who have often been marginalized from the canon. On a personal note, I came to anthropology through the work of Black women anthropologists like Zora Neale Hurston, Katherine Dunham, Pearl Primus, and others. At some point along my journey, I came across a beautiful quote by Cole: "To be a Black feminist anthropologist means to bring into one's inquiry about the human condition, an analysis that is informed by a sense of the importance of 'race' and of gender. And it means to participate in some way in the struggle against racism, sexism and all other systems of inequality" (Heyward-Rotimi 1998, 4).

These words have guided me as I have navigated my way through anthropology and the academy. However, in the same interview with a Spelman alumna, Cole pointed out the ironic situation in which "Spelman students, like many students of color found feminist anthropology engaging, important, and convincing when it was not defined as feminist" (Heyward-Rotimi 1998, 5).

Sara Ahmed writes that "to work as a feminist often means trying to transform the organizations that employ us" (2017, 89). Cole has been doing this important work for decades. In a 1987 *Essence* magazine article, Paula Giddings (1987) asked Cole, "What will the Spelman campus be like in the year 2010?" Her response was prescient: "There will be an archive that houses the papers of distinguished Afro-American women as well as other scholars throughout the world. Spelman students . . . will have a familiarity with the world. They will know what a young Japanese woman of roughly the same age is about. They will be familiar with what's going on in South America. And they will not be at all surprised to hear someone talking about English-speaking Black people on the Atlantic coast of Nicaragua—they will already know about them." It seems that Cole was able to predict the future because this is the Spelman College that I know and love! To be sure, Cole has cemented her legacy as a trailblazer, leader, thinker, and model for the field. In a 1987 interview published in *Change: The Magazine of Higher Learning*, she stated: "One of these days, somebody is going to have to figure out how to get rid of racism and sexism—and that's an intellectual's job" (Bernstein 1987, 53). As a public intellectual, Cole has been "interested in communicating in large circles with stuff that anthropology can teach" (Yelvington 2003, 287). The path that Cole has charted in her career since earning her PhD in 1967 illustrates Ahmed's point that "feminist theory is what we do when we live our lives in a feminist way" (2017, 11). What are we doing to ensure we also live our lives in a feminist way?

NOTES

This chapter appeared in a somewhat different form as Erica L. Williams, "The Practical Ethics of Johnnetta Betsch Cole: The Life of a Black Feminist Anthropologist," *Feminist Anthropology* 1, no. 1 (May 2020): 118–28.

1. The DK Summer Institute was the third in a series organized by the Democratizing Knowledge team, which consisted of Chandra Talpade Mohanty and Linda Carty at Syracuse University, Sherri-Ann Butterfield at Rutgers University–Newark, and Beverly Guy-Sheftall and Erica L. Williams at Spelman College. The first DK Summer Institute took place at Syracuse University in 2016, and the second one took place at Rutgers University–Newark in 2017.

2. This is presented in the documentary film *Herskovits at the Heart of Blackness*, directed by Christine Herbes-Sommers, Llewelyn Smith, and Vincent Brown (2009), as well as in the Yelvington interview (2003).

3. Founded in 1881, Spelman College had four white female presidents and two Black male presidents before Cole: Sophia B. Packard, Harriet E. Giles, Lucy Hale Tapley, Florence M. Read, Albert E. Manley, and Donald M. Stewart. According to Susan McHenry (1987), none of the white female presidents had doctorates. The two male presidents had doctorates but were fundamentally administrators. In a *New York Times* article (Collins 1987), Cole even described herself as not a "safe choice" for president since she was a divorced woman with progressive politics.

4. Other awards include the Barnard Medal, the Alexis de Tocqueville Award for Community Service from United Way of America, the Joseph Prize for Human Rights presented by the Anti-Defamation League, the Uncommon Height Award from the National Council of Negro Women, the John W. Gardner Leadership Award from the Independent Sector, and the Lenore and George W. Romney Citizen Volunteer Award from the Points of Light Foundation. In November 2018 she was appointed national chair and seventh president of the National Council of Negro Women (Levitan 2018).

5. Spelman College Archives, Box 7.

6. Spelman College Archives, Box 7.

7. Cole worked with the Venceremos Brigades (Dizard 1988).

8. According to Jewish Voices for Peace, Canary Mission is "a malicious website that seeks to vilify principled activists for Palestinian human rights with targeted campaigns of misinformation, bigotry and slander."

9. Audre Lorde (1934–92) was a Black lesbian poet and mother who published several collections of poetry, as well as a novel and prose.

10. In another part of the interview, Cole describes how her great-grandfather, Abraham Lincoln Lewis, traveled on a steamer to Egypt with his second wife in 1937. Thus, she grew up "with an atypically positive notion about the continent of

Africa." She also describes going to Liberia for her fieldwork as a "profoundly important and unsettling experience because . . . enslaved people from Liberia brought
to the US went back to Liberia and set themselves up in positions of privilege and
power vis-à-vis those who had never had the experience of being enslaved in the US.
So that two-year period was one that forced me, as someone who had been victim-
ized by racism, to acknowledge that all people have the ability to victimize."

11. Ericka Huggins joined the Black Panther Party at eighteen years of age and
became a leading member of the Los Angeles chapter along with her husband, John
Huggins. In 1969, her husband was killed shortly after the birth of their daughter.
She also led the Black Panther Party chapter in New Haven, CT. She was a political
prisoner and went on to become an educator, poet, and human rights activist.

12. Bateson is an anthropologist and the daughter of Margaret Mead and Gregory
Bateson.

13. John Hope Franklin (1915–2009) was a distinguished historian who earned his
PhD from Harvard University in 1941. He taught at Duke University, Howard University, and the University of Chicago.

14. Richard Kurin is an anthropologist with a doctorate from the University of
Chicago who specializes in the study of South Asia. He is the Smithsonian Distinguished Scholar and Ambassador-at-Large.

15. Wayne Clough is a civil engineer who served as president of Georgia Institute
of Technology from 1994 to 2008 and was the twelfth secretary of the Smithsonian
Institution.

16. Founded by Howard Ross and Dottie Cook in 1989, Cook Ross, now known as
Be Equitable, "is a full service consulting firm with 32 years of experience addressing
the most challenging issues facing organizations in the areas of inclusion, diversity,
equity, and accessibility."

17. Cole writes about her prominent family in "Will the Circle Be Unbroken?" in
Conversations: Straight Talk with America's Sister President (1994).

18. Cole also writes about her sister in "Will the Circle Be Unbroken?," in *Conversations*, 14–15. Her sister is profiled in the *Smithsonian* magazine article "Beach
Lady" by Russ Rymer (2003) and in the biographical entry "MaVynee 'Beach Lady'
Betsch" (n.d.) on the History Makers website. In the Q&A portion of the conversation, Cole elaborated on her sister:

> You also asked about my sister, the only blood sister that I have. Well first of
> all she was a sight to behold. In her first rendition of life she was a double major
> in voice and piano at Oberlin College, an incredibly gifted musician. She went off
> to Paris and studied with a renowned African American musician. She ended up
> singing lead roles in German state opera. And when she came back to the US,
> I don't know all that went on in Germany, but she obviously went through some
> very serious emotional challenges. So, my sister comes back and moves to the
> beach, grows her dreadlocks—she was six feet tall and she had one dreadlock
> from the top of her head to her feet. And on that dreadlock were more but-
> tons than you can imagine. When she passed away, the major environmentalist
> organizations made beautiful gestures—one sent a huge basket of butterflies,

which we released on the beach. There is a white whale named for my sister. For a long time I kept her answering machine. She lived on the beach despite everything I tried to do to get her to stop literally sleeping on the beach, and I finally did get her to move into a structure. So, she had an answering machine and you would call and it would say "Hello. This is the beach lady. I'm sorry I'm not here. I'm probably on the beach, where I have turned into a butterfly." My sister had a love affair with the environment. And while there were these very creative expressions of it, she was very serious about environmentalism as a Black woman's issue. And the extent to which it is no accident where the most pollution takes place.

19. A February 12, 2020, Facebook post on the Gullah Geechee Cultural Heritage Corridor National Heritage Area page documented this story, and references an article by Daniel Schaeffer, "Anna Madgigine Jai Kingsley: African Princess, Florida Slave, Plantation Slaveowner." See also Schaeffer 2018. As the descendant of the Kingsleys, Cole was invited by the National Park Service to give a keynote speech on February 15, 2020.

20. In the interview, Cole mentioned that she was in the process of publishing a children's book of African proverbs with a Lebanese illustrator and friend, Nelda Lateef. The book, *African Proverbs for all Ages*, was published in 2021.

Interview 2

· · · · · · ·

JOHNNETTA BETSCH COLE AND THE
ART OF SPEECHIFYING

CELESTE WATKINS-HAYES

From the stage of the Democratizing Knowledge Summer Institute held at Spelman College to the dining room table of the Virginia home where she dwelled during her directorship of the Smithsonian's National Museum of African Art, Johnnetta Betsch Cole demonstrates the power of deep introspection about her life and career. The following conversation captures an informal exchange between mentee and mentor, as Celeste Watkins-Hayes visited her as she prepared to return to her home state of Florida. Sorting through papers, books, artwork, and clothing that would later be archived at Spelman College and housed with dear friends and family members, Cole and Watkins-Hayes paused for tea to discuss the Art of Speechifying.

CELESTE WATKINS-HAYES: Dr. Cole, how do you view speeches as a medium of communication, as a mode of influence?

JOHNNETTA BETSCH COLE: I have asked myself why I am so enamored with this form of communication. And when I think about it, it's not surprising that I go back to my own childhood. I remember being fascinated by the minister of Mount Olive Church, Reverend Walker, who to me had a power that nobody else had in my community. It was because of the way he did a sermon. Granted, that is a specific form of speechifying, but I've often thought that like any good Black preacher, Reverend Walker would tell you what he was gonna tell you, he would then tell you, and then finally he told you what he just told you. A fundamental way of organizing a speech. Storyteller par excellence. Inspirational as well as knowledge giving. So, I give the Black church a lot of credit for teaching me how to do a speech.

I also want to lift up that back in the day when I was an undergraduate at Oberlin College, you did not graduate without a course in speech. It's a requirement we don't see as often anymore, in part because it is a less frequently used form of communication. Not just speechifying, simply speaking. We communicate through electronic devices, through texting and emailing. It's not the human voice. At Oberlin, one of my major extracurricular activities was the debate team. And I am convinced that those two sources still resonate in my speechifying. Debating teaches you how to organize the compelling argument. Then it teaches you how to deliver that compelling case.

Speech, as a course, taught me how to organize, how to present. So I've always, since I was knee high to a duck, been enamored with speaking and speechifying.

Early in my career as a professor, I began to sense that the key to being good at this was figuring out how I communicated that information. Yes, I had to control the information, yes, I had to master the field. But if I couldn't *deliver it* in that classroom—and yes, the form that we most often use is the lecture—then I wasn't gonna be successful. So from the Black church, to Oberlin, to early professor days, you see a pattern now where I'm just increasingly falling in love with speechifying.

Early in my career, I'm then invited to give a keynote at a gathering of anthropologists. Later on, as I chaired the board of United Way of America, I did several speeches. And so there hasn't been any time in my adult life when I haven't seen speechifying as a major professional field activity.

CELESTE WATKINS-HAYES: What are the components of a great speech?

JOHNNETTA BETSCH COLE: I would say, Celeste, two things. To instruct and to inspire.

CELESTE WATKINS-HAYES: Absolutely.

JOHNNETTA BETSCH COLE: All right?

CELESTE WATKINS-HAYES: Absolutely.

JOHNNETTA BETSCH COLE: You can instruct without inspiring. How many students are willing to testify about the classroom experience of instruction without inspiration? Yes, I think you can inspire without simultaneously teaching, but not really. Not really. I think you gotta do both. Who are the great speechifiers? Dr. Martin Luther King Jr. masterfully taught us, but he simultaneously inspired us, and in fact inspired us to action. Now for me, because I self-define not only as an academic, but as a social justice activist, that third component is something that is always a goal for me.

You gotta instruct or teach, you gotta inspire in general. But, ultimately, can you inspire someone enough that they take action?

CELESTE WATKINS-HAYES: Why do you think that speechifying is such an important tool for social justice? People can write books and have influence in all kinds of other ways. So why is speech, from a social justice perspective, one of the most important tools in the arsenal?

JOHNNETTA BETSCH COLE: First of all, I wanna situate myself within the African American experience, where during enslavement, the ability to *write* was punishable. The ability to *read* was punishable. These horrific individuals didn't want enslaved people who could read or write. So not surprisingly, a form of communication centered in traditional African culture emerged, where we have the griot.

Speaking became an important instrument not only of communication, but of activism.

And obviously as an enslaved people, you can enslave the body, but ultimately you can't really enslave the mind and the spirit if it wants to be free. It will find a way. So creatively then, we begin to use songs, like "Follow the Drinking Gourd." The African American preacher then becomes a very central figure in the movement for social justice. And what he—unfortunately it is almost exclusively he—does is deliver the social justice message through that story of freedom out of Egypt. So the very circumstances of seeking social justice almost begs for the speechifying.

But, second, if you're trying, in the sense of a movement, to instruct, inspire, and lead to action, you're a fool if you're standing up there reading a book.

What else would you do if not deliver? And so some of the great, great orators that we think about are grounded in the African American experience. We think about Sojourner Truth. We think more recently about Stokely Carmichael, who had some issues on the gender question there, but he was an extraordinary orator. We think about Malcolm X as an orator.[1] Think about our own sorority sister, Dorothy Irene Height. Think about Mary McLeod Bethune. So I'm saying that still, within the social justice journey of African Americans, speechifying has been incredibly essential in this movement.

CELESTE WATKINS-HAYES: Yes, absolutely. Absolutely. Tell me about being a woman at the podium. In what ways is there a relationship between speechifying and authority as a woman? Speechifying and storytelling, speechifying and social justice, from a feminist perspective?

JOHNNETTA BETSCH COLE: From a feminist perspective one of the first things we have to say is that when the great orators that we think about, from a Sojourner Truth, to a Dorothy Height, to a Mary McLeod Bethune, to the most recent examples that we would come up with, it was never easy for them to have that podium. Certainly in the religious realm, so many of these denominations, these sects, these whatever you want to call them, literally deny women, or have denied women the right to be in the pulpit. They can speak from the floor, but that pulpit belongs to men. So interestingly I'm saying that as an orator, as a speechifier, women were having to fight their way to be able to do that. Dorothy Height may have been up there with the Big Six, but they weren't allowing her to speak.[2] Rarely is she given the podium. It's the other Big Six. But when women have developed the ability to really speechify, it has made them even more effective as social activists. In my view, Marian Wright Edelman is an amazing and grace-filled orator. Her command of the data, her ability to rattle off the statistics, and then to inspire us, as she would say, to "take care of all of our children."[3]

When I think of other great women orators, I think of very different styles. Gloria Steinem to me has an incredibly effective style.[4] Very different from Marian Wright Edelman. But no less effective. If I move into the Latina community, listening to Delores Huerta, and what the extraordinary Cherokee chief, Wilma Mankiller, was able to deliver. Even when we go and say in a sense, a less dramatic form of speechifying, but nevertheless effective, someone out of the indigenous community like a Joy Harjo. These women are very, very powerful as social activists. In their toolbox, along with being good at tactics, being good at strategy, having determination not to give up, having an incredible network, in that toolbox is speechifying. So in the feminist movement, I can't think of anyone who I would say has profound respect, status, and effectiveness, who isn't also a good orator. She's gotta be.

CELESTE WATKINS-HAYES: Tell me about speechifying as an auditory experience. One of the distinguishing characteristics of your speechifying is your voice, and the depth of your voice. And your cadence tends to be—

JOHNNETTA BETSCH COLE: Quite slow.

CELESTE WATKINS-HAYES: Quite slow. Tell me about that. And is it deliberate? Is it strategic? What work does that do?

JOHNNETTA BETSCH COLE: I'm tempted to say all of the above. But I begin with having learned it. I'm not sure how I learned it. But I learned to articulate very, very carefully. I learned not to rush. And even to use the *pause* as an instrument in speechifying. The deliberate pause. I haven't forgotten what I wanted to say. I am purposefully pausing right now.

CELESTE WATKINS-HAYES: To let silence reign.

JOHNNETTA BETSCH COLE: To let silence be effectively in charge. I know that I not only articulate carefully, but that I speak slowly, and it's got a challenge. Because a speech has got to not go on forever. I think the easiest mistake that orators make is in speaking too long. Well if you speak rapidly, you have a whole lot you can say in 20 minutes, that is gonna take me easily 25, probably 30 minutes to say. So time is something that I'm always very, very conscious of. And I try to be respectful when I am asked as a part of my contract with the speakers bureau, and I am represented by one of the major firms in this country. Mine is the American Program Bureau.[5] "Dr. Cole, you're asked to give a keynote in such and such a situation, this is the suggested topic, this is the time." To go over that time is disrespectful. It's just not fair. You've been asked to give a 20-minute talk, it's 40 minutes and you're still up there.

CELESTE WATKINS-HAYES: Right.

JOHNNETTA BETSCH COLE: And especially in African American communities of a certain era. It is not always the case that folk are respecting that time limit. I won't do it. And the one time that I still think of as a speech that I am not proud of, it was around time. I went on too long.

CELESTE WATKINS-HAYES: How did you know? How could you tell?

JOHNNETTA BETSCH COLE: I could just feel, I could feel the audience. I knew myself, I looked at my watch, I had my script, I'm doing a Power-Point. It was too long. Once I recognized that, now I'm trying to speed up, but it didn't work.

CELESTE WATKINS-HAYES: I asked you last night if you had ever bombed?

JOHNNETTA BETSCH COLE: I'm willing to call that a bomb.

CELESTE WATKINS-HAYES: I think those stories of when it didn't go well can be just as instructive.

JOHNNETTA BETSCH COLE: So instructive. When it didn't go well. So yes, I'm so glad you're doing this book, Celeste. Because it's a huge part of my life.

CELESTE WATKINS-HAYES: And as I'm listening, I'm seeing how it's all coming together and the really important role that speechifying plays in your career, but also in the historical trajectory of social justice. Particularly for Black people, women, it's really significant.

JOHNNETTA BETSCH COLE: Any underrepresented community.

CELESTE WATKINS-HAYES: Right. It's so significant but taken for granted in a lot of ways. I also want to talk about speechifying as your introduction to a community. You talked about the classroom setting, when you were primarily an instructor. Then you came into a presidency at Spelman College. And speechifying becomes a primary way, a key tool to connect with this new community.

JOHNNETTA BETSCH COLE: Yes.

CELESTE WATKINS-HAYES: Tell me about that, take me back to that.

JOHNNETTA BETSCH COLE: Well it's easy for me to recreate being in Sisters Chapel during that first presidency, and beginning almost to paint my presence as the president. I'm not sure when the first time was that I said from the podium in Sisters Chapel, "My Spelman Sisters," but I didn't say that. I said, "My . . . Speeeeeel . . . man . . . Sisters."

CELESTE WATKINS-HAYES: And was that planned? The way that you slowly draw out, "My . . . Speeeeeel . . . man . . . Sisters." It became iconic. It still is iconic. Anyone who hears the phrase said in that way is reminded of you and that period in the history of the college.

JOHNNETTA BETSCH COLE: I don't remember planning that. But I know that when I'm in the middle of an airport and I greet one of our sisters, that's how she wants to be greeted. She wants to be greeted as "My . . . Speeeeel . . . man . . . Sister." So repetition, when not over-used, is an incredibly important device in speechifying. The repetition within a speech, if you're able to find a thread that you can repeat, but also repetition over the course of speechifying. So, my use of "My Sisters and Brothers All"—and interestingly now being conscious of gender identity, I will say, "My Sisters, My Brothers, My Siblings All."' Cause some folk don't identify as a sister or a brother. But they can be a sibling. So, Spelman clearly enhanced both my interest in, and I think my effec-tiveness as, a speechifier.

How many times did I have to get up in Sisters Chapel to speak? And so it became really a joy. It wasn't just a responsibility, it was a joy to cre-ate the most effective moving expressions. At the same time that I was learning, or getting better at that medium, in the confines of the presi-dency, I was also—because of Spelman, and I fully admit this—going onto a national stage that then called for my speechifying beyond Spel-man. It continued.

And then, I think it was 2002 when I joined a speakers bureau—and I remain under contract, but it is a nonbinding contract. If I get a request to do a speech that doesn't come to the American Program Bureau, I can accept it.

But I largely work with them because of the logistics. . . . And, in fact, speechifying has not only been an instrument in my social justice work. I'm being very honest to say it has also been a source of financial compensation.

CELESTE WATKINS-HAYES: Can we pause on that? Because I think it's really important, and it's a really important point because I can imag-ine a lot of readers, particularly who are thinking about this medium, are sometimes reluctant to talk about being financially compensated for speaking or to ask for more. We know that women and underrepresented minorities particularly struggle with this. I was just recently asked for my fee, and I struggled with, "Well, the fact that they're asking me is the honor. Maybe I just need to do it for free because I know the person who referred me or to promote one of my projects." And you talk yourself through this, and what I'm hearing you say is that you're actually under-valuing something that is of great value.

JOHNNETTA BETSCH COLE: Absolutely. But at the same time that I will receive a hefty amount of money for giving a speech, I know I have done the *work* to prepare a good speech.

CELESTE WATKINS-HAYES: And it is work.

JOHNNETTA BETSCH COLE: But, second, I know how many times I do a speech for absolutely no compensation. How could I ask for compensation from some community group that is asking me to speak? I would be embarrassed to take those funds. So, you know, I think you work it out but you make sure that you're not undervaluing yourself as an African American woman, or as a woman of another community that is underrepresented.

CELESTE WATKINS-HAYES: I think that's really important. We can't be so excited to be invited into the room that we undervalue our labor.

JOHNNETTA BETSCH COLE: This is an art and a science. Real speechi-fying is an art and a science. Now, do I think it deserves to have the same recognition that Elizabeth Catlett receives for her art? That James Baldwin receives for his writing?[6] No. I just don't. It's not of that level. But it's not to be dismissed. It's not to be dismissed. And we both know Dr. King's words to us: "If it is your road to be a street sweeper, then sweep streets like Michelangelo painted." And he goes on, and the last line is, "Sweep streets so that all will say, 'There goes the best street sweeper.'" I think you have to see this as work. It's also an art. And doing it well requires a kind of science. But you've got to do it well.

CELESTE WATKINS-HAYES: What is the science of a great speech?

JOHNNETTA BETSCH COLE: What makes it a science to me is the same thing that a chemist does. You've got to do the research. You don't stand up there to give a speech on the need for greater diversity, equity, accessibility, and inclusion in the world of art museums if you don't know anything about art museums. If you haven't read the Mellon Foundation's demographic survey of art museums, where is the research? What's the data? And, like in a scientific exercise, you are in many ways saying, "This is my hypothesis. It is my hypothesis that museums will not do well in the coming years if they do not have greater diversity. That's my hypothesis. Here's the experiment. Look at what happened at this museum where they didn't have diversity. Look what happened at this one when they did." Am I not bringing you the evidence to support my hypothesis? All right, there are differences, but it's fundamentally the same process.

CELESTE WATKINS-HAYES: What's the art of a great speech? Is it the inspiration?

JOHNNETTA BETSCH COLE: The art of it is how you create it. You can have the best hard data in the world. You can have a righteous cause, but how you create a speech, that's the art. As I shared with you last night, I'm an old-school speechifier. Yes, sometimes I will go to the computer. But most times, I write it with my hand. And I don't know, maybe it's my own little indulgence. I don't paint. I don't write poetry. But writing a speech really satisfies my creative juices. So yes, I see it as an art form.

CELESTE WATKINS-HAYES: Are great speakers or speechifiers born or made? I can imagine a lot of people would look at you and say, "Born. She just has it." But as I listen to you, I hear the hard work that you put into it, and I think that for a lot of people that's going to be helpful to hear.

JOHNNETTA BETSCH COLE: I'm going to come down and say it's the way I come down on almost any issue. Leaning more toward "made" than "born." And one of the things that I bring forth to support this is people are taught to be good speakers. Now, I've never gone to Toastmasters, but I know folk who say, "You can literally improve your speechifying." What I do think one is born with is the set up for the experiences that you've got to draw on in the storytelling. And so for me, being born cis-female and Black has a set of experiences, which if I draw on them carefully, are so important in the speechifying. That's what I think is the set up at birth, but you learn this. You develop this. And that also leads me to say what we were saying last night. That is the centrality of storytelling in good speechifying.

CELESTE WATKINS-HAYES: Can you say a little bit more about that? And particularly the centrality of storytelling, not only in terms of telling your own story, but also having the license to tell the stories of others.

JOHNNETTA BETSCH COLE: There are wells from which I think a good speaker dips, and dips from constantly. Telling one's own story is the most powerful because it is one that cannot be challenged. It's your story, and if you tell it well, watch this: it becomes the story of others. When we think about a good biography, certainly when we think about a good autobiography, what is the most attractive to us is that in reading the life of this person, I see reflections of my own or contrast with my own. Yes, it wasn't written all about me, but look, if I'm going to really gain from this book, there's got to be some of me here.

The same with speechifying. When you're telling your story, it shouldn't be, "Let me tell you about my story." Rather, "This is my story. Do you see any reflection of yourself in my story?"

Telling the story of others, I think ultimately has its greatest power when you, the storyteller of the story of others, connect it back to yourself. So, it's the same process again. It's always about broadening the community.

CELESTE WATKINS-HAYES: What do you want to know about an audience before you speak?

JOHNNETTA BETSCH COLE: Very good question. And certainly, when I am speaking for the American Program Bureau, but also when I am speaking for what I do professionally, because having been a principal consultant at Cook Ross, a good deal of my work was as a keynote speaker.[7] American Program Bureau sends me the demographics. I know how many men, how many women. I ask them to tell me as much as they can, including racial demographics. "Is this an audience largely of college-educated folk?" You've got to know as much as you can about who it is you are *speaking with*. A better term than speaking to. The more you know, the more you figure out the most effective way to both teach and inspire.

CELESTE WATKINS-HAYES: Talk to me about the impromptu speech. You are so extraordinary at that, and I think that is a huge area of intimidation for people. How do you get in front of a crowd and know just the right words to say at that moment, and put together a whole composition by just talking without the preparation?

JOHNNETTA BETSCH COLE: Drawing on all of those times when it wasn't impromptu helps. So, when we say impromptu it's as if I've never given a speech before, and I'm just going to get up. But I think of the hundreds of times that I've prepared and given a speech. So now not knowing I was going to be called on, my immediate thought is, "I'm going back to everything I know about speechifying anyway. Don't get up there and go too long. Make your audience feel comfortable immediately." The role of my frequently stated phrase, "My Sisters and Brothers All" at the beginning of my talks. Have something, for lack of a better word, that is catchy. Is it a proverb? Is it a story? I don't tell jokes. I think that's just not me. But increasingly, I am using proverbs. Or is it a little saying out of the book that you have? So, again, it may look like I'm getting up there and it's impromptu, but I'm pulling from those hundreds of experiences that have taught me: don't go on too long, make sure you connect with that audience, and find something catchy that is meaningful and that will be remembered.

CELESTE WATKINS-HAYES: Wow. Very helpful. What about recalibration during the speech: How do you read the room and how do you make those in-the-moment adjustments?

JOHNNETTA BETSCH COLE: Well, I will tell you reading the room has become a lot easier since we became so technologically dependent. If during the introduction, I look around and I see a whole bunch of folk who are texting, reading emails, doing whatever they're doing, it means the person introducing me or whoever spoke before me hasn't engaged that audience. A lot of times I'm speaking in a football stadium, or in a huge auditorium, and you can't see that far. But come on, I can see at least the folk fairly near me, and I don't want to see people disengaged. Also, I work the hardest at the beginning of a speech. My energy has got to be really, really up because if I can't engage that audience quickly, it's going to be hard to do it later on. And so I think in many ways I'm at my best at the beginning of a speech. If, though, I begin to sense that what I had prepared is just somehow not the absolute best, I will switch in the middle.

And let me say this, Celeste: I rarely get up without the speech on paper. You are with the evidence. There are four hundred and some odd speeches in file boxes. But I don't read the speech. I *deliver* the speech. So, I've got the speech printed. It's there. I know it well enough to be able to look down and see where I am. But I'm delivering. I'm not reading. And because I'm delivering, because I'm watching, because I'm aware, if I'm not getting the full buy-in—pardon that expression—then I'm going to switch it up. Then I need to insert something out of my own experience. Even if I'm in the middle of a huge setting, I may need to do something to get audience engagement. I may decide to say, "Like Fannie Lou Hamer would have said, 'I'm sick and tired of—'" and I'll go like this [*gestures*] to hear the audience come back and say, "—being sick and tired."[8]

So, I'm not minimizing techniques. But basically, I don't want to give the impression that it's all technique. You know? It's still art. It's more than anything else a belief in what it is you're saying. Because I think most of us, particularly when we look at speechifying in the political realm, we can say, "You don't really believe that. You're saying that to get some votes."

If I ever feel that I am giving a speech about something I don't really believe, I'm gonna be terribly ashamed of myself.

CELESTE WATKINS-HAYES: It's interesting that you talk about the devices. Because, in this age of technology, technology is a distraction. But I'm learning increasingly that technology is a tool during the speech. So, I've given talks where people are tweeting quotes from my speech. So they're listening and they're engaged, and then they're tweeting out aspects of the speech.

What's been your experience with that? Are you on social media?

JOHNNETTA BETSCH COLE: And I can see that. But it's one thing when somebody is tweeting, it's another thing when somebody is sitting there, and you can—

CELESTE WATKINS-HAYES: And you can tell the difference.

JOHNNETTA BETSCH COLE: Oh, come on, they're reading emails! They're reading emails. There's almost a look on the face of tweeting, "Dr. Cole just said, 'dididididi.'" First of all, how many characters have you got? Okay? So, we're not talking about sitting there, you can almost, there's a look of, "I am reading my emails."

CELESTE WATKINS-HAYES: Of disengagement as opposed to, "Oh, let me tweet that."

JOHNNETTA BETSCH COLE: Absolutely, yeah.

CELESTE WATKINS-HAYES: How do you feel about this new era in which people can record your speeches and your words can instantly go beyond the room?

JOHNNETTA BETSCH COLE: Well, first of all, I have always tried to never give the exact same speech twice. Yes, there are fundamental points of the speech. But now, with technology, not only are people tweeting catchy phrases, we are now at a point where I give a speech, it has gone viral in its entirety because "so-and-so" has put it up on their website.

This is a real challenge. And I can't afford the wardrobe that says, "Oh, she was in that outfit when she gave that speech which I saw online." So the need to, in a sense, customize the speech for that particular audience because you dare not give the exact same speech. You just gave that speech.

Now, I've got to tell you quickly because I've never forgotten it. I had given a speech, and I had to give another speech the next day. I'm sitting the next day waiting to give this speech. An African American sister comes up to me and says, "Oh, I'm so excited to hear you. And you know, I was really pleased to hear the speech you gave yesterday." I said, "Oh, my goodness." I said, "My sister, I rarely do this, but I am going to give fundamentally the same speech today that you just heard. And I want to apologize to you." She said, "Don't apologize. Listen to me. When you give speeches, you really do educate people. And what you've got to remember is when it comes to education, repetition is good for the soul." I still didn't feel that great giving fundamentally the same speech because I knew she was out there, but I have never forgotten her.

And so when I read Dr. King's speeches, when I read Malcolm X, when I read Dorothy Height, when I read Marian Wright Edelman, there is a lot of repetition because it is good for the soul. If you found an effective way of saying it, then it behooves you to do it again, unless you have found a more effective way to say it.

CELESTE WATKINS-HAYES: How do you deal with perfectionism? Getting off the podium and not feeling like you stuck the landing in the way that you wanted to? Or the concern that you had about, "Oh, she's heard this speech again." How do you not overanalyze the work that you've done?

JOHNNETTA BETSCH COLE: Well, I do care a lot. I know when I've pretty much given a good speech, and it's not just in the standing ovation, although who doesn't want a standing ovation? You know, you know in the same way that I knew in the classroom when that fifty minutes had gone well. You know it. Same as when I went to try to get somebody to give some money to Spelman College or to Bennett College or to the National Museum of African Art, you know when you have done the case well. But what I do think is important is self-criticism. I think it's something you've just got to do. And so I do spend time at some point thinking about the speech I have given and I try to do self-correction. Otherwise, I'm not going to get better at this. I'm going to be stuck. The ability to say, "That was a daggone good speech. Now what could I have done to make it even better?" That's what I try to do.

And I often have my trusted other voice. JD, my husband, is so good. First of all, over the last year, he's been fundamentally working as my executive assistant as he's going through his own career change and moving into executive coaching. But at Cook Ross, where I work with all of these millennials, nobody has an assistant. All right? I'm eighty-one years old. I have lived the last phase of my life with assistance. So who is my assistant? Literally, JD is my executive assistant. He has word processed every one of my speeches. He knows the speeches. And when it's time to give a speech, I will sit with him and say, "Here is the engagement. Here's what's requested. Here's what I need to do. Do you have any thoughts?" He's a wonderful sounding board. Not always, but sometimes he's present when I give a speech in which case, he can participate in my self-criticism and he's very, very helpful in critiquing the talk.

CELESTE WATKINS-HAYES: What was your favorite speech? You've given, we are estimating probably close to a thousand. But is there one that you say—I know it's hard to narrow it down, but one that you say, "That is one of the best representations of who I am and what I do?"

JOHNNETTA BETSCH COLE: Certainly, on the list would have to be the Spelman College inaugural address. It would have to be. The stakes were so high, the emotion was so deep, and the expectation was off the chain. So that's certainly on the list.

CELESTE WATKINS-HAYES: Can you break down each of those: What were the stakes, why was the emotion so deep, and why was the expectation so high?

JOHNNETTA BETSCH COLE: Because, yes, I was the one—but far, far, far, far more importantly—I was that somebody, who after 107 years, was going to be the first Black woman president of this historically Black college for women. It was historic, it was "herstoric." You remember those days. I do. This is now the front page of the *New York Times*. This is being talked about in places outside of the United States. I happened to be the one, but this was a moment, and while it belonged to Spelman women, that appointment belonged to all Black women—in concentric circles—then it belonged to all women, and then the next thing you knew, it belonged to all underrepresented communities.

And I would easily say that I was not the obvious choice in the eyes of a lot of people: a divorcee following a man who was there with a very beautiful family. I had a pretty clear reputation as a social justice activist following a president who was not known in those terms. Even the fact that I wore a natural hair style was for some Spelman folk a question to be debated. So when you put all of that together—plus I didn't come out of a presidency into a presidency, I came out of the classroom. Granted, I'd been an associate provost, but I was basically seen as a professor. And then the most challenging of it all, could I raise the money? And I don't know if you know, but I almost lost the Spelman presidency. I had done well in all of the on-campus interviews and then I got to the faculty, the last of the interviews before I would go downtown and meet then–board of trustees chairperson Bob Holland at the Ritz Carlton.[9] And I thought, "Whew, I'm so relaxed because I'm a faculty member."

CELESTE WATKINS-HAYES: These are my people. [*laughs*]

JOHNNETTA BETSCH COLE: [*laughs*] These are peeps. And I'm sailing through and then Hayward "Woody" Farrar Jr., professor of history, raised his hand and said, "Dr. Cole, if you come into the presidency, how will you do with fundraising?" In my usual "be honest" medium, I said, "Well, Professor Hayward, I have raised money, but really as an academic, as an anthropologist raising funds for my research. I've had research grants, but the kind of fundraising you're talking about, I'd say I haven't raised a dime. But I think I'm capable of raising millions because I think the key to effective fundraising is passion for what it is you're raising funds for. And I am passionate about the education of Black women." Well, it didn't go over well. By the time I got down to the Ritz Carlton, Bob Holland's phone was jumping off the hook. I walked in and he said basically, "Oh, why did you blow it?" I mean, that's not what he said, but that's what he said. He said, "The faculty. I've gotten these calls. They're upset that you won't be able to raise funds. You won't be able to fundraise."

As you know, at my inauguration, Bill and Camille Cosby announced that gift. So it became the most wonderful joke between me and the faculty members. I would see Professor Hayward and I'd say, "Twenty million? Is that enough?" and we would laugh and we would hug. So I was not the ideal candidate for that presidency, but in contrast to all of that was the deep belief on the part of a lot of people that I really was *the Esther* for such a time as this.[10] So I don't remember a time of greater emotion surrounding speechifying and coming into that Spelman presidency. And in a sense, every time I got up to speak, all of that was there again. All of what was there in being inaugurated was there again, every single time.

NOTES

Celeste Watkins-Hayes interviewed Johnnetta Betsch Cole at her home in Virginia on July 10, 2018.

1. Stokely Carmichael (1941–1998), who later adopted the name Kwame Turé, was a leader of the Student Nonviolent Coordinating Committee (SNCC) as well as an "honorary prime minister" of the Black Panther Party and leader of the All-African People's Revolutionary Party. In the mid-1960s he was quoted as saying, "What is the position of women in SNCC? The position of women in SNCC is prone."

2. The Big Six refers to prominent Black male leaders of the civil rights movement, including James Farmer, Martin Luther King Jr., John Lewis, A. Philip Randolph, Roy Wilkins, and Whitney Young. In James Farmer's autobiography, *Lay Bare the Heart* (1985), he did not include A. Philip Randolph in his list of the "Big Six," instead listing Dorothy Height, president of the National Council of Negro Women, as the sixth member of the group.

3. Marian Wright Edelman is founder and president emerita of the Children's Defense Fund.

4. Gloria Steinem is a writer, lecturer, political activist, feminist organizer, and cofounder of *Ms.* magazine.

5. The American Program Bureau was founded by Robert Walker in 1965.

6. Elizabeth Catlett (1915–2012) was an African American sculptor with degrees from Howard University and the University of Iowa. She taught at the National School of Fine Arts in Mexico City for nearly twenty years. James Baldwin (1924–1987) was an African American writer and activist who spent many years living in France.

7. Founded in 1989 by Howard Ross and Dottie Cook, Cook Ross is a full-service consulting firm that addresses organizational development issues, including deep expertise in the role of unconscious bias in the workplace.

8. Fannie Lou Hamer (1917–1977) was a civil and voting rights activist from Mississippi. She was an organizer for the SNCC and cofounded the Mississippi Freedom Democratic Party in 1964.

9. Robert Holland Jr. (1940–2021) was the first Black partner at the consulting firm McKinsey & Company and the first Black chief executive officer (CEO) of Ben & Jerry's. He served as chair of the Spelman College Board of Trustees.

10. This refers to the biblical story of Esther, who was eventually chosen to be queen of Persia and was integral in delivering the Jews from destruction. Esther 4:14 states, "For if you remain silent at this time, relief and deliverance for the Jews will arise from another place, but you and your father's family will perish. And who knows but that you have come to your royal position for such a time as this?" The Bible makes it clear that Esther was placed in her influential position so that God's purpose could be accomplished.

The Speeches

. . . .

1. Origin Stories

Johnnetta Betsch Cole's journey from an upper-middle-class childhood in Florida to becoming a public anthropologist, corporate board member, and college president shows that you don't know where you're going unless you know where you've been. Rather than presenting the speeches in chronological order according to the date of the speech, we present them in order of the origin stories contained within the speeches. For instance, in "My Story and Yours: Empowering Meaningful Change Together," her 2015 speech to Medtronic's African Descent Network, Cole shares lessons learned from her childhood in segregated Jacksonville, Florida. In "Defining Moments: Lessons learned from Anthropology," her 2013 acceptance speech for the Northwestern Alumnae Award, she discusses her initial exposure to anthropology through George Eaton Simpson at Oberlin College, as well as her graduate training with Melville Herskovits and Jim Bohannon. We also learn about her early fieldwork experience in Liberia, which was the first place where she was exposed to African art. In her 2007 speech "Three Stations along My Journey as a Citizen Volunteer," she reflects on her family history of service as well as lessons learned from her experiences in the public sector. And in her 2017 speech "The Continuing Significance of President Lincoln's Gettysburg Address," Cole traces her ancestry back to a woman from the African continent in order to reflect upon the continuing significance of this famous speech. This speech showcases the power of a brief rather than a long-winded speech. Ultimately, the origin stories revealed through these speeches exemplify the feminist adage that "the personal is political."

FIGURE 1.1 Johnnetta Betsch's Oberlin College yearbook photo, 1957. Courtesy Oberlin College Archive.

Johnnetta Betsch
Sociology

My Story and Yours

EMPOWERING MEANINGFUL
CHANGE TOGETHER

Medtronic's African Descent Network, Minneapolis, MN, August 15, 2015

My Sisters and Brothers All: Good morning! And as one would say in the southern Black church that I grew up in, it's a great "gettin' up" morning! Why? Because we are gathered here at this eleventh national meeting for Black employees of Medtronic around a truly important theme—namely: *empowering meaningful change together.*

Dr. Bartley suggested that I share with you some lessons learned from my journey. In sharing passages from "My Story," I hope to make connections with your stories—and in the process, we all might gain a little more clarity on how your work here at Medtronic can and should be a part of the journey that we are on that will ultimately take us to the day when our differences no longer make any difference.

Lesson one. I grew up in Jacksonville, Florida, in those horrible days of legal racial segregation. Those wretched days in a southern city where, like every African American girl and boy, the day came when my parents had to help me to grasp a totally unjust reality that was nevertheless essential for me to know. Namely, that because of the color of my skin, there was "an official narrative" that said that I was and always would be a second-class citizen. An "official narrative" that said that no matter what I did, I could never be as good, or go as far, or accomplish as much as a white person.

Indeed, my parents had to answer a haunting question that Margaret Burroughs, artist, writer, and cofounder of the DuSable Museum of African American History in Chicago posed in her famous poem, "What Shall I Tell My Children Who Are Black?"* My parents, and other family members, my pastor, my Brownie and Girl Scout leaders, my teachers—all of the adult folks in my community in that segregated town of Jacksonville, Florida, had to instruct me in the basic rules of racism and racial segregation. That is, there were laws that said I had to sit in the back of the bus, go to schools for Black children, and only drink from water fountains marked "Colored."

But how fortunate I was, as were countless Black girls and boys of that era, that my kin folks, and my community folks insisted that there was another narrative, a narrative in total opposition to the "official" one of the segregated South. That counter narrative said that I, and all who were of the darker hue (to use W. E. B. Du Bois's term) were made by the same God, had the same rights, and could accomplish as much or more than anyone who was white. And (and this is the extraordinary lesson that I was taught by the folks who "grew me up") that in concert with others, I had a responsibility to do all in my power to help to change that unjust and horrific system of racial segregation.

Yes, the lesson of my childhood that remains a fundamental lesson for each of us *today* is captured in a call for justice and equality for all people. As Marian Wright Edelman, president of the Children's Defense Fund puts it: If you don't like the way the world is, then change it; even though you will have to do it one step at a time.† And so, My Sisters and Brothers All, here we are in 2015, and we are still in a struggle for racial equality. It is as simple, yet complicated, as urgent, yet as long standing, as the struggle in Ferguson, New York, Cleveland, and Baltimore. It is the struggle that must be waged in every city, every school, every workplace across our country. It is a struggle that is summarized in three powerful words: *Black lives matter!*

A lesson learned from my childhood that has a renewed importance today is quite simply that each of us has the responsibility to speak up, and to stand up for justice and equality. *And*, while each of us must do that, we are the most

---

* See the full poem at the Poetry Foundation website, https://www.poetryfoundation.org/poems/146263/what-shall-i-tell-my-children-who-are-black-reflections-of-an-african-american-mother, accessed December 28, 2022. See also Burroughs 1963.

† Marian Wright Edelman founded the Children's Defense Fund in 1973. For more information, see "About the Children's Defense Fund," https://www.childrensdefense.org/about-cdf/, accessed December 28, 2022.

effective when we do that *together*. Of course, that is the great lesson of the civil rights movement. And our ongoing movement for freedom for our people. There is an African saying that makes this point: "If you want to go fast, go alone. If you want to go far, go together!"

Lesson two. There is a second lesson that I learned early in my life that has been reinforced every step of my ongoing journey. I heard it in language that my parents, grandparents, and great-grandparents would say to me. But, far more importantly, I saw it in how they acted in the African American community of Jacksonville, Florida, and beyond. And this lesson was certainly preached from the pulpit of the African Methodist Episcopal Church where our family worshiped. It was a part of what my teachers in the colored schools of Jacksonville taught. Yes, repeatedly I heard, "Doing for others is just the rent you must pay for your room on earth." At the base of this call to action is the fundamental notion that each of us can and must engage in actions that can create positive change.

Dr. Martin Luther King so believed in the importance of service to others that he said this: "Life's most persistent and urgent question is: What are you doing for others?" [King 1957]. When I was a youngster, one of my sheroes was Dr. Mary McLeod Bethune, the founder of Bethune–Cookman College—now a university—and the founder of the National Council of Negro Women. In connection with her work with Black women, Dr. Bethune gave a lot of speeches, many at lunches. The club women would come to those luncheons wearing hats, gloves, pocketbooks, and pearls. Dr. Bethune would look out at such a gathering of "high saditty" Black women and say, "My sisters, you have got to stop playing so much bridge and start building bridges back into the communities that you come from." She would go on to say, "It is fine for you to be successful, to climb to the very top of your professions." But, Dr. Bethune would say, "You must lift others as you climb!"

My Sisters and Brothers All, is that not a charge to each of you and, yes, to me as well? While you are here at Medtronic, doing fairly well, is it not your responsibility to reach out to folks who are not doing so well? To become a big brother or a big sister to a youngster who really needs you; to volunteer in a shelter for women who are the victims of domestic violence; to volunteer in a soup kitchen. That is how change can and does occur in our communities.

Lesson three. We were three children in our nuclear family. My older sister and younger brother and I joked that we had pushy southern Black parents who believed in education like the devil believes in sin. They were atypical folks for their era in the sense that each had a college degree: my mother from Wilberforce College, now a university; and my father from Knoxville College. I am proud that my mother and my father were graduates of historically Black colleges. So there was no question about the Betsch children going to a college or university. The only question was which one. At age fifteen, I went to Fisk University in an early entrance program, and then on to Oberlin College where I discovered cultural anthropology. From Oberlin, I went to Northwestern University for my masters and doctorate in anthropology, with a focus on African studies.

To obtain a doctorate in anthropology, I carried out fieldwork for two years in the West African country of Liberia. Armed with a PhD in anthropology, I went on to a career in the academy, teaching cultural anthropology, African American studies and women's studies. When I think back over the more than four decades in which I taught in American colleges and universities, *and* participated in social justice movements, here is the most important lesson that I learned.

Namely, that each of us has multiple identities, and while one may relate most strongly to one of those identities, it alone cannot fully define who you are.

Audre Lorde, who I came to know well when we were both on the faculty at Hunter College, had a humorous but very profound way of making this point. When she would stand to do a reading of her poetry, she would often begin by saying, "I am Audre Lorde, a Black, woman, lesbian, mother, poet, professor, warrior! And do not try to deny me any of my identities. You see, I do not wake up in the morning and say: It is 8 o'clock. So, from 8:00 to 9:00 a.m. I will be Black. But on the stroke of 9:00, I will become a woman. But only for an hour, for at 10:00 a.m., I will turn into a lesbian—at least for sixty minutes." And on and on she would go, making the point that she could not be defined by any one of her multiple identities.

Connected to this basic point that each of us has multiple identities is the reality that one can be oppressed on the basis of one of one's identities *and* exercise power on the basis of yet another of one's identities. For example, while I have and continue to experience the bitter sting of racism and sexism, I have power and privilege as someone who is in the upper-middle class, someone who is a heterosexual, someone who is an able-bodied person, and someone who is a Christian in a world where anti-Semitism and Islamophobia are alive and well.

So, one can experience oppression on the basis of one identity, and then oppress someone else on the basis of a different identity. For example, white women who are the victims of sexism can turn and use white skin privilege as the basis of oppressing Black folks. An African American can be the victim of racism, and then succumb to homophobia and practice heterosexism. Let me put the pieces of this lesson together by saying that each of us needs to acknowledge our multiple identities. We also need to own that we may be subject to bigotry and discrimination based on one of our identities and, at the same time, we can hold bigoted ideas and engage in discrimination against someone based on one of their multiple identities. Understanding this lesson will not make all of the *isms* in our world disappear. But such an understanding can be a first step in seriously wrestling with the power of privilege—whether that privilege is rooted in racism, sexism, heterosexism, ableism, classism, or any other system of inequality.

Lesson four. In 1987, I had the extraordinary honor and joy of being selected as the first African American woman to serve as the president of Spelman College, a historically Black college for women. I know, one has to ask why it took so long for a Black woman to lead a Black women's college! Some years later, I was appointed to the presidency of Bennett College, the only other historically Black college for women in the United States. I like to tease that I want my page in the *Guinness Book of World Records* because I am the only person who has served as the president of our nation's only two historically Black colleges for women. Being at the helm of those two colleges taught me an enormous amount and reinforced what I knew from experience about the trials and tribulations of Black women and, yes, about the triumphs of my sisters as well.

But surely the single most important lesson that I saw, experienced, and carry with me to this very day has to do with the importance and the power of true sisterhood. The dictionary says that sisterhood is the solidarity of women based on shared conditions, experiences, or concerns. That will do for a definition. But here is what I really want to say. When the young women at Spelman or Bennett looked out for each other, that was the sisterhood at work. When a student at one of these colleges got the math lesson the professor was teaching, and she then offered to work with a group of students who did not get it, that's the sisterhood at work. When students at Spelman or Bennett would band together around an important cause, something would happen that would otherwise never happen.

Lesson five. The final lessons I want to lift up here were taught to me during the period in my life when I served on the boards of a number of corporations: Nations Bank South, Home Depot, Merck, and Coca-Cola Enterprises. It never occurred to me to take the position that I was simply like any other board member. No, I always felt that it was my responsibility to bring forth my experiences, insights, and understanding that were a result of my being an African American woman. And so, I took a special interest in issues of diversity and inclusion at those companies on whose boards I served. The lessons I learned from those corporate boards about what is required to truly advance diversity and an inclusive culture will not surprise you. But they are worth repeating.

First, a commitment to diversity by the top leader of a company is necessary, although not a sufficient condition for genuine change in a company.

Second, there is great value in having affinity groups in a company, for they create safe spaces where employees who share a principal identification can feel safe and valued. Third, if diversity is to be advanced in a company, measurable goals must be set. And there must be rewards when they are met, and consequences when they are not met. Fourth, the most difficult struggles around advancing diversity in a company often take place among middle managers, where the straight white men who occupy those positions have to somehow arrive at the point where they see value in creating a climate where they and everyone feels the advantage of finding a place for everyone at the table. And if the table is not big enough for everyone to be there, then it is important to build a bigger table.

And the final point in this group of interrelated lessons is that while there is clearly a moral reason for promoting diversity and inclusion—it is simply the right thing to do to give an opportunity to all who are qualified to compete for positions at a company. It is also the smart thing to do. For when employees from different backgrounds and conditions come to a company, they bring their diverse experiences and ideas with them. And it is that diversity of ideas that helps to make a company truly competitive in this global economy.

It is now time for me to begin to wrap up this talk that has centered on some lessons learned along my journey that are hopefully of some use to each of you. If there is one central theme in all that I have said this morning, it is surely the importance of our working together in the interest of positive change. In the words of one of my favorite African sayings, "When spider webs unite, they can even tie up a lion."

Defining Moments

LESSONS LEARNED FROM ANTHROPOLOGY

Northwestern University Alumnae Award, Evanston, IL, October 24, 2013

I want to acknowledge and thank all of the administrators and faculty who are here. From my days in the academy, I well know that a college or university cannot excel without highly professional, dedicated, and productive colleagues like all of you. Any award from Northwestern would mean the world to me. But to receive an award from the alumni of my university—why that is truly special.

Having served as the president of our nation's only two historically Black colleges for women, oh do I know how important alumnae are to the health and well-being of an educational institution.

And I also know that the education of women and girls is an especially important process if a nation is to truly soar to the height of its possibilities. This truism is captured in an African proverb that says: "When you educate a man, you educate a man. When you educate a woman, you educate a nation."

I also want to acknowledge and sincerely thank outstanding Northwestern alum, Stu Bohart. Stu is the chair of the national advisory board of the museum where I have the honor and the joy of serving as the director of the Smithsonian's National Museum of African Art. I could not ask for a more effective, dedicated, and generous leader of our board. Stu, if my gratitude could be converted into a monetary form, you would be an incredibly rich man.

I was asked to briefly share with you a few of my experiences at Northwestern and to note a few highlights from my career that followed those days when I was a graduate student. For each of us, there are defining moments in our lives. Coming to Northwestern University was one of those defining "moments" for me.

The road to my arriving at Northwestern began "way back in the day" where I grew up in the segregated southern city of Jacksonville, Florida. The official message of most white folks at that time was that no matter what I did, I would always be a second-class citizen in my country. But my parents, my family, and my community had a different message. Namely, that such a proposition was morally wrong and legally indefensible, *and* I had the responsibility to do whatever I could to help to rid my country of unjust laws that were predicated on racism. The folks in Jacksonville who "grew me up" explained that in order for me to do what I could and should do in the world, I had to secure a quality education. That is why I was sent off to Fisk University, on to Oberlin College, and then to Northwestern University.

It was during my undergraduate days at Oberlin College that professor of sociology and anthropology, George Eaton Simpson, introduced me to the field of anthropology and prepared me for graduate studies here at Northwestern.[*] I was so smitten by anthropology—a field I had never heard of before Professor Simpson's class—that after I graduated from Oberlin in May of 1957, I began graduate studies at Northwestern that summer.

Why did I come to Northwestern? Because Professor Simpson told me to do so! I was not only sent to Northwestern, but I was also sent to study under the direction of Professor Melville J. Herskovits.[†] As many of you know, Professor Herskovits was a mighty force in the fields of cultural anthropology and African studies. Here at Northwestern, he founded the department of anthropology in 1938, and the program of African studies in 1948. He was largely responsible for the development of a distinguished Africana collection at Northwestern, a collection that today is housed in the Melville J. Herskovits Library of African Studies at Northwestern and is the largest separate Africana collection in existence.

---

[*] George Eaton Simpson (1904–1998) was an anthropologist whose focus was on the various social aspects of Caribbean religions. He wrote over sixty articles and books, and taught sociology and anthropology at Oberlin College from 1947 to 1971. See "Preliminary Guide to the George Eaton Simpson Photographs, 1936–1964," Smithsonian Online Virtual Archives, https://sova.si.edu/record/NAA.PhotoLot.93-14, accessed December 28, 2022.

[†] Melville Herskovits (1895–1963) was an anthropologist who traveled and conducted research throughout Africa and the African diaspora. He published several books, including *Myth of the Negro Past* (1941), *Suriname Folklore* (1936), and many others.

Herskovits was an intellectual giant who was greatly admired, and at times feared, by his colleagues and his students. The extraordinary accomplishments of Professor Herskovits are chronicled in an award-winning film: *Herskovits at the Heart of Blackness*.* This film, in which I am one of the "talking heads," also gives insight into the complexities of this world-renowned Northwestern scholar/professor who was profoundly important in my intellectual development and the intellectual development of many distinguished Africanists.

Professor Herskovits made a special effort to encourage African American students to come to Northwestern to pursue graduate work in anthropology and African studies. He also strongly supported bringing women to his department and the African studies program—an effort that was fueled, no doubt by the fact that as a student of Franz Boas, he was associated with women anthropologists like Ruth Benedict, Margaret Mead, and Hortense Powdermaker. So, not only was I one of Professor Herskovits's students, I felt that I might even have been among his favorite students, for I was a "twofer," that is an African American and a young woman.

Professor Herskovits was the chair of my master's thesis committee. For a reason that I could not understand, he continued to put off signing off on the research I proposed to do for my MA degree in anthropology. After all, I proposed to do research that was solidly in the theoretical and ethnographic traditions that were associated with Professor Herskovits. Namely, that enslaved Africans did not leave their culture on the shores of Africa, for like any other people, they brought their culture with them. And, thus, it was possible to identify the retention of African cultural patterns in New World Black societies. My thesis would explore the retention of African religious rituals and practices at Greater Harvest Missionary Baptist Church where Rev. Louis Boddie was the founding minister.

A day or so before the deadline for securing his signature on my master's thesis proposal, I had an appointment with Professor Herskovits. As I always did when I went into his office, I sat down as soon as it was appropriate for me to do so. As a five-foot, eight-inch-tall graduate student, I saw no advantage in towering over my "vertically challenged" professor. Only after he had signed off on my research did I ask Professor Herskovits why he had been reluctant to

---

* This documentary, which premiered in February 2010, was made by Llewelyn Smith, Christine Herbes-Sommers, and Vincent Brown. In this film, "intellectuals and historians discuss the vast impact and heated debate Herskovits continues to inspire around our modern perception of cultural identity." *Herskovits at the Heart of Blackness*, PBS, http://www.pbs.org/independentlens /documentaries/herskovits-heart-blackness/, accessed December 28, 2022.

do so. Because, he said, he feared that as I carried out that research, Rev. Boddie might gain a parishioner and he might lose a graduate student.

There were two "camps" in the anthropology department when I was a student: cultural anthropology and social anthropology. As I began working toward my doctorate, I took several courses with social anthropologist professor Paul J. Bohannan, became one of his students, and he chaired my dissertation committee. However, I never ceased to identify myself as a student of Professor Melville J. Herskovits.

A quick story. One day when I was in the lounge where we graduate students hung out, we heard Professors Herskovits and Bohannan in a heated discussion. At one point, Professor Herskovits said: "The problem with you Jim Bohannan is that you have no sense of history." To which Professor Bohannan retorted, "The problem with you Mel is that you have no sense of society." A graduate student among us then said, so that only we students could hear him: "And we students say a plague upon both of your theoretical houses."

It was here at Northwestern that I met my late husband Robert E. Cole who was a graduate student in the economics department and the African studies program. The two of us, and another graduate student in economics and African studies, Robert P. Armstrong, were given the exceptional opportunity to work on a project with a team of distinguished Northwestern University economists that included professors Robert Clower, George Dalton, and Mitchell Harwitz. The project involved an economic survey of Liberia that led to the publication of the book *Growth without Development: An Economic Survey of Liberia* [Northwestern University Press, 1966].*

The three of us had permission to use some of the data we collected for our doctoral dissertations. Robert Cole and I lived and worked in Liberia from 1960 to 1962, and our first son, David Cole, was born in Monrovia.

I want to say quite explicitly that being a graduate student at Northwestern clearly prepared me for all of the professional positions I would assume in the academy, and now in the world of museums.

First, I received stellar training in anthropology and in African studies at Northwestern from professors Melville J. Herskovits, Paul J. Bohannan, William Bascom, Alan Merriam, Gwendolyn Carter, and others. Those major scholars prepared me to teach at Washington State University, the University of California at Los Angeles, the University of Massachusetts–Amherst, Hunter College, and Emory University.

---

* *Growth without Development* was authored by Robert W. Clower, George Dalton, Mitchell Harwitz, and A. A. Walters.

Second, I drew on the pioneering work in the study of the African diaspora done by Melville and Frances Herskovits as I developed my interest and expertise in African American studies. I am convinced that there is a line that can be traced from my training in African studies and anthropology that led to my scholarship and activism in the Black studies movement.

Third, lessons learned in anthropology at Northwestern certainly influenced my explorations, as a teacher and scholar, of various systems of inequality, especially those based on notions of gender, race, and sexuality. Whether they knew it or not, my Northwestern professors laid the groundwork for my intellectual explorations into feminist thought and practice, and my teaching and publications in the field of women's studies. Without such a feminist perspective, I surely would not have assumed the presidency of Spelman College and Bennett College for Women.

My first trip to Africa solidified my commitment to the fields of anthropology and African studies and fueled my interest in African art. Since that first experience on the continent that is the birthplace of humankind, I have been privileged to go many times to many of the fifty-four African countries. If I had not been a student of anthropology and African studies here at Northwestern, I would surely not have the position I currently hold as the director of the Smithsonian's National Museum of African Art—an important cultural institution where we collect, conserve, exhibit, and educate about the diverse and dynamic visual arts of Africa and the African diaspora.

I thank all of you for this opportunity to look back on some of my experiences as a Northwestern graduate student. Doing so affirms the message of *sankofa*, a Ghanaian adinkra symbol. *Sankofa* is most often pictured as a bird whose head and long neck are looking back over its body. The message of *sankofa* is: "look back in order to go forward." The old folks in Jacksonville, Florida, the community where I grew up, would put it this way: "You can't know where you are going if you don't know where you have been." I'm really glad that I've been at Northwestern and had the kind of experiences that helped me to know where I was to go.

Three Stations along My Journey as a Citizen Volunteer

Acceptance Speech, George and Lenore Romney Citizen Volunteer Award,

presented at the National Conference on Volunteering and Service,

Philadelphia, PA, July 16–18, 2007

My Sisters and Brothers All: Good afternoon!

I address you as my sisters and my brothers to lift up the basic yet powerful reality that we are "kin folks" in the sense that we are bound together in a belief in the necessity of service to others. We are indeed connected to each other through our practice of volunteering.

And so, My Sisters and Brothers All, please bear with me when I express my gratitude for being singled out for doing what everyone of you does to some extent, in some way, every day.

What an honor it is, what a privilege it is to receive an award that bears the name of George and Lenore Romney—a hero and a shero in our extensive extended family of volunteers in the service of others.

I am particularly humbled by this award because it is associated with the Points of Light Foundation, for I had the privilege and the joy of serving as a founding member of the board of that organization.*

---

* Founded by former president George W. Bush in 1990, Points of Light is an international nonprofit, nonpartisan organization dedicated to engaging more people and resources in solving serious social problems through voluntary service.

Last night, Bob Goodwin, the retired brother president and CEO of the Points of Light Foundation and I were reminiscing about the early days of this organization that has come to play such an essential role in our movement for volunteering and service.

Throughout that conversation and, indeed, throughout this conference, I decided to interrogate myself about my own journey in volunteering and service, and in doing so to ask the question that is so important in the world of education: So, what have these experiences taught me? What can we all learn from these experiences?

Ever so briefly, let me take you to three stations along my ongoing journey as a citizen volunteer—each of which highlights a fundamental lesson we all need to pay attention to as we collectively work in the interest of an even better America and a far more peaceful and just world.

Station number one. I grew up in a southern Black family and community during the awful days of legal segregation. There was so much around me as a youngster that was unjust and irrational and just plain wrong: What else can you say about the idea that God has a preference for people of a certain color— that white folks are born superior to Black folks?

But as I grew up, there was also all around me the righteous, the wonderful, the powerful notion that doing for others is just the rent you must pay for living on earth.

From my mother and father, my grandfather, and my great-grandfather, I heard over and over and over again that I had the responsibility to "make something of myself," but I absolutely must lift others as I climbed.

I saw them doing just that and I also saw that the leaders in my community in Jacksonville, Florida, were leaders because they served others.

What is the fundamental lesson we should draw from my experience?

Quite simply, that there is great value in introducing volunteerism and service to young people.

For doing so can set the course of their lives.

Station number two. As you know from the program, I have been in the world of education all of my life—as a student, as a professor, and a college president.

What is clear to me is that the particular sectors of the academy in which I have worked have "a culture of volunteerism and service" that has deepened values I first learned from my family and community.

Historically Black colleges and universities were founded out of deep notions of doing for others. And today in the 105 public and private historically Black colleges and universities, the culture of civic engagement is promoted.

Of course, my own experiences as a president of colleges have been in the two historically Black colleges for women in our nation: Spelman College and Bennett College for Women. And we all know of the long history—or better put, "herstory"—of women and community service.

However, the basic lesson I have learned from my experiences in the world of higher education is that it takes more than a belief in doing for others to create effective change.

If higher education is to be a major force in making our communities, our nation, and our world better places for all of us, then service must be chiseled into the very mission of our colleges and universities. We must say and believe that the role of education is not only to help one understand the world better but also to help make the world better.

And higher education must align its systems of instruction, recognition, and rewards to reflect an endorsement of the importance of volunteering and service.

Station number three. A third station in my ongoing journey has involved participation in some of the most respected organizations in the world of civic engagement and community service.

As I mentioned, I was a founding board member of the Points of Light Foundation. Since 1987, I have been deeply involved with local United Ways and, since 2002, I've served on the board of United Way. In 1997, I became a big sister to Miranda Smith through the Big Brothers and Big Sisters program in Atlanta, Georgia. Miranda and I are still in each other's lives. And today I'm privileged to be on the advisory committee of America's Promise.

What is the single most important lesson I have learned from engagement in these organizations?

There are three.

First, the attitude that a volunteer takes into a community sets the stage for failure or success. The notion of "bringing light and salvation to poor people who have no authentic leaders or community assets" is, unfortunately, not dead. Each of us must continue to not only say but genuinely believe that as volunteers in service to others, we will gain as much as we give, we can learn more than we teach, and we can be as effective as followers as we think we can be as leaders.

The second lesson I've learned from working in "our world" of volunteerism is the importance of collaboration and partnership. While each of our service organizations can do no good if it does not believe in its own mission, strategy, and programs, it can do the most good when it acknowledges that it is not the only organization involved in civic engagement and community service. The more we collaborate, the more we build partnerships in the not-for-profit and for-profit worlds, the more effective we become in identifying the root causes of problems and making a serious impact on eliminating those problems.

The final lesson I have learned from my years in the volunteer sector is that we make a monumental mistake whenever we ignore issues of diversity and inclusion. In the work that each of us is committed to, we have got to bring to the table folks who come from the range of attributes, experiences, and life-styles that make up a community. And I am fond of saying, "If the table isn't big enough to accommodate all of these folks, then we will just have to build a bigger table."

Our boards, our staff, and our strategies and programs *must* reflect the great diversity in our nation in terms of race, gender, class, sexual orientation, religion, age, and physical and mental ability.

The Continuing Significance of President Lincoln's Gettysburg Address

Lincoln's Birthday National Commemorative Committee Luncheon,

Alexandria, VA, February 12, 2017

Good afternoon, and what a special afternoon it is as we continue the 2017 Lincoln's Birthday festivities in commemoration of President Abraham Lincoln's 208th birthday. Two years ago, I had the extraordinary privilege of reading President Lincoln's Gettysburg Address during the Memorial Program that is held annually at the Lincoln Memorial. As the first woman and the first African American to do so, it was one of the great honors of my life.

I chose as the topic of my remarks, "The Continuing Significance of President Lincoln's Gettysburg Address." Permit me to first address that topic by sharing with you a passage from my own life—the story of a man who was my maternal great-grandfather. His name was Abraham Lincoln *Lewis*. Of course, my great-grandfather was one of many African American men who bore the name of the president they said had "freed the slaves."

Indeed, Abraham Lincoln Lewis and countless Black people of his generation were devout members of the Republican Party, and they referred to it as "Lincoln's Party." In addition, Black folks in the South during that era wanted nothing to do with the Democratic Party as it was organized in the southern states, for that party was strongly identified with the legacy of slavery. The truth is that neither the Republican nor the Democratic parties have a good history of supporting civil rights, but it was a deeply entrenched notion among Black folks of my great-grandfather's era that Lincoln freed the slaves. Lincoln was a Republican. Therefore, Black people should be Republicans.

To share with you the story of Abraham Lincoln Lewis, I must begin with the story of Anta Madjiguène Ndiaye, who was also known as Anta Madgigine Jai Kingsley. Born on June 18, 1793, in Senegal, West Africa, at the age of thirteen this girl was captured from her family and Wolof ethnic group, sent through the Door of No Return on Gorée Island, and put in shackles on a slave ship. After surviving the horrors of the Middle Passage, she was put on an auction block in Cuba.

Zephaniah Kingsley, a slave owner and trader who was born in Bristol, England, had traveled to Cuba from what was then the Spanish owned territory of Florida for the purpose of buying slaves. He would later declare that he fell in love with Anta when he first saw this thirteen-year-old girl and wanted to marry her. But the laws of that day did not permit such a marriage. Zephaniah Kingsley studied the customs of the Wolof (Anta's ethnic group) marriage and they took their vows according to that custom.

Anta was brought back to the Kingsley Plantation on Fort George Island, Jacksonville, Florida, where she lived in "the big house" with Zephaniah Kingsley. Kingsley freed Anta and all of their four children. After her freedom, she was given a Spanish land grant of five acres and she held twelve slaves. Kingsley traveled a great deal and he put Anta in charge of much of the running of his plantation. Over the course of his life, Kingsley had four wives and nine mixed-race children.

When the United States took possession of Florida, the attitude toward a mixed-race family, such as the Kingsleys', was definitely not accepted. And so, Zephaniah, Anta, and one of their four children moved to Haiti. In 1843, during one of his trips to New York, Kingsley died and was buried there. Anta returned to Florida where she won the court case that affirmed Zephaniah Kingsley's will that left much to her and her four children. Anta Kingsley and her four children became union sympathizers when the civil war broke out. She died in 1870 at the age of seventy-seven.

Today the Kingsley Plantation on Fort George Island is under the care of the National Park Service. Every year those of us who are descendants of the Kingsleys—and come from different countries and different "races"—gather on the plantation.

Now I share with you that Mary Kingsley Sammis, the great granddaughter of Zephaniah and Anta Kingsley married my great-grandfather, Abraham Lincoln Lewis [Mary Sammis Lewis, 1865–1923; A. L. Lewis, 1865–1947]. The life and work of Abraham Lincoln Lewis is an extraordinary story of triumph over obstacles; indeed, it is a story that speaks to what one African American accomplished following President Abraham Lincoln's "freeing of the slaves."

On January 1, 1863, President Lincoln signed the Emancipation Proclamation. That was two years before Abraham Lincoln Lewis was born in Madison, Florida. In 1880, he moved to Jacksonville, Florida, where he went to school in between working at a Jacksonville sawmill and lumber yard. A. L. Lewis, as my great-grandfather was most often called, never went beyond an elementary school education. However, he went on to become an exceptionally successful businessman, a respected civic leader, and a pillar in the Mt. Olive AME Church.

In 1901, A. L. Lewis and six other African American men met in Jacksonville, Florida, to discuss how they could create a business that would assist Black people in their community when they faced the trying circumstances of illness and death of their loved ones. Those seven men formed the Afro-American Industrial and Benefit Society. The building in which this new business began was destroyed by the fire that swept through Jacksonville in 1901. And their business was moved to the home of Abraham Lincoln Lewis. He then named the business the Afro-American Life Insurance Company. "The Afro," as everyone called it, was the state of Florida's first insurance company. And Abraham Lincoln Lewis went on to become the state of Florida's first Black millionaire.

In 1935, Abraham Lincoln Lewis responded to the laws of segregation in Jacksonville that denied Black people access to any beaches. He said, "Black people deserve recreation without humiliation." And he used money from the Afro-American Life Insurance Company Pension Bureau to buy a stretch of land on the Atlantic Ocean—and he named it American Beach. Today, there is still a vibrant community on American Beach, thanks in large measure to my sister's successful effort, the beach is now on the US National Register of Historic Places.

In 1990, responding in part to competition from other insurance companies, the Afro-American Life Insurance Company closed its doors and was subsumed by the Atlanta Life Insurance Company.

The extraordinary life of Abraham Lincoln Lewis ended in 1947; but he is still remembered in Jacksonville, Florida, and beyond as a great man who carried with distinction the name of President Abraham Lincoln.

I turn now to state in very specific terms "The Continuing Significance of President Lincoln's Gettysburg Address." In doing so, I am fully aware that I am "preaching to the choir," for I am here in a setting where each and every one of you knows more about President Abraham Lincoln—including his famous

Gettysburg Address—than I will ever know. But as a colleague once said to me: "When it comes to education, repetition is good for the soul!"

President Lincoln was invited to make remarks on November 19, 1863, in Gettysburg, Pennsylvania. The occasion was the dedication of the Soldiers' National Cemetery, the final resting place for union soldiers who were killed at the Battle of Gettysburg. That was the bloodiest battle in the Civil War. On this occasion, the featured speaker was Edward Everett, former president of Harvard University, a leading academic and popular orator.

In a speech lasting approximately two hours, Everett spoke angrily about the great division between the union and the confederacy. In his "remarks" that are only ten sentences long, 270 words, delivered in two minutes, Abraham Lincoln never mentioned the union, the confederacy, the Emancipation Proclamation, or slavery. Instead, President Lincoln spoke of the universal values and ideals of devotion, sacrifice, democracy, and human equality. Thus, he stressed the importance of healing the country and working together toward the ideals laid out in the Declaration of Independence. When comparing their two speeches, Everett said this: "I should be glad if I could flatter myself that I came as near to the central idea of the occasion, in two hours, as you did in two minutes" [Everett 1863].

In very specific terms, what is the continuing significance of the Gettysburg Address? I think the answer is captured in the first and last lines of this two-minute speech. I will focus on the significance of the first line. President Lincoln marked the Battle of Gettysburg as a turning point in the Civil War and he reframed the war as a struggle for human rights and the principle upon which our nation was founded. Thus, he made it clear that the many who had died in the battle had sacrificed their lives in support of the principles of human equality and self-government.

Beginning with the words, "Four Score and Seven Years Ago," Lincoln lifted up the bold—indeed the bodacious—proposition in the Declaration of Independence that "all men are created equal." Remember: slave owners argued they had a constitutional right to own slaves. Thus, in the Gettysburg Address, President Lincoln implied that the constitution had to change in order to bring forth "a new birth of freedom."

Let me stress that in this famous address, Lincoln called the idea that all men are created equal a proposition, not a self-evident fact. For what was self-evident to the writers of the Declaration of Independence was challenged and rejected by slave owners.

I want to take a few moments to make it clear that President Lincoln had conflicting ideas about slavery and enslaved African Americans. During the

1858 debates with Stephen Douglas, Lincoln said he believed whites were superior to Blacks, he opposed "miscegenation," and he opposed having Black people serve as jurors. However, three years into the Civil War, in April 1864, Lincoln said this: "I am naturally anti-slavery. If slavery is not wrong, nothing is wrong. I cannot remember when I did not so think and feel" [Lincoln 1864]. Thus, Abraham Lincoln could view Black people as inferior to white people and still view slavery as wrong.

The historian Eric Foner [2011] has written that while Lincoln was against slavery, he didn't know what to do with that unjust system. His first idea was to send enslaved people back to Africa, specifically back to the West African country of Liberia. Then, for well over a decade, Lincoln advocated repealing slavery gradually—perhaps, he thought, slave owners should be compensated for their losses. It was not until the Emancipation Proclamation that Lincoln publicly rejected his earlier views. Foner says that what turned Lincoln's views was his observation of the role that Black soldiers played in the Civil War. By the end of the Civil War, 200,000 Black men had served in the Union army and navy.

Thus, Foner says, Lincoln came to see Black folks in a different light, and he could imagine an interracial society. This happened in the last two years of his life. Indeed, it was his support of Black suffrage that led John Wilkes Booth, a staunch supporter of slavery and the confederacy, to assassinate President Lincoln in the Ford Theater in Washington, DC, on April 14, 1865.

Clearly, President Lincoln's support of the proposition that "all men are created equal" is one expression of the continuing significance of the Gettysburg Address. I hope that were he alive today, President Lincoln would have said, "All men and women are created equal."

It is my view that so much of the trouble and turmoil in our country and our world results from the reality that too few people adhere to this proposition and thus the struggle continues for equal rights of all people, regardless of their race, gender, religion, nationality, age, class, sexual orientation, abilities, and disabilities.

As I move toward closure, let me ever so briefly note the last lines in President Lincoln's Gettysburg Address: "that this nation, under God, shall have a new birth of freedom . . . and that, government of the people, by the people, for the people, shall not perish from the earth." What an extraordinary statement about and in support of democracy!

As Doris Kearns Goodwin, the masterful historian, has said of the Gettysburg Address: "Lincoln had translated the story of his country and the meaning of the war into words and ideas accessible to every American . . . [he] had forged for his country an ideal of its past, present, and future that would be recited and memorized by students forever" [Goodwin 2005, 587].

As a descendent of an enslaved woman, Anta Madjiguène Ndiaye, and a slave owner, Zephaniah Kingsley, and as the great-granddaughter of Abraham Lincoln Lewis, I can testify to the continuing significance of President Lincoln's Gettysburg Address. Thank you for listening.

2. The Importance of Historically Black Colleges and Universities

As president of the nation's only two historically Black colleges for women—Spelman College and Bennett College for Women—the following speeches affirm the importance of HBCUs.

Upon assuming the presidency of Spelman College in the 1988 inaugural address, "Another Day Will Find Us Brave," Johnnetta Betsch Cole shares her vision for Spelman as a "mecca of Black women's studies." This is a pivotal speech that launched her to national prominence. In this speech Cole also affirms the importance of increasing the number of Black faculty in the United States and emphasizes the necessity of community service. This inaugural address showcases Cole's brilliant ability to weave poetry and sociological concepts to bring her audience a message of hope and optimism that captures the importance of the liberal arts and prioritizes the education of servant leaders. In her 2012 speech "Straight Talk on HBCUs: Implications for Economic Transformation," at the North Carolina Institute of Minority Economic Development HBCU Forum, she discusses the accomplishments of HBCUs and the various factors that make them successful. Turning to the challenges facing HBCUs, including harsh economic constraints, she mobilizes the metaphor of the family to build intimacy with her audience before offering innovative suggestions for HBCUs to move forward. Likewise, her 2012 Howard University speech, "It Is Going to Take Faith and Action: A Call to Support Our HBCUs," contemplates HBCUs' history and origins, as well as their impact on African American communities and the world. Here she uses creative colloquial phrases like "carry on

FIGURE 2.1
Commencement
speech, Spelman
College, Atlanta, GA,
circa 1990s. Courtesy
Spelman College
Archive.

and carry out" with regard to one's responsibilities to community. Taking cues
from the Bible and the speechifying practices of preachers, she emphasizes the
importance of both faith and action. She also invokes the term "straight talk"
to establish intimacy and familiarity with her audience. Finally, she closes this
speech by lauding distinguished alumni, singing a "praise song" for HBCUs,
and encouraging her audience to take action to support HBCUs. We close this
chapter on the importance of HBCUs with an archival document—a 1988 interview between Cole and Paula Giddings—that captures the special moment
in history of her becoming the seventh president of Spelman College. This interview offers a candid discussion of the significance and impact of Spelman,
Cole's role as a nontraditional president, and her vision for the future of Spelman College.

Another Day Will Find Us Brave

President's Inaugural Address, Spelman College, Atlanta, GA,

November 6, 1988

With a profound respect for Spelman's past and an undaunted optimism for her future, I greet you.

Greetings to the members of the academic community who have come to join in this wonderful rite of passage.

Greetings to our guests from all walks of life: the various professions, the corporate world, foundations, and government. Your presence signals a belief in the necessity of partnership between what you do, and what we do at Spelman College.

My friends, former students, colleagues from many institutions and organizations, hometown folks: thank you for making the special effort to share this day with us.

And greetings to each group within the Spelman College family.

My Spelman sisters: I greet you, students of the greatest women's college in America!

My colleagues, the faculty: I acknowledge the centrality of your work in bringing the college to the point where a recent issue of *US News and World Report* lists Spelman among the top colleges and universities in America.

I also offer greetings and appreciation to every member of the staff for all that you have done, and will continue to do, to make Spelman College a financially stable, efficiently run, and attractive institution.

Our alumnae: how warmly I greet you. Representing the more than six thousand women who are in our alumnae family, hear my thanks and appreciation for all that you have done for "your school." Under the leadership of Dr. Mary Brookins Ross, last year you raised the largest sum the alumnae have ever raised in the history of the college.

Members of the Board of Trustees: thank you for your encouragement and support as I try to follow the very course you have set.

This day marks a juncture along a remarkable journey which began on April 11, 1881, when Sophia B. Packard and Harriet E. Giles founded Spelman College in the basement of Friendship Baptist Church. And we recall and celebrate the support of Rev. Frank Quarles in the work of our founders.

This is a day to celebrate and to enhance the Spelman tradition. It is a tradition molded by women and men who know how to do so much with so little. I embrace the Spelman tradition. I am compelled to honor that tradition and to advance it by helping to institute the kinds of changes that are required of us if we are to prepare Spelman women for meaningful lives in the coming century—lives characterized by professional accomplishment and service to others.

To focus my comments during this inaugural address, I turn to a poem written by Clarissa Scott Delany, a Black American woman born in 1901 in Tuskegee, Alabama.* Though privileged with a "middle-class" background, a Wellesley college education, a job as a social worker, a marriage to a prosperous attorney, and the publication of her poems in several books and journals, Clarissa Scott Delany was still not able to escape the harsh realities of being Black and female in America. She endured constant bouts with racism and sexism, and she finally lost a six-month battle against illness and died at the age of twenty-six.

The Clarissa Delany poem [Delany n.d.] I've chosen as a centerpiece of my comments is entitled "Interim":

The night was made for rest and sleep,
For winds that softly sigh;
It was not made for grief and tears:
So then why do I cry?

The wind that blows through leafy trees
Is soft and warm and sweet;
For me the night is a gracious cloak
to hide my soul's defeat.

---

*Clarissa Scott Delany (1900–1926) was a poet, essayist, educator, and social worker associated with the Harlem Renaissance.

Just one dark hour of shaken depths,
Of bitter Black despair—
Another day will find me brave,
And not afraid to dare.

Clarissa Delany, today we hear you; for indeed, these days there is so much to cry about. In his recent publication *The Truly Disadvantaged*, William J. Wilson [1987] points out a worsening plight for an "underclass" that is disproportionately Black and Hispanic. These are our fellow Americans who are haunted by chronic unemployment, welfare dependency, inadequate food and shelter, teenage pregnancies, poor educational achievement, drug abuse, and crime. There is an increasing isolation of this "underclass" from the mainstream of American life.

Perhaps even more frightening is the recognition that the "underclass" is identified as only the bottom rung along a ladder of impoverishment in America. Perhaps more devastating yet is the fact that at a time when we need to nurture all of our talent and potential to address the problems of our land, too much of it will go wasted. Human minds and bodies are indeed terrible things to waste. Let us return to the last two lines of Delany's poem:

Another day will find me brave,
And not afraid to dare.

In these lines, we hear a wish, a hope, an intuition about the future as Delany speaks not just for herself, but for all women, especially for Black women. And to the extent that she speaks for those who have received the least among us, she speaks for us all.

I share the hope and optimism in Delany's last lines. Much of my optimism stems from a belief in education as a powerful instrument for change. But I mean a particular kind of education—the kind of education that prepares students to understand themselves and their world; the kind of education that inspires students to help change the world for the better and thereby transform themselves. In Spelman's second century that is the kind of education we will pursue.

At Spelman, we will continue to guide students into intellectual confrontations with themselves and with the world around them—and we will continue to use the liberal arts curriculum as the major force that demands that confrontation.

But as we continue to embrace the liberal arts tradition, we must dare to critique it—not for whom and what it has traditionally included, but because of all of the peoples and realities that have been systematically left out. We cannot claim to understand our world or ourselves if we fail to consciously include in our analyses the realities of half of the world's people—women—and over two thirds of the earth's inhabitants, people of color.

The serious and demanding study of the history, literature, psychology, and spirituality of Black women is a task for all intellectuals. It must be a special task for us at Spelman College.

How much easier it will be to do this task because of the extraordinary gift, the unprecedented gift, we have received from Dr. Bill and Mrs. Camille Cosby. As we accept this gift from America's beloved family, we join them in hoping that others will give to our historically Black colleges and universities in proportion to what they have. Sisters and brothers, we must tithe for our churches and our schools.

At Spelman we will take this magnificent gift from the Cosbys, combine it with our intellectual energies, and make Spelman College the mecca of Black women's studies.

As we pursue academic excellence in the interdisciplinary field of Black women's studies, we will continue to develop the fine arts, social sciences, natural sciences, humanities, and education at Spelman.

And because we are a strong undergraduate college, we accept the challenge of helping to increase the number of Black professors in America.

At Spelman College, we must indeed manage to more fully understand the world—including who we are within it. But, if we do nothing to improve our world, then we cannot call ourselves educated women. How can we call ourselves either educated or leaders if we turn away from the very reality that a third of Black America lives in poverty? Do we dare call ourselves educated if we lift not a finger to prevent our Black babies from having babies? Can we be satisfied with our own schooling when we recall that a quarter of the adults of the state of Georgia can neither read nor write? So the new day for us must surely include a sense in which Spelman women stretch the power of their leadership through expressions of genuine service.

The new day, then, must find us recreating the old traditions of scholarship at Spelman and daring to invent new ones. The new day must also find us acknowledging the great tradition of service at Spelman. We recall our history of close association with missionary activity in Africa. We remember our very founding in the basement of a church, a site where the notion of doing good for others was surely present. We acknowledge the fact that today there are various forms of community involvement and service at Spelman. But, in the new day, we must organize and intensify our efforts for a better nation and world. We must build sturdy Black bridges into the very communities from which we have come and into those that surround us. For if we do not build those bridges, then we will surely drown in our own selfishness and inaction.

This is a day when we at Spelman College must begin with great humility, to search for and find our role, our social responsibility, in every community in which we are located. This is the moment for us to say that at Spelman College we move toward opening an Office for Community Service.

On this special day, this new day, we recommit ourselves to the education of servant leaders! We will continue to teach and learn in ways that help us to fully understand the issues and the problems of our times and indeed to address them. And we will feel and care in ways that lead us to help solve those very problems.

In a spirit of collaboration, we at Spelman College reach out to other educational institutions at all levels, to the community of Atlanta, to our people everywhere, to Black women, wherever they may reside. We are committed to taking a courageous stand for a better world, and we take great comfort in knowing that by your presence here today, you endorse our efforts and join us in this righteous quest.

Let each coming day find us brave, and not afraid to dare.

Straight Talk on HBCUs

IMPLICATIONS FOR ECONOMIC
TRANSFORMATION

*Twenty-Fifth Anniversary of Executive Networking Conference, North
Carolina Institute of Minority Economic Development, Durham, NC,
June 21, 2012*

Sister President Andrea Harris, members of the Board of the North Carolina
Institute of Minority Economic Development, My Sisters and Brothers All:*
Good afternoon! It is an honor for me to be with you for NCIMED's twenty-fifth
anniversary executive networking conference.[†]

For a quarter of century, this nonprofit organization has worked to build the
asset base among limited resource populations across the state of North Carolina. In connection with that mission, NCIMED has called us together to engage
in straight talk about our historically Black colleges and universities. We are
challenged to wrestle with implications of economic transformation on HBCUs
here in the state of North Carolina.

There are ten public and private HBCUs in North Carolina—the largest number in any state in our country. Understanding the strengths and the

---

* Andrea Harris cofounded the Durham-based nonprofit North Carolina Institute of Minority.
† The NCIMED was founded in 1986 in Durham. The name of the organization has been since
changed to the National Institute for Economic Development.

weaknesses of these institutions will teach us a great deal about the rest of the 103 historically Black colleges and universities.

And so, colleagues all, here we are once again, challenged to engage in the kind of straight talk that family members have behind closed doors. But, before we do so, like any family let us give voice to our accomplishments and tell some of our success stories.

We are truly proud that many of our nation's African American heroes and sheroes graduated from HBCUs: Dr. Martin Luther King Jr., Marian Wright Edelman, John Lewis, Jessye Norman, Andrew Young, Barbara Jordan, Ralph Ellison, Oprah Winfrey, Thurgood Marshall, Regina Benjamin, Vernon Jordan, Toni Morrison, Langston Hughes, and Nikki Giovanni.

In total, HBCUs are 3.3 percent of American colleges and universities, but they generate 50 percent of African American teachers. More than 70 percent of African American doctors and dentists earned their undergraduate degrees at HBCUs. Over 40 percent of all African Americans who receive degrees in physics, chemistry, mathematics, biology, and environmental sciences graduated from HBCUs. Three-quarters of all African Americans who hold a PhD in any field did their undergraduate work at an HBCU. These realities make us feel mighty proud.

We take pride in the fact that at our HBCUs, we not only educate academically gifted women and men, we bring onto our campuses women and men who have not received the kind of preparation for college that they need and deserve. We believe in such students, we provide remedial work for these students, and we stick with these students until they make the kind of progress that leads to their graduation.

We are certainly proud that at HBCUs, students are taught that education is not only about coming to understand the world better, it must also involve honoring one's responsibility to help to make the world better. For as Dr. King said about service, "Life's most persistent and urgent question is: What are you doing for others?" [King 1957]. And, in the words of Dr. Mary McLeod Bethune, we must lift others as we climb.

The successes of our HBCUs are the result of a complex of factors. However, the obvious ones are: the absence of the kind of blatant racism that is still present on too many of our nation's predominantly white higher education institutions; the presence of a faculty that sets high expectations of every student *and* provides the kind of close attention to students that helps them to succeed; day-to-day efforts of staff that encourage each student to engage in the kinds of activities that lead to their students' personal development; and the ongoing support and involvement of students' parents, surrogate parents, and members of their religious and civic communities back home.

The impressive accomplishments of our nation's historically Black colleges and universities beg the questions: Why is it that these higher education institutions do not receive the credit they deserve? Why is it that when one of our HBCUs is faced with a serious challenge, we hear this question more frequently than usual: Do we still need HBCUs? Is such a question posed about all PWIs [predominantly white institutions] or all Catholic colleges when one of them has a serious challenge? Of course not!

But, rather than concentrating on the things that are unfair about how our HBCUs are judged, views that we can't change or fix, at least not in the short run, we need to concentrate on the things that we can control, things we can change, things we can fix about our public and private historically Black colleges and universities.

If we are honest with ourselves, the kind of honesty that can take place among family members behind closed doors, then we will own the fact that so many of the issues, problems, and challenges that we talked about during the 2008 HBCU symposium have not gone away. Indeed, they have worsened. In many cases this has happened because of circumstances associated with the dramatic downturn of the economy in our country and around the world. But we must face the truth that many of these problems are also tied to poor leadership, ineffectual management, and outdated business practices.

We are living in unusual economic times. And such unusual times require unusual responses. We have got to think and act differently about the financial state of our HBCUs if they are to not only survive but thrive—that is to create the kind of solid financial conditions that will make it possible for these institutions to fully prepare students to make a good living and to live a good life in this highly technological, fast moving, and demographically diverse world of the twenty-first century.

The president of Liberia, Ellen Johnson Sirleaf, the first woman president of any of the fifty-five countries of Africa and the recipient of a Nobel Peace Prize has said this: "If your dreams do not scare you, they are not big enough" [Sirleaf 2011].

Let me say in the same spirit that if our responses to the current financial state of many of our HBCUs, including those in the state of North Carolina, do not scare us, they are not bold enough to be effective.

Here are five proposals, some of which, if not all, could be big and bold enough to contribute to putting some of our institutions on a more stable financial path.

One. We all know that strong and effective leadership of our colleges and universities is a necessary, though not a sufficient factor for creating and sustaining financially viable institutions. What does it say about this question when we note that fifteen of our HBCUs are currently without a "permanent" president and, in our schools, presidents are staying in office for far fewer years.

I think it is time to explore the possibility of different kinds of leaders, and different leadership models. For example, would it benefit some of our HBCUs to create an organizational structure that more definitively acknowledges the need for a leader whose focus is on raising money and relating to external constituencies, while the "internal" leader is charged with keeping the internal academic and organizational matters in order?

Many of our schools say that they operate with that model, but because of the tradition of focusing on the title and the authority of "the president," the authority of the inside leader—often called the provost or vice president for academic affairs—is minimized.

Specifically, I am suggesting an out of the box idea of "co-presidents" so that each of the two top leaders carries the "magical" title, and in their different but related spheres of work they are seen as equals.

While the "inside co-president"—and I do appreciate that we need to find better language for these positions—would need to have the skills and attributes that have long been associated with a provost, the "outside co-president" as the principal leader for friend raising and fundraising could be a seasoned businesswoman or -man.

In terms of campus leadership, I would also suggest the appointment of an individual whose responsibility is very much that of a COO [chief operating officer]. For if we cannot start to run our HBCUs like well-organized businesses, we risk not having institutions to run at all.

Do these ideas scare anyone?

Two. The composition of and functioning of the boards of our HBCUs—especially those of our private institutions—present yet another set of challenges. The criticisms most often heard are that board members meddle too much in the day-to-day operations of a campus and give too little money in support of the institution.

The proposal I make in response to these concerns is quite simply this. Where best practices in terms of board governance are at least on the books, somebody or somebodies must make sure that they are adhered to. Where they do not exist, then somebody or somebodies must bring them forward, and work to institute them.

Surely such an idea will scare someone!

Three. Do we dare take a page from American business practices in terms of how we should respond to the reality that a number of our schools are in very precarious financial conditions? This is especially the case with private church-related institutions. Yes, I am talking about the "M" word.

Rather than continuing to keep several private church-related institutions alive, why not initiate a process to explore the possibility of a merger that would result in fewer schools, but the few would be financially viable and academically strong?

Does this idea scare anyone?

Four. In the interest of creating and sustaining more stable financial conditions on our campuses, we need to explore greater collaboration in terms of purchasing products and carrying out services. This is of course an idea that will work easiest among institutions that are in fairly close geographical proximity.

When I was at Spelman college, I could never understand why our institutions in the Atlanta University Center could not have a consolidated office for purchasing the standard products that all of the institutions used. Nor could I understand why some of the back-office operations that each institution had could not be merged.

How do you respond to these ideas?

Five. Suppose a number of prosperous American businesses developed a partnership with a number of our HBCUs. Each of these partners has a need that the other could address. American businesses continue to need well-educated employees that bring diverse experiences to the organization. And our HBCUs need to operate ours like a good business.

What I am suggesting is that a given HBCU would benefit from learning and instituting best business practices, and the American business would have special "access" to the graduates of the new and improved HBCU.

Is this a scary idea?

It Is Going to Take Faith and Action

A CALL TO SUPPORT OUR HBCUS

Nation's Football Classic Weekend, Rankin Chapel, Howard University,

Washington, DC, September 2, 2012

My Sisters and Brothers All: Good morning! And what a great "gettin' up" morning it is as we gather here in Rankin Chapel on the campus of Howard University, culminating four days of diverse, intense, serious, and fun activities—all of it under the banner of the second annual Nation's Football Classic weekend.

It has been a weekend where a rivalry between two of our stellar historically Black colleges and universities took place on the football field and in a student debate. It has been a weekend when folks from many of our HBCUs came together to *carry on* at parties, mixers, and tailgate gatherings. But let it be known that folks have also *carried out* their responsibility to seriously discuss and promise to take action on issues of vital importance to our community.

This annual Morehouse–Howard classic weekend lifts up great traditions in our historically Black colleges and universities. And our presence in this chapel is all about one of those traditions. For at an HBCU, women and men are not only prepared to make a good living, but to live a good life. And that means that serious attention must be given to the development of one's mind, the care of one's body, and the feeding of one's soul.

When our brother, Dean Richardson, asked me to bring the message on this special Sunday morning, I instantly felt the need to speak quite specifically about our historically Black colleges and universities. The title of the message I will bring is this: "It's going to take faith and action: A call to support our historically Black colleges and universities."

It will not surprise you that the inspiration for this title comes from powerful words in the book of James. From the African American Jubilee Edition of the Holy Bible.

The message I want to develop from that passage in James will be in the spirit of messages that Black preachers are delivering all over our country on this Sunday morning. And, interestingly, it will resonate with what rabbis say in synagogues on Shabbat, and imams say in leading Islamic worship services.

That is, while these messages occasionally tell us something we did not know, their basic purpose is to remind us of what we already do know, to reinforce very basic beliefs, and, importantly, to issue a charge for us to do the right thing!

There is something else about what I am going to do here this morning that I hope is characteristic of our Black churches. And that is they must be places where it is not only alright, but also the expectation, that there will be a whole lot of straight talk . . . that from up in the pulpit parishioners are going to hear the truth; and, in fact, some dirty laundry might get aired!

Let me turn now to this morning's message. You know, my sisters and brothers, we believe in our historically Black colleges and universities. In fact, we know that if they did not exist, it would be necessary to invent them. These special mission institutions were born out of a troubled past in American history and herstory. A past when African women and men were enslaved and brought to the so-called new world to give free labor and to receive some of the most horrific treatment that any group of people has ever been subjected to.

Let us be clear, HBCUs started before, during, and after slavery in response to the fact that Black folks were denied education in America's colleges and universities.

And so, righteous Black and white folks did what was necessary to create for African Americans what they knew was a path to true liberation. Namely, an education.

A Mississippi slave owner understood this fact when he said: Knowledge and slavery are incompatible.

Oh, and in terms of where our HBCUs are today, *look where he's brought us from!* Today, our 105 private and public HBCUs graduate upward of 370,000 students. That is a significant share of all African Americans who receive degrees.

Hear me: these colleges and universities that we call historically Black produce approximately 23 percent of all bachelor's degrees earned by African Americans, 13 percent of all master's degrees, and 20 percent of all professional degrees.

No wonder we believe in and have faith in our HBCUs. They produce 50 percent of Black public-school teachers, 70 percent of Black dentists and physicians, and three-quarters of all African American PhDs did their undergraduate studies at an HBCU.

I know you will understand how proud I am of the fact that Spelman College and Bennett College for Women produce over half of the African American women who go on to earn doctorates in science fields. Indeed, these two historically Black colleges for women produce more women who go on into science fields than the seven sister colleges combined.

Over half of the Congressional Black Caucus members went to HBCUs. And, Xavier University produces more successful African American medical school applicants than Johns Hopkins, Harvard, and the University of Maryland combined.

You know, My Sisters and Brothers All, when we look at the distinguished African Americans who have graduated from our HBCUs, it makes you feel mighty proud.

Look at the two colleges that were in the spotlight this weekend, Morehouse and Howard. Among the major figures in American and global affairs who graduated from Morehouse is of course Dr. Martin Luther King Jr. And, indeed, Martin Luther King Sr. and Martin Luther King III are also graduates of that institution.

To name only a few other distinguished graduates, let me call the names of Calvin Butts, Dr. David Satcher, Howard Thurman, Spike Lee, Reverend Otis Moss Jr., and Maynard Jackson.

From a very long list of distinguished graduates of Howard University, I will mention just a few: Andrew Young, Elizabeth Catlett, Ossie Davis, Jessye Norman, Paul Lawrence Dunbar, Toni Morrison, Ralph Bunche, Patricia Roberts Harris, Vernon Jordan, Zora Neale Hurston, Adam Clayton Powell, and Vashti Murphy McKenzie.

We are certainly proud that at HBCUs, students are taught that education is not only about coming to understand the world better, it must also involve honoring one's responsibility to help to make the world better. For as Dr. King said about service, "Life's most persistent and urgent question is: What are you doing for others?" [King 1957]. And in the words of our shero, Dr. Mary McLeod Bethune, we must lift others as we climb.

Another way to look at our nation's HBCUs is to note the impact these higher education institutions have within African American communities, in their local and state environments, in our nation and the world.

The most often noted impact is the economic one. For example, the *economic impact* of the ten HBCUs located in North Carolina on that state is upward of $1.6 billion.

Not as easily calculated, but no less important, we can note that HBCUs have a *definitive impact* in the sense that there is a relationship between the number of college-educated individuals and the stability and overall advancement of a given community, city, state, our country, and the world.

We might also speak of the *psychological impact* of HBCUs on African American and wider communities. It is always to the psychological good of Black youngsters when they are made aware of the presence of our HBCUs— something we can do by bringing our young people to our campuses for visits and, even better, for specific educational programs.

The nation's HBCUs have always had a *cultural impact* on African American communities and beyond. Of course, during the period of legalized racial segregation, our HBCUs were usually *the* places where Black folks went for musical and dance concerts, theatrical performances, and art exhibitions. Today, when there are many opportunities for such cultural enrichment beyond our HBCU campus, our colleges and universities remain important sites for such artistic performances.

Today, as I work in the field of the visual arts, I am keenly aware of the stellar art collections on HBCU campuses, including, of course, the priceless works of art here at Howard University. I cannot resist making a plea that we care for, teach from, and never sell these priceless treasures.

My Sisters and Brothers All, I have sung a praise song about our HBCUs. But now I must say something else that you surely know. Namely, that today, in some measure in response to the dramatic downturn of the economy in our country and around the world, some of our HBCUs are not doing so well. Too many are suffering from fiscal instability. Enrollments are declining at many of our Black colleges and universities. And the problem of deferred maintenance is widespread. One shocking index of what is going on in the HBCU community is the fact that, at this very moment, there are a dozen or more HBCUs that are searching for a president.

Now, here is where truth telling comes in, here is where we have got to be willing to air some dirty laundry. Let me say it: Some of the challenges our

HBCUs are facing are tied to poor leadership, ineffectual management, troublesome governance procedures, outdated business practices, and insufficient support from alumni.

And what have these problems got to do with you and with me?

Everything! For saying that we love our Black schools, that we believe in our Black schools, that we have *faith* that our HBCUs will continue to be a major force in preparing countless numbers of Black people for the future—saying all of that, but doing nothing to address these problems, is shameful!

And so, My Sisters and Brothers All, here we are on a Sunday morning that culminates a weekend that was steeped in HBCU traditions, filled with pride in Morehouse College and Howard University. Indeed, over the course of this weekend we have repeatedly said how much we love the HBCU we graduated from, we have talked about how special all of our HBCUs are, and we have declared over and over again our faith in these institutions. *But what actions will we take to support our historically Black colleges and universities?*

Will we create new and effective ways to prepare a new generation of HBCU presidents and chancellors?

Will we do far better at making sure that the current leaders of our HBCUs do what they are supposed to do according to their legal contracts *and* in terms of the moral and ethical contract they should have with our community?

Will we raise our voices to local, state, and federal agencies—and individuals—who are cutting the financial support our HBCUs desperately need?

And then will we put our votes where our voices are?

Will we do all that we can to encourage new and better ways of selecting the boards that govern our HBCUs—and then will we insist that these trustees abide by correct governance procedures?

Through our alumni associations, forums held at our alma maters, and conversations with administrators and faculty, will we insist on the kind of academic curriculum that will prepare our students for the highly diverse, technologically driven world that they will live in?

In whatever ways that we can, will we stand for zero tolerance of racism, sexism, heterosexism, and any other system of inequality on our HBCU campuses?

And here comes the question that you know I will ask: Will we start financially supporting our HBCUs to the very best of our abilities? Certainly not at all, but at so many of our HBCUs, the percentage of alumni who give is pathetically low. This must change if our HBCUs are to not only survive but thrive. And yes, it can be done!

A Conversation with Johnnetta Betsch Cole

PAULA GIDDINGS

PAULA GIDDINGS: What was it like growing up in Jacksonville, Florida?*

JOHNNETTA BETSCH COLE: I grew up in an especially warm Black family; but I also grew up in the 1940s in the typical South. So, on the one hand, I remember that my daddy was a very open, affectionate person. I have that image on the one hand and then, on the other, I can remember nights when we would be in the car with my father, and I prayed that we wouldn't run out of gas if we were going on a trip. I remember just thinking, I've gotta go to the bathroom again, because if I don't go to the bathroom now, I know there's going to be no place for me to go.

I don't think this is peculiar to me. I think this is what it meant to be Black and to grow up in the South in the 1940s; and even if you didn't have a father and a mother there was for most of us some kind of warmth in a Black family.

We moved at a certain point, and each and every day when I walked out of the back door of our house, I looked at the most gorgeous park, beautiful swimming pool, and wonderful swings—and the whole thing was for white folks. So, there was that segregation on the one hand and, on the other, I was a part of a family that had built a Black institution. My great-grandfather, who had a sixth-grade education, had started an

* This interview originally appeared as Paula Giddings, "A Conversation with Johnnetta Betsch Cole," *Sage: A Scholarly Journal on Black Women* 5, no. 2 (Fall 1998): 56–59.

insurance company. So, when I think about growing up in the South, I think about that kind of duality.

PAULA GIDDINGS: What kind of impact does that have on your thinking now?

JOHNNETTA BETSCH COLE: I find myself thinking about returning to the South, because it is a different era and, because so many of my thoughts are of another era, I'm trying to bring how I feel about the South into alignment with what it is now.

PAULA GIDDINGS: You started in Jacksonville in the South, and then to Fisk [University] for a year—how was that experience?

JOHNNETTA BETSCH COLE: Like many Black kids in this country, I had pushy parents; and you know, I'm convinced that if there is one avenue that our folks have consistently felt is the way, it is education. And this message was delivered to me very, very concretely. The way is education! So, they made me take this exam. I passed, and I ended up at Fisk. Fifteen years old!

Among my memories there is the librarian, Arna Bontemps.* I knew that he not only put books on shelves, he wrote them. That to me was just mind boggling. You know, I had never had any sort of just daily contact with someone who wrote. Sure, I knew James Weldon Johnson wrote the Negro National Anthem, and he came from Jacksonville. And I had read Langston Hughes—but I did not personally know them. The world of the intellectual is what Fisk really did trigger for me. On the other hand, it was very confusing to be in the middle of a profoundly social life that I was too young for. I was also very struck by the materialism and classism of many of the students. But Fisk was also . . . being away from home. In many ways, I think I was too young for it. And yet, I don't regret having gone to Fisk at fifteen years old. I left at the end of one year, out of me-too-ism, because my sister had gone to Oberlin. Everything that child ever did I wanted to do—including playing the piano, which I could not do; including sewing, which I never will be able to do. But she was at Oberlin, so why shouldn't I go?

PAULA GIDDINGS: How much older was she?

* Arna Bontemps was a poet, novelist, and librarian. For more information, see "Arna Bontemps, 1902–1973," Poets.org, https://poets.org/poet/arna-bontemps, accessed December 29, 2022.

JOHNNETTA BETSCH COLE: Eighteen months.

PAULA GIDDINGS: What is it about Oberlin that creates so many Black women leaders?

JOHNNETTA BETSCH COLE: It seems to me the first thing one's got to say is, if you let us in, we're going to do it. And Oberlin did in fact open its doors, as the first institution in our country, to Black folk and to women. So, I credit Oberlin for certainly opening that door. However, I have a concern about Oberlin now, because there may be fewer Black students than when I graduated in '57. I understand that it's hard to attract students—and that it's isolated, but Oberlin has a real special responsibility.

PAULA GIDDINGS: There's a diminished number, as you know, of Black college students nationally. What can we do about that, particularly as it concerns women?

JOHNNETTA BETSCH COLE: With desegregation, we've lost all of those special things about being educated in our own community. I may have told you the story about Bunny Vance because I can't get her out of my head. I remember the first day in first grade, and Mrs. Vance asked me my name. I mumbled it, and that woman screamed at me—and I have not mumbled my name since. That woman told me to stand up, look her in the eye, and *say my name!* Call it imprinting; call it mentoring; call it socialization. It is what makes a society work well when those who know more spend time helping those who know less. And I don't see that happening now.

PAULA GIDDINGS: How would you define a well-educated person?

JOHNNETTA BETSCH COLE: For me that means if there are courses on world history and US history and no courses on Black history, that you can't be well educated, especially if you're Black. In the same sense that someone who is Native American who understands everything about the Second World War, but knows nothing about the Trail of Tears, isn't well educated. And since it seems to me that what happened, all that wretchedness that happened to Black folk, did not happen to Black folk in isolation from white folk—I don't see how white folk can be well educated unless they have Black history too. So, a well-educated individual has a sense of the world in relationship to himself/herself.

I also think one ought to be able to communicate well—but to communicate well in relationship to where one is sitting. For example, an individual who is able to speak in very complex terms but is unable in a community setting to describe her own emotions and to relate to folk who are there, to me, is not well educated. Communicating doesn't mean controlling language skills—it means understanding and being understood.

PAULA GIDDINGS: How do you teach that?

JOHNNETTA BETSCH COLE: I think a piece of it has got to involve communicating a sense of social responsibility that ought to put educated Black folk into some kind of ongoing relationship with our communities. I can't think of any motivation other than a sense of responsibility, which has *got* to be different from charity—I am *not* talking about charity work. I am not talking about Black people pulling up in a van and loading it up with a bunch of little kids to take them off to the zoo for one day.

Responsibility may just take the form of someone who in fact works in a corporation but goes to a YWCA every Saturday and puts in two hours in a tutoring program. That's that old-fashioned kind of stuff that Black women always nurtured, socialized, taught, trained.

I think an individual is not well educated who only knows theory and never engages in any kind of action. I don't think you can know theory without putting it to some kind of a test. And so that brings us full circle back to this notion of social responsibility where, if one has really studied and understood society, then one ought to be doing something within that society.

And if we had the means, it seems to me that we would make that a part of a college education. Whether it is that every student is engaged in some kind of a tutorial program, or that every student is involved in an internship somewhere—but, to move away from the sheer language of the classroom and into the reality of communities is something I think we've got to figure out.

PAULA GIDDINGS: Why did you choose teaching as a profession?

JOHNNETTA BETSCH COLE: I was supposed to be a doctor, because that's what you strive to do when you're a little, middle-class Black kid from Jacksonville, Florida. But a liberal arts education says that you have got to expose yourself to the breadth of human knowledge. So, I ended up in this class—I don't know why, except it fit into my schedule fairly well. The professor starts talking about anthropology and jumping up and down and talking about Jamaica, and the retention of African culture in the New World. And the next thing I knew, I could not wait to get back in that classroom again and hear more! I had never in my life seen the letters strung out that spelled anthropology: I was in college! That word was not a part of my vocabulary.

I became an anthropologist in a sense then because I was *exposed* to a possibility, because there was an option out there that I had never even dreamed of. And because my interest was so strong, I just decided that's what I was going to do. What you do with this stuff becomes an issue later. I remember as if it were yesterday the day that I went home to Jacksonville, Florida, and my grandfather said, "All right, what do you want to do? What are you going to be? I mean, you're going to come into the insurance company, right?" And I said, "Papa, I want to be an anthropologist." And my grandfather looked at me, and he said, "What's *that*?!"

PAULA GIDDINGS: You were how old?

JOHNNETTA BETSCH COLE: I must have been seventeen. I said, "Well, Papa, you know, an anthropologist is somebody who studies people and understands us and goes away and lives with these people and in my case it would be to go to Africa, and understand Africa. And then to finally understand what happened to us here." And he started to laugh. And he told me that was the craziest thing he'd ever heard of. And how was I ever going to make a living doing something like that! And I can remember just absolutely bursting into tears. And you know, I also remember that my grandfather comforted me and said he was sorry and he didn't mean to hurt me—but I'd better figure out how I was gonna make a living.

PAULA GIDDINGS: That's very poignant.

JOHNNETTA BETSCH COLE: I remember my mother serving as the translator of that conflictual situation. She said that I had to understand that my grandfather was concerned about me, that I did have to take care of myself, that I should not think that somebody would always take care of me, and that it was my responsibility to work and have a career. And then she looked at me and she said, "But if you do work that you hate, you will be miserable for the rest of your life. Find work that you love."

PAULA GIDDINGS: As a divorced woman, who has been primarily a college professor, you are nontraditional. How much of it is the times that have allowed that to happen? Is this a special time? Or would it have happened before? Should it have happened?

JOHNNETTA BETSCH COLE: Let me respond by saying what I really honestly believe. At any moment in time, it is possible for the nontraditional to take a form that is unproductive, that is eccentric. It is equally possible for the nontraditional to be the only mode that will create change.

I mean, for Ida B. Wells to be standing somewhere with a pistol strapped around her body was not exactly what you would call traditional. Rosa Parks, in many ways, did a nontraditional thing. The tradition was to get to the back of the bus but refusing to get up the *way* she did has been so embedded in our reality. And it's hard to imagine anything else that would've worked. I think that a presidency with someone like me is possible because presidencies, when they're done well, really involve fairly complex, team-orchestrated activities. Leadership is not only whatever I bring, but a number of modes, some of which are very, very traditional. I can't imagine it in any other way because it's not going to work any other way.

PAULA GIDDINGS: What will Spelman be like, say in the year 2021?

JOHNNETTA BETSCH COLE: In one sense, a person walking on Spelman's campus in 2021 should basically see what you can see right now—"together" Black women.

PAULA GIDDINGS: What do you mean, "together?"

JOHNNETTA BETSCH COLE: What do I mean by that? I mean women who look you straight in the eye and who present themselves with a dose of confidence that is not the same as arrogance. I mean women who seem to me to be comfortable with being women. But I think that by the year 2021 Spelman women will need to be familiar with what the world is like. The world needs Black women who not only feel centered in themselves but know who they are vis-à-vis what a young Japanese woman of roughly the same age is about: Black women who are very knowledgeable about what's going on in all of South America, Black women who would not be at all surprised to hear somebody talking about English-speaking Black folk on the Atlantic coast of Nicaragua. The world needs Black women who have a worldliness beyond the comfort of being Black and a woman.

I would hope that the year 2021 would have us talking about Spelman alumnae who have not only gone off to be great surgeons, who have not only invented complicated biomedical machinery, but who are with a team that is finally getting on top of the problem of homelessness in the United States of America. Or imagine that there is some Spelman alumna who is actually writing the most definitive work that has ever been written on systems of inequality. Black women are going to be great discoverers because discoveries are often made by folk who see out of more than one eye. Black women see out of their Blackness, out of their womanness, often out of their poverty. It's that ability to move around any given issue or problem and see it that sometimes helps you learn how to conquer it.

So, I would think that in the year 2021 when we walk around campus, we'll see people from all over the world. They'll be on our campus because we are the world's center of scholarship on Black women. I'm really serious. At the Atlanta airport there will be signs that say, "This way to the Center on Black Women's Studies." I can imagine a woman flying in from India to study and compare the historical violence against Black and Indian women.

At Spelman there will be significant archival holdings because distinguished Afro-American women would give their papers to Spelman. And there will be a serious think tank of Black women, and men too, where people begin to imagine and to think and to dare to invent around serious social and political questions. I love dreaming. Imagine it is August at Spelman College and you look up and here are these little eight-year-old kids sitting at their computers because they have come for the Spelman summer splash in education. And these kids may have come out of schools that are still not preparing young Black youth for the twenty-first century. They are coming to Spelman to get an infusion of summer skills and inspiration. And they're going to walk out of here at the end of August having signed a contract that says, "If I can keep on top of my studies, even though I am eight years old, when I get to be eighteen, I'm coming to Spelman."

And then someone says, "Where does the money come from?" and there is a slogan that keeps going in my head. The slogan is, "Each one, give one." If every Spelman alumna gave no less than a hundred dollars each year, there are very few of our dreams that we could not at least begin to construct. I know all of the standard sources and we have got to systematically, creatively, sensitively, respectfully pursue every one of them. From filling out every possible grant application, going for every federal program of support, asking every single corporation that's engaged in any kind of program, to put us on their list. But we have also got to learn to "do for self." If there's one thing anthropologists know, it is that giving is important because it establishes, reinstitutes, and deepens a relationship. And when all sorts of alumnae give, they are in a relationship with their school.

PAULA GIDDINGS: Why should those who have probably more associations with places like Sarah Lawrence and the "Seven Sisters" and Ivy League schools or who are white support a place like Spelman?*

JOHNNETTA BETSCH COLE: Gloria Scott, president of Bennett College, said something the other day that impressed me a great deal. Gloria was responding to a question somewhat like yours that Ethel Payne had put to her.† And basically, what she said was, "You know, you can't run this country well without us. You can well educate every white person in America, but until you learn to educate Black folk, the ship is not going to sail. It's as simple as that."

I really think that Gloria was right; it is as simple as that. Until we [Black people] are also well educated, this society will never be whole. It will never be fully healthy. So, it seems to me, that white America has an enormous stake in Black education. Most folk don't see it that way—obviously. If they did, Black education would not be in the state that it is in.

PAULA GIDDINGS: Let me take the question one step further: Why support a school, a college, of Black women?

JOHNNETTA BETSCH COLE: I'll tell you one thing: Black schools may have only roughly 14 percent of the Black college students, but Black schools graduate somewhere around 37 percent of all African Americans who graduate from an undergraduate institution. Now, Black institutions are doing something that is right. And we think we know what it is. We may not have the most fabulous libraries, we may not have chemistry labs with the most up-to-date equipment, but we've got a climate that says, "You are Black and woman—I do not assume you are stupid."

And there is something about the atmosphere in which Black women go to school at a place called Spelman that permits them to succeed. Because they're sitting in classrooms not having to prove every day that they're not second to men or white folk. They do not spend the first half

* The Seven Sisters is a consortium of prestigious East Coast liberal arts colleges for women that originally included Mount Holyoke College, Vassar College, Smith College, Wellesley College, Bryn Mawr College, Barnard College, and Radcliffe College.
† Ethel Payne (1911–1991) was a journalist and civil rights activist who came to be known as the "first lady of the Black press."

hour of every intellectual encounter dealing first with racism and sexism. It is marvelous to be in a setting where, from your president to the sister who is serving your meals, you are mirrored. I think that for the majority at Spelman, the assumption is that Black women can do anything. So, you know, the record tells us that we'd better continue to support Black schools, because that's where Black graduates come from.

PAULA GIDDINGS: Thinking back over your life, who are the people who've influenced your direction in life?

JOHNNETTA BETSCH COLE: I tell you, Bunny Vance, my first-grade teacher, stays on my case! I think of a series of Black women teachers, librarians, and even a college president. That's the first set of folk that I think of. I think of Bunny Vance, my first-grade teacher. I think of my mother's closest friend and the head librarian of what was the "colored" branch of the Jacksonville public library, Olga Bradham. It was Olga Bradham who first gave me a love of books. A righteous librarian is a powerful being. And then it goes from Olga Bradham to one of my mother's closest friends, the librarian for *years* at Bethune–Cookman College, Martha Berhel. And I knew who Mary McLeod Bethune was when I first knew that one ought to know about somebody. And I also was very, very fortunate—I actually heard her tell the story of how she founded Bethune–Cookman College and became its president.

PAULA GIDDINGS: You're talking about Bethune?

JOHNNETTA BETSCH COLE: Oh, yeah! So I really was "set" by Black women school teachers and librarians, and a college president! My mother continues to influence me although she is no longer alive. As long as I can remember, she worked. And like many of her generation and of her means, she went to college. My mother graduated from Wilberforce. I have strong memories of my mother as a schoolteacher. She was a fancy schoolteacher—which meant she taught college—at a place called Edward Waters College in Jacksonville, Florida.

PAULA GIDDINGS: What have been highlights of your life?

JOHNNETTA BETSCH COLE: I can at this moment recreate the moment in 1965 when I was named the outstanding teacher of the year at Washington State University. I was so profusely pregnant that in order to give me the award, the person almost had to come to the side of me. You see, I think of myself still, as a teacher.

And I also think of myself in the most expansive sense of the word "mother." And the reason I put it that way is that I am extremely concerned about mandates that say each and every woman must be a mother in the most literal sense of motherhood: she is to produce a child. I honestly think that that is not instinctually what every woman has to do. But I do think there is something in that very role that in its largest sense is the ability to teach. I think it is the ability to socially reproduce; it is not just biological reproduction. And for Black folk that means the necessity to socially reproduce some things like resistance and protest and a thirst for justice.

My mother images include someone like Ida B. Wells on an anti-lynching crusade; Mary McLeod Bethune with one of those fine outrageous hats cocked to the side of her head, calling for quality education for Black youth; Marian Wright Edelman telling us that we must defend our children because they are our tomorrow; and Winnie Mandela doing all in her power to bring full freedom to our sisters and brothers in South Africa.

Now. You know, it's my problem, I guess, to figure out why those are my images of mothers. But I guess what I'm trying to say without getting too sentimental is that I think if you take that role and that tradition and that concept, and extend it as far as it goes, it is really the ultimate in social responsibility. That's what I think motherhood is—being an agent of change.

PAULA GIDDINGS: Any other highlights?

JOHNNETTA BETSCH COLE: Of course, there is another one, a big one. I will never as long as I live forget waiting for the board of trustees to make their decision on who would be the seventh president of Spelman. And once that decision was made, I will never, ever forget the complex of emotions that I experienced. I felt proud yet humble, joyous yet nervous, ready to take it on yet overwhelmed by the magnitude of it all. So, the Spelman presidency is, you know, one of *the* highlights of my life. It's a little frightening in the sense that you can no longer find even a little sliver of space between yourself and one of the most crucial activities in Black American life. I am now so embedded in the very question of Black education that there's something very unnerving about it—and also very exciting.

3. Higher Education

Johnnetta Betsch Cole's commitment to education, including higher education, shines through this collection of speeches reflecting on the state of higher education in the United States over a twenty-year period. In her speech "Look for You Yesterday, Here You Come Today," delivered sometime between 1968 and 1970, she discusses the history of the creation of the Black Studies program at Washington State University. She reflects on misconceptions, problems, and solutions regarding Black Studies. In her inauguration remarks for President Jane Dammen McAuliffe at Bryn Mawr College in 2008, she sings a "praise song for women's colleges," and emphasizes the need for universal education of women and girls throughout the developing world. It is interesting to witness how Cole invokes the memories of historic figures such as Sojourner Truth, Helen Keller, Mary McLeod Bethune, and Martin Delany to underscore her powerful message. This can be identified as one aspect of her speechifying practice.

In her 2012 speech at Williams College, "Difference Does Make a Difference: The Struggle for Diversity and Inclusion in American Higher Education," she opens with an African proverb and by situating her personal connection to Williams College—her eldest son attended Williams College and she was a 1989 honorary degree recipient. In celebrating the accomplishments of two Black Williams College alumni, W. Allison Davis and John Aubrey Davis, she weaves together a discussion of the similarities between her journey and theirs.

Boldly situating herself as a public intellectual and activist "committed to the struggle for racial equality," she urges her audience not to fall victim to

FIGURE 3.1 Speaking with Spelman College students, circa 1990s. Courtesy Spelman College Archive.

the lures of thinking we are living in a "post-racial" America after the election of President Barack Obama. Cole then weaves together a discussion of struggles over affirmative action and the need for diversity in curricula to build a case for diversity and inclusion in higher education. Lastly, in her 2017 speech "The Future of African American Education," at the College Board's A Dream Deferred and HBCU conferences, Cole offers key lessons for successfully educating African American students. By this time, she was working in the field of African art, and she was the recipient of the Asa G. Hilliard Model of Excellence Award. She draws upon the adinkra symbol of *sankofa* to reflect on her career trajectory, arguing for the importance of parental involvement in education. This speech invokes the names of James Baldwin and Mary McLeod Bethune, and also quotes a Spelman student and an African proverb to underscore her message about the need for empathy in education. For instance, she states, "As an anthropologist, here is a question that I would pose to white educators involved with Black students: To what extent are you learning about the realities of your Black students through a fundamental human process called empathy?" Ultimately, these speeches on higher education are presented in chronological order to showcase the breadth of her expertise on various aspects of higher education, but also to highlight some of the strengths of her speechifying techniques, including the use of personal narrative, African proverbs and symbols, and historic figures.

Look for You Yesterday,
Here You Come Today

Washington State University, Pullman, WA, circa late 1960s

I'd like to entitle this talk after a LeRoi Jones poem, "Look for You Yesterday, Here You Come Today," because the issue is not why Black Studies, but why has it taken so long for Black Studies to be, why has it been so many years for the history, culture, psychology, and arts of Black America to become a part of the university curriculum?*

The answer to that question is not a pleasant one. Indeed, it is a powerful blow, for you see, universities, no less than other institutions of this society, have been the victims of racism. The hurt is severe, however, when it comes to universities, for they have been billed as the seekers of truth, the storehouses of knowledge, the vanguard of change. And yet, until last year or so, when Black students, joined in many cases by whites, took up the demand for Black Studies, universities simply ignored 12 percent of the American population. That's not quite fair—most universities did recognize us—there was a course in race relations in the sociology department and, in such courses, we Black people were always the problem.

So in Black colleges as well as white ones, in Black and white public schools, Afro-Americans were mentioned as the problems in civil rights, with perhaps

---

* LeRoi Jones (1934–2014) was a Black poet and founder of the Black Arts Movement. He changed his name to Amiri Baraka after the assassination of Malcolm X in 1965.

a word or two on slavery and maybe that George Washington Carver invented peanut butter.

In 1967 and 1968, as the Black liberation struggle took on stronger and stronger direction, Black students began to question the university fathers: Why is it that only white people appear in textbooks, why only the Russian, the Asian, at times even the African could have studies? The irony is severe—African studies is okay but not that of Black America.

At this university, the Black Student Union, in 1967, made a request to the administration for Black Studies. The idea was picked up by a university committee, the Social Responsibility committee, and then a Black Studies committee was appointed to work out the details of a proposed program. In each of these capacities, students worked hard and well—Black students and white students demonstrated that they not only care about their university but wish to be involved in its actions.

Those of you who are freshmen missed the stuff when it came down last year. With an academically sound program to consider, many students and faculty began to say no, they said there is no need for Black Studies, or they said— now watch this—they said, "Well, we will not have Black Studies, only Ethnic Studies." It's at times like this that Blacks almost lose all faith—for Black students had worked hard and, I might add, peacefully, for Black Studies, a sound academic program, and the response was, "Let us submerge you in some entity called Ethnic Studies."

The final outcome was that Black Studies did pass the faculty, as one of three or four degree-granting programs in the program in American minority studies. Black Studies is now a reality at this university and there are committees working on Mexican American studies and American Indian studies.

Enough of the history, what about now? What is Black Studies at this university and at the other one hundred or so universities in this country?

As you know, many universities responded to the sincere and legitimate cries for Black Studies—some responded slower than others.

Today there are still questions, of course, about the nature of Black Studies. Let me run down how I see Black Studies, run through some of the misconceptions about Black Studies, and end with a few problems and possible solutions.

But first, Black Studies, it seems to me, is one of the most crucial symbols that a university can have. Let me run that down in some detail, for I want to suggest that Black Studies is symbolic in several ways.

Black Studies symbolizes the recognition of Black America. Investing in Black Studies says that we not only acknowledge the presence and contributions of Black America but we also label these significant.

I think it's quite simple. A university could bake a cake, but it is not a baker by trade. A college could commission a great artist to write an opera, singing praises of Black America and that narrates the complexities of Black culture. But colleges are more than creators and patrons of the arts.

In this context, the significant thing is that university is a degree-granting institution and it can demonstrate its recognition of Black America by offering a degree-granting program in Black Studies.

Black Studies is symbolic of the students' cry for a relevant curriculum that deals with relevant issues. Students say:

"We know about Athens and the ancient Greeks. Tell us about Bronzeville and the Central District of Seattle and the Black man of today."

"We know all about the War of 1812. Please tell us what you know about the Vietnam War and how it relates to Black people."

"We read Hemingway and Milton. What about Don Lee? What of Gwendolyn Brooks? And Mari Evans?"

"I can get a degree that will permit me to design bridges, vaccinate cows, or teach sociology. Could I please also learn to understand the social problems that face my country?"

This relevant issue is why I see Black Studies primarily for the student body at large. Not the majors in the program. Not so much for the minors. That is, being an education major and Black Studies minor. Though, this is terribly exciting. I see Black Studies creating its greatest impact through service courses.

Black Studies is symbolic of the interdisciplinary approach. It is so unfair to train undergraduates strictly in terms of disciplines—for people do not live by disciplines and departments. Life consists of issues and ideas. Black Studies is such an idea with issues.

One of the major criticisms of Black Studies is that it does not have academic depth: "What do you do after the Afro-American history course?"

If we become creative and move beyond the bounds of our narrow disciplines, there are many, many avenues. At Washington State University, we have standard courses: Afro-American history, sociology of Black America, Black American music, Black politics, literature of Black America. But also we have other courses: Black theater, Black subcultures, and athletics and Black community. And we plan to move into still other areas, like nutrition. Black Studies permits us to go across the bounds of universities wherever there is data on and about Black folks.

Finally, in terms of symbols, Black Studies is symbolic of a new day in American education. A frequently voiced criticism is that Black Studies programs will not be like traditional departments. My response is, "I sure hope not." If

Black Studies is to be like any other department, why bother? We must be innovative, experimental, and creative.

Next, in this talk, I would like to deal with some misconceptions about Black Studies. First, and perhaps the most explosive misconception, is that Black Studies is simply a segregated program to keep the militant Blacks happy. There are Black Studies programs of all types in the United States now— programs exclusively for Blacks because the university or college is exclusively or almost exclusively for Blacks, such as Federal City College in Washington. There are programs that are almost exclusively for whites because the college is pretty much for white students.

And then there are those like at WSU where the program is clearly aimed at both sets of students. It is highly symbolic of our program to note that we now have four declared majors in Black Studies: they come in two colors and in two sexes. In the six courses currently offered in the Black Studies program, there is a combined enrollment of 424 students. There is nowhere close to 424 Blacks on this campus, so some whites must be sneaking in.

Second, there is the misconception that Black Studies is a useless major. My response to this is twofold. First, most undergraduate degrees are useless. There is no BA degree in history, anthropology, economics, English, etc. that is the desire of every employer. Most simply put, employers care that you majored in something to get out with a college degree. However, and this is my second response, if one is going to major in something, Black Studies is perhaps the most marketable major when it comes to the social sciences and humanities. The demand for teachers and social service personnel is particularly great and will continue to increase as Black Studies programs spread from universities into high schools, the problems of minority education and life in the cities receive increased attention, and as new government programs are initiated and old ones are expanded.

Certainly, the student who majors in Black Studies can undertake graduate study in one of the social sciences or humanities, enter the teaching or business professions, or begin careers in social work.

A third misconception is that Black Studies is just like any other ole department—maybe just a little more work. Well, it is true that Black Studies is work. However, we are fighting like crazy and will continue to fight to keep it from becoming just like any other department. In the Black Studies program, we do not have faculty meetings. We have program meetings, where we emphasize good teaching. That's not to say that research is not important, but teaching is what students are here for. In Black Studies, we are trying to be creative in our approach to the program.

Once there is Black Studies on paper, what are the kinds of "problems" created and where might we look for "solutions?" Note the "quotes" because not all are truly problems.

One so-called problem is that the program or degree is majored predominantly by whites—that is, that the Black students who fought so hard for Black Studies continue to major in sociology and English literature. The obvious solution here is not to view this as a problem . . . since Black Studies is a symbol, it does its job for Blacks by having whites major in it.

Second, the problem of where to get Black faculty? One assumption about Black Studies is that faculty should be predominantly, and some say completely, Black. If we have departments and an administration willing to hire Black faculty, where do you find them? And if you find them, how do you afford them? I have two specific suggestions. One, we've got to be a lot looser on our uptight "qualifications." Second, we should consider the possibility of exchange programs with Black colleges and universities.

If You Educate a Woman

Inauguration of President Jane Dammen McAuliffe, Bryn Mawr College, Bryn Mawr, PA, October 4, 2008

Sister President Jane Dammen McAuliffe; first brother of this college, Professor Dennis McAuliffe; the past leadership of Bryn Mawr, brother president and Senator Harris Wofford; Sister Presidents Nancy Vickers and Pat McPherson. I also greet Bryn Mawr's trustees, faculty, staff, students, alumnae, alumni, parents, and friends. And to be fully inclusive, let me say Sisters and Brothers All of the Bryn Mawr family: Good afternoon.

And what a great "gettin' up" afternoon it is as we gather for the inauguration of Dr. Jane Dammen McAuliffe as Bryn Mawr's eighth president.

It is an honor and a joy for me to participate in this glorious celebratory weekend, and it feels mighty good to be at Bryn Mawr, a women's college! I strongly believe in the power and the promise of education, and I can testify about the importance of educating women and girls, and how effectively that can be done at a women's college.

There is a saying in the Women's College Coalition, an organization of the presidents of our nation's women's colleges. The saying is this: "At a women's college, we are never against men, but oh, are we for women!"

I want to center my remarks on the importance of women's colleges, and the role of institutions like Bryn Mawr in helping women to heed the call of the great abolitionist and feminist, Sojourner Truth. At a gathering of suffragettes, Sojourner Truth said this: "If one day, in a garden, one woman turned the world upside down, then all of these women ought to be able to get it right side up again" [Truth 1851].

My sisters, given the current state of our economy and the range of other challenges in our communities, our country and around the globe, with men who are our allies, we've got a lot of work to do to get this world right side up again.

I often lift up a praise song about women's colleges. But it seems particularly appropriate to do so today as we celebrate the inauguration of Sister President McAuliffe, who is a graduate of a girls' school and Trinity College, a women's college. And now, Dr. McAuliffe is charged with providing leadership at Bryn Mawr, a highly selective women's liberal arts college that continues to deserve the description given by Katharine Hepburn, one of the college's famous alumnae: "Bryn Mawr isn't plastic, it isn't nylon, its pure gold" [Hepburn 1953].

Many words have been penned about the importance of educating women. But I must say I am particularly drawn to words spoken by a man, Martin Delany, an abolitionist who was arguably the first proponent of American Black nationalism, and the first African American field officer in the US Army. Here are his words: "If you educate a man, you educate a man. If you educate a woman, you educate a nation."

Today, years after Delany offered those provocative words, they still ring true. For while many men are waking up to the joy there is in socializing children, that difficult yet pleasurable responsibility is still most often in the hands of women. And women far more often than men are teachers in the early grades, where so much of what youngsters need to learn and how they need to continue to learn is set forth.

If for some unexplained reason I was granted the power to make just one thing happen throughout the developing world that would transform those societies, I would not hesitate to say: provide universal education for women and girls. For when girls and women are granted the right and have the means to go to school, many things that are good begin to happen, things that are good, not only for them, but for their communities and their nations. Girls and women pay more attention to the importance of fetching clean water; they place more emphasis on practices that lead to better overall health for themselves and their families; they practice family planning more often; and schooling enables women to earn income for themselves and their families.

Here in the United States, if every girl and woman wanted to attend girls' schools and women's colleges, the existing single-sex educational institutions could not accommodate them all. But for those who do choose a woman's college, we know that it can be and most often is a life altering experience.

The Women's College Coalition, drawing on the results of a survey done by the National Survey of Student Engagement, lists the benefits enjoyed by students who attend women's colleges. As you listen to this list, I am sure you will recognize what your Bryn Mawr daughters, granddaughters, students, and alumnae say about their women's college.

> At a women's college the students are more engaged than their peers at coeducational institutions.
>
> At a women's college, the students are more likely to experience high levels of academic challenge.
>
> Students at women's colleges engage in active and collaborative learning to a higher degree than women at coeducational institutions.
>
> At a women's college students take part in activities that integrate their classroom and outside of classroom experiences more than their counterparts at coeducational institutions.
>
> Students at women's colleges report greater gains of self-understanding and self-confidence.
>
> At a women's college, students are more likely to graduate, and more than twice as likely as women graduates of coeducational colleges to earn doctoral degrees and to enter medical school.
>
> Women at women's colleges earn more after graduation than their coed counterparts because they often choose traditionally male disciplines, like the sciences, as their academic major. Women's colleges continue to graduate women in math and the sciences at 1.5 times the rate of coed institutions.

As I listen to these benefits of attending women's colleges, benefits I have certainly witnessed at both Spelman College and Bennett College for women, it is clear to me that at these very special institutions, women learn to heed Helen Keller's advice: "One can never consent to creep when one feels an impulse to soar" [Keller 1903].

There is an additional benefit of a women's college education that I want to add to the list I just shared with you, a benefit not only to the students of these special institutions, but a benefit to so many others.

Graduates of a women's college are twice as likely as women graduates of coeducational colleges and universities to be more involved in philanthropic activity. How good it is when women give, and give generously, of their time, their talent, and their treasure in the interest of improving conditions in their communities, their country, and their world.

Of course, we want the graduates of women's colleges to do well; but how much better it is when they do well and they "do good." Dr. Mary McLeod Bethune, one of my sheroes who founded Bethune–Cookman College, now Bethune–Cookman University, often spoke to this duality when she would address African American club women. She would say, go on and climb, climb to the top, but you must remember to lift others as you climb.

Surely these words of Dr. Bethune have a familiar ring here at Bryn Mawr, because on this large hill there is a strong ethic of community service and civic engagement.

I want to issue a challenge to the Bryn Mawr community and to all women's colleges. In your curricula, in extracurricular activities, indeed chiseled into the fiber of your institution, there should be a commitment to valuing diversity and promoting a culture of inclusion.

Whatever their race, ethnicity, class, sexual orientation, age, religion, physical ability or disability, women experience sexism. Some bad news that follows this fact is that being the victim of one form of discrimination does not prevent a woman from participating in the discrimination of others. The good news is that because bigotry is learned, it can be unlearned, and a liberal arts education can be very effective in helping an individual to do just that.

How fortunate Bryn Mawr is to have in Sister President McAuliffe an individual who has a long-standing commitment to programs that support the notion that the best educated and prepared students are those who experience on campus the same multicultural world that lies beyond.

Sister President McAuliffe is an internationally respected specialist in Islamic studies who understands the importance of these words in the Quran: "We are made into nations and tribes that we may know and love each other" [Quran, sura 49, verse 13].

As I bring closure on my remarks, I turn very directly to you, Sister President McAuliffe, to offer my hearty congratulations and sisterly support as you accept the awesome and joyous responsibility of leading an institution that must educate women well so that they can help to educate *and* to change their nation and their world.

Difference Does Make a Difference

THE STRUGGLE FOR DIVERSITY AND INCLUSION IN AMERICAN HIGHER EDUCATION

Naming Ceremony for the W. Allison Davis and John A. Davis Center,
Williams College, Williamstown, MA, October 20, 2012

I begin by acknowledging our most honored guests: the Davis family. Brother President Falk, Williams College faculty, staff, students, alumni, members of the Williamstown community, and, to make sure I have been truly inclusive in my greetings, Sisters and Brothers All: Good evening!

Please know that it is both an honor and a joy for me to be with you this evening and to offer the keynote address that is a part of the weekend of celebration, rededication, and naming of the Williams College Multicultural Center for two of the college's mighty, distinguished, and courageous alumni, W. Allison Davis and John Aubrey Davis.

I feel deeply connected to the Williams College community. There is an African proverb that captures this notion of connectedness that we can and should have with each other: "I am because you are. You are because I am."

In very specific terms, here is how I am connected to Williams. My oldest son, David Kamal Betsch Cole, who is here with me tonight, is a 1984 graduate of Williams. Among his proudest accomplishments is that he joined with Robin

Powell and Byron Walker in founding the Williams College Black Alumni Network. I am grateful to Williams for the many ways that being here helped David become the very special person that he is. It was here that David fully embraced two passions that remain so important in his life and work: ice hockey and art. David, the fact that you majored in art here at Williams and you continue to make sure that art is a force in your life influenced my decision to get a third F-minus in retirement and assume the position of the director of the National Museum of African Art at the Smithsonian. I, too, am an alum of this ever so special college, having received an honorary degree from Williams in 1989.

There are more ways in which I am because you are. On April 12, 2004, in Brooks-Rogers Recital Hall, I was privileged to deliver the annual Allison Davis lecture. I entitled my talk, "On Being a Public Intellectual: Lessons from Allison Davis."

And during two different winter terms, January 1984 and 1985, I was a visiting professor of anthropology here at Williams College. I was a Luce professor. That's Luce *not* loose!

Relevant to why we are gathered here tonight, I am connected to Williams because I feel a deep kinship with two extraordinary men of Williams: Allison and John Davis. Like William Allison and John Aubrey Davis, I grew up during the days of legal segregation. In Washington, DC, where they grew up, and Jacksonville, Florida, where I was born and raised, as youngsters we had to learn that water, bathrooms, schools, libraries, lunch counters, and, yes, cemeteries, came in two basic colors: they were white and colored.

Also like the Davis brothers, I grew up in a family where I was taught that the behavior associated with the racist belief that all Black people are inferior to all white people is wrong. And, importantly, I had a responsibility to join with others in the struggle against bigotry and racial discrimination.

While my accomplishments are certainly not of the order of magnitude of those of Allison and John Davis, like each of them I am a social scientist. As an anthropologist, I came to look at the world and try to understand the world as Dr. Allison Davis did as a noted social anthropologist and psychologist, and as Dr. John Davis did as an esteemed political scientist.

Allison and John Davis spent many years of their professional lives in the academy. So did I. And like professors Allison and John Davis, I have had strong ties to historically Black colleges and universities. Dr. Allison Davis taught anthropology at Dillard and Hampton; and Dr. John Davis taught at Howard and Lincoln universities. And I had the amazing and grace-filled experience of serving as the president of each of our nation's HBCUs for women: Spelman and Bennett College.

Again, like the Davis brothers, I, too, have taught at predominantly white institutions. And while I was never turned down for a faculty position because of my race, like Allison Davis was denied a junior faculty position in the English department here at Williams, I, too, have known the bitter sting of racism— and of sexism, too, in the American academy.

I think the most significant way in which my journey is like that of Allison and John Davis is that like those distinguished Williams College alumni, I am also a public intellectual, I am also an activist, I am also committed to the struggle for racial equality.

I turn now to offer my perspective on where we are in the struggle for racial equality, and more broadly for diversity and an inclusive culture in the American academy.

There has clearly been progress on these questions since the days when Allison and John Davis were students here at Williams College.

Indeed, it is widely held that Williams has shown a consistent and genuine commitment to diversity in its curriculum, and among its faculty, students, and staff. And it is said that there is an ongoing effort to create and sustain an inclusive culture on the Williams College campus.

But the struggle continues! Indeed, we are still a very long way away from the day when all schools, colleges, and universities reflect the diversity that makes up America. And we have certainly not arrived at the point where individuals of all races, genders, sexualities, ages, religions, nationalities, abilities, and disabilities can bring their whole selves to their college or university.

I must make the obvious point that the academy does not exist in isolation from what goes on outside of the so-called ivory tower.

Of course, there is a world of difference between where we are on "the race question" now and in the days before the civil rights movement. But we are still a mighty long way from the day when no one is judged by the color of their skin, the shape of their body, who it is that they couple with, which supernatural force if any they worship, how much money they have, and ways in which they are able or differently abled.

The election of the first African American to the highest political office in the United States was clearly an extraordinary expression of change in the racial dynamics in our nation. What a moment in history and herstory that was. People of my generation wept as we said, "I never thought I would see this my lifetime." But because it happened does not mean that we now live in a post-racial society.

At the risk of oversimplifying what are complex dynamics, I remind us of the disrespect that is often shown to our president; and, indeed, statements that are publicly made about President Barack Obama that are simply racist.

And surely I do not have to remind us who are here that our society continues to deny African Americans and other people of color equal access to a quality education, to decent housing, to affordable health care, and to a pathway to social mobility.

Anyone who thinks that we have dealt with the race problem has only to note that the Supreme Court of the United States is now hearing the case where Ms. Fisher, a white woman, is claiming that she was denied entrance to the University of Texas because of her race.

If affirmative action is overturned, state universities and colleges will have to adjust their admission policies, and diversity on these campuses will definitely decrease.

In 1996, when California passed a ballot initiative barring any consideration of race in admissions in higher education, the results were not good. Two years after that ballot passed, admissions of minority students fell at all California campuses; and at UCLA and UC Berkeley, African American, Latino, and Native American first year applicants and admissions dropped by 50 percent.

Clearly not in every institution of higher education, but in many colleges and universities there is a myth that just will not go away. Rarely spoken out loud, but clearly in force is a belief among many that excellence in education cannot coexist with diversity.

I am convinced that excellence in education is only possible if there is diversity in the curriculum and among the participants in the process of teaching and learning.

I want to make two points in this regard. The first is that through study, and ideally through human interactions, a well-educated person must be informed about the diverse peoples and cultures throughout human history and herstory *and* in today's world.

With respect to diversity in curricula in the academy, again, we can clearly see some progress, but as Dr. Beverly Guy-Sheftall, one of my colleagues at Spelman college puts it, the curricula in American education, including higher education is still too much about the three Ws: that is, it is largely Western, white, and womanless.

We cannot imagine that a well-educated person would not know who William Shakespeare was and have some knowledge of his works. Shouldn't a well-educated person also know of and have some knowledge of the works of some of the extraordinary writers who are women of color?

I know my understanding of myself, of American culture, and indeed the world has been enormously enriched by reading the works of great American women of color.

I refer to writers such as Maxine Hong Kingston, a Chinese American who blends history, myth, legend, and autobiography into her writings; Chicana novelist Sandra Cisneros whose writings are influenced by how she grew up in a context of cultural hybridity and economic inequality; Native American Joy Harjo who is Muscogee (of the Creek Nation), an accomplished author, poet, performer, and educator; and Audre Lorde, the most acclaimed Black lesbian poet, essayist, and novelist of this era.

My second point is this: the great human process of teaching and learning soars toward excellence when the participants in this process are of diverse backgrounds.

How well I know that even on the most progressive of campuses, it is not easy to attract and keep a multicultural, multiracial, multi-ethnic faculty.

I also know that taking a business-as-usual approach will never bring people of color in meaningful numbers to predominantly white faculties.

At the same time, white faculty members must also struggle to raise their own consciousness and engage in the kind of human empathy and purposeful self-reflection and education that will prepare them to teach and treat students of color effectively and fairly.

As an anthropologist and as a practicing human being, I am convinced of the power of human empathy. As one of my sheroes, Audre Lorde, frequently said, "If Black professors can learn to teach Shakespeare, then White professors can learn to teach James Baldwin." But while they do, we must still have as one of our most urgent priorities the creation of communities of diversity, and this means increasing the number of faculty of color as well as students of color on our campuses.

In terms of college and university staff, let me say clearly and strongly: I see staff as critical partners in the great project called education.

It is staff at any higher education institution that are instrumental in helping students to acquire knowledge and skills outside of the classroom—including learning about and respecting people from diverse communities.

It makes a huge difference to have staff of diverse backgrounds engaging in this highly important work.

Among the reasons it is so important to have a diverse student body is that a great deal of what every student learns is learned from other students.

I am sure that at least someone among you is asking how I justify the ongoing existence of historically Black colleges and universities, Hispanic serving institutions, tribal colleges, and, yes, women's colleges.

While these special mission institutions inevitably have faculties and staff that are far more diverse than the predominantly white institutions, the student bodies are predominantly of one community of color or are all women. Of course, within a community of color, there is substantial diversity. And, if you have seen one woman, you haven't seen us all. Thus, in terms of students, it is clearly a tradeoff. For on these special mission campuses, students do give up the advantages of racial or ethnic or gender diversity in order to study, learn, and live in an environment that is close to being free of racial, ethnic, and gender bias.

Now let me play professor and pose and answer my own question. Why bother? Why should American colleges and universities put in the time and genuinely hard effort to not only increase the diversity on their campuses, but to build the kind of inclusive culture that makes diverse folks want to remain in that academic community?

Just as folks in the corporate world talk about a moral and a business imperative for diversity and inclusion, the same is true in the academy.

In the business world, the moral imperative means there must be an equal opportunity for all qualified people to not only enter the enterprise but to advance in that enterprise, because that is the right thing to do.

The same is true for the academy. Making sure that qualified people of underrepresented groups have an equal opportunity to be employed as staff, to join the ranks of the faculty, and to matriculate at a given college or university—that is simply the right thing to do.

But enlightened leaders in corporations go on to say that there is a business case for diversity. That is, if a business is to compete effectively in this global economy, it must have within its company people of diverse backgrounds who will bring different and innovative ideas to the table.

There must also be employees who command the language and have cultural competencies that reflect the diverse people, languages, and cultures of their customers.

There is also a business case for diversity in the academy. Of course, the business of the academy is education, and students cannot be fully educated in this era without serious exposure to the diverse people and cultures of a world that is increasingly like a global village.

In short, quality teaching and learning flow far more easily when the participants in the process bring to the discussion different ideas, different experiences, different "truths" that flow from their diverse attributes.

Today, the population of our country is far more diverse than it was "back in the day" when Allison and John Davis were students at Williams, and I was a college student at Fisk University and then Oberlin College.

In 1970, 4.7 percent of Americans were born outside of the United States. In 2010, 13 percent of Americans were born in another country.

Today in the United States, one-fourth of all children under eighteen have at least one parent who was born in a country other than the United States.

Today, one-third of the population of the United States is of a "minority" group.

Of course, since humankind began on the African continent, there have been women and men! But today, there is far more consciousness about inequalities between "the sexes" and the extent to which these categories are biological *and* social constructs.

The same can be said about individuals in LGBT communities. That is, diversity in sexuality is not some twenty-first-century phenomenon. But the struggle for the rights of lesbian, gay, bisexual, and transgender people is today a far more open and winnable struggle.

There is another reality that has always been with us but has only recently been articulated and understood.

Again, back in the day, and still to a large extent, we tend to describe and "deal" with each other as if we have only one identity. We say, "That person is Black." We refer to someone as "gay." We identify someone as "a Muslim."

Identifying an individual, and worse still, treating that individual as if he or she has only one identity is not only common, but also a gross and dangerous distortion of reality.

There are two very important realities that flow from the fact that each of us has multiple identities. First, let me use the term that Kimberle Crenshaw, a legal scholar, brought forth: "intersectionality." We cannot deal with bigotry and discrimination without confronting the reality of the intersectionality of *isms*: racism, sexism, heterosexism, classism, and all other systems of inequality.

The second reality that flows from the fact that each of us has multiple identities is this: while there are some groups that have been systematically subjected to bigotry and discrimination, it is hard to find someone who does not have some form of power and privilege.

I certainly know what it is like to be a victim of white skin privilege and power. And I know what it is like to be a victim of male privilege and power. Because of my multiple identities, I can also exercise power and privilege that is based on my class, my religion, and my sexual orientation.

I certainly want to resist putting forth simplistic ideas about how in the academy and, indeed, in our nation and around the world we can make greater progress in dealing with all of the *isms* that continue to haunt us.

But I cannot resist saying that there are three things that each and every one of us could do. First, learn how you learned your prejudices. Each of us should interrogate ourselves about our particular journey around questions of human differences. When did you first notice your homophobia? Have you started to have feelings and ideas that might indeed be expressions of Islamophobia?

Second, each of us can get in touch with our multiple identities. And, once you do so, you must never let others relate to you in terms of only one of your attributes.

And third, each of us can and should honestly examine our own power and privilege. For, if I am to avoid using my power and privilege in ways that exploit and oppress others, then I must be in touch with what power and privilege I do have, the basis of it, and how it can be used in positive ways.

The Future of African American Education

College Board's A Dream Deferred Conference, Washington, DC,

March 20, 2017

Sister and Brother Educators: Good morning! There is something so very special about receiving the Asa G. Hilliard Model of Excellence Award. First, because I see myself fundamentally as a teacher and as a learner. And so, to be acknowledged in this setting where the power of learning and teaching are so appropriately acknowledged is indeed an honor.

Let me also share with you that I had the privilege and the joy of knowing the good doctor, Asa G. Hilliard.* He was unrelentingly committed to educating African American students, and he understood and practiced how a knowledge of and respect for the continent of Africa could contribute to the education of Black people, indeed all people! Today, as I work in the field of African art, I not only remember brother Asa, I continue to be inspired by his model of excellence.

I have been asked to look back over my many years in the field of education. And, specifically, the education of students whom W. E. B. Du Bois would have called students "of the darker hue."

---

* Asa Hilliard III (1933–2007) was an educational psychologist who taught at San Francisco State University and Georgia State University. Hilliard's career was dedicated to exploring ways to better educate children and to teach the truth about the history of Africa and the African diaspora. He developed African-centered curricula and often led study groups to Egypt and Ghana.

Let me look back in the spirit of *sankofa*, an adinkra or symbol among the Ga-speaking communities of Ghana in West Africa. *Sankofa* is presented most often as a bird, using its long neck to look back over its own body. The message of *sankofa* is looking back in order to go forward. Or, as the elders in the community where I grew up would say, "You can't know where you're going if you don't know where you've been!"

Looking back, I see that in my first teaching position at Washington State University, I joined with Black students and students of other colors in demanding a Black Studies program. Looking back, I recall joining the W. E. B. Du Bois Department of Afro-American Studies at the University of Massachusetts where the groundwork was laid for what is today a highly acclaimed doctoral program. Looking back, I recall my years at Hunter College where I was a full professor of anthropology with foci in women's studies and Afro-American and Caribbean studies. During my time at Hunter, I assumed the role of a student as my shero, Audre Lorde, who was also a professor at Hunter, taught me how to confront my heterosexism.

As I look back, of course I will never forget the experiences of serving as the president of our nation's only two historically Black colleges for women: Spelman and Bennett. During those magical years, I witnessed everyday what was possible when African American women believe that they can fly! They do! They soared toward the height of their possibilities.

In the spirit of *sankofa*, looking back at all of those experiences, I see lessons for today and for the future—lessons in how you and I can more effectively educate African American students.

So dear colleagues, here is what I propose to do. First, drawing on lessons from my many years as an educator, I want to quietly reference three fundamental requirements for the successful education of Black students. You are fully aware of each of these requirements. Then why am I taking time to tell you what you already know? Let me answer by recalling an experience that I had.

Some years ago, just before I was to give a talk, an educator came up to me and said how much she looked forward to hearing my talk. She said that during the previous week she had also been present at a talk that I had given. I responded by sharing with this sister educator that I was so concerned that she would shortly hear the same points that I had made in the speech she had recently heard. I said that it was my pattern to craft each speech specifically for the audience that I would be addressing. And that it was rare for me to give fundamentally the same speech on two different occasions.

This is what the sister educator said to me: "Not to worry, Dr. Cole. Remember, when it comes to education, repetition is good for the soul."

So let me repeat by simply listing what you know are three basic requirements for the successful education of African American students.

First, there is the importance of early childhood learning. While successful early childhood learning encompasses many components, including universal pre-K education, I want to lift up something that is so profoundly basic. That is the educational and emotional impact of reading out loud to young children.

There are numerous studies that have shown the critical importance that reading aloud plays in developing young minds. Thus, it should come as no surprise that one of the most accurate predictors of academic success for children as they enter primary school is the size of their vocabulary. In the landmark Hart and Risley [2003] study, children who grew up in households where their parents were more affluent heard thirty million more words by age three than children who grew up in families that were economically poor.

Colleagues all, we as educators of Black students at all levels must be aware of this reality and address how we can work with our students to address today what they missed years ago.

A second requirement for fully educating African American students, and it is certainly connected to the first one, is this. While a student is the focus in primary and secondary educational processes, there must be the engagement by a student's parents, or surrogate parents, or some significant adults in that student's life. There is overwhelming evidence that parental or surrogate parental involvement is associated with children having better grades, better school attendance, higher test scores, and effective social skills.

However, when African American parents are not engaged in their children's education, let us not immediately assume that the reason is that these parents do not care about their children's education. For it is often the case that parents who are poor or working more than one job to support their family may simply feel that they cannot miss going to work at night to attend a PTA meeting. Teachers need to be sensitive to such situations and do whatever is possible to help parents in these circumstances to be as engaged in the education of their children as possible.

That may mean, for example, a phone conference that substitutes for a one-on-one parent–teacher conference.

Ideally, the parents or surrogate parents of every Black student need to not only be active participants in their child's learning at school, but involved in fostering educational experiences outside of the formal classroom. As you and I know so well, Black children, like all children, can benefit so much from trips to libraries, zoos, museums, and other cultural institutions.

What do I see as the third requirement for the effective education of Black students—again one that you're fully aware of? It is this: dreams of African American students will continue to be deferred as long as here in America, the richest nation on earth, insufficient resources are allotted to their schools—these ever so important places where students not only are to learn how to make a good living, but how to live a good life.

While our nation spends more per student than almost every other country, this spending is not being distributed equally to poor communities and communities of color.

According to the Organisation for Economic Co-operation and Devolvement, we are one of only a handful of advanced economic countries that provides more funding to affluent districts than to poorer districts. As educators, all of you understand that districts and students who are struggling need more resources, not less.

President Obama's former education secretary Arne Duncan made this point when he stated: "What it says very clearly is that we have, in many places, school systems that are separate and unequal. . . . Money by itself is never the only answer but giving kids who start out already behind in life, giving them less resources is unconscionable and it's far too common" [Watson 2016].

I turn now to two additional points, points that are no less relevant, but are not as often referenced in discussions about the education of Black students as the three I just lifted up.

My first point is poignantly made in these words of the great African American, openly gay writer, James Baldwin. He said: "You cannot teach children that you do not love."* That was James Baldwin's way of saying that the prevalence of racism, sexism, yes, heterosexism, and all forms of bigotry are severe obstacles to the education of students.

If one either openly or silently does not see Black students as potentially as capable as their white counterparts, that expression of racism will damage the possibility of a Black student ever reaching his or her potential. A student at Spelman said to me when I asked why she had chosen a historically Black college for women: "Dr. Cole, I did not want to go to a college where some professor would ask openly or subtly 'Honey, are you sure you can do physics?'"

The days of legal segregation, of open statements in support of the myth of white supremacy are over. And yet, throughout our country, including in

---

* This is a paraphrase of "A child cannot be taught by anyone who despises him, and a child cannot afford to be fooled" (Baldwin and Cazac 2018).

our educational system, there is a legacy of viewing all African Americans as second-class citizens.

Having low expectations of Black students is a subtle yet damaging expression of racism, including when a teacher thinks that he or she is being supportive of Black students by allowing them to aim low.

The second and final requirement for successfully educating Black students that I want to lift up is captured in an African proverb. This proverb says: "She who learns must teach. And she who teaches must learn."

Specifically in terms of educators working with Black students, this proverb reminds us that as educators we must keep on learning about, keep on asking questions about, the realities in the lives of young Black folk.

And so I would ask those of you who have the sacred responsibility of educating Black students: What have you read recently, whether fiction or nonfiction, that captures the realities of young Black people in today's America? What have you been learning about the major issues and concerns in today's African American communities that range from gated communities of upper-middle-class and upper-class Black folk to economically challenged Black communities where so many African American students live?

As an anthropologist, here is a question that I would pose to white educators involved with Black students: To what extent are you learning about the realities of your Black students through a fundamental human process called empathy?

It is time now to bring closure to my remarks. I do so by once again invoking *sankofa*. But this time I want to look way back beyond my experience as an educator to those days in Jacksonville, Florida, where I grew up under the scourge of legal segregation and ubiquitous racism.

There was a dominant narrative that said this: no matter what I did and no matter how hard I worked, that I, as an African American, would never be as smart and as successful as a white person.

But thank goodness for the counternarrative that was no less present in my early life. That counternarrative was convincingly taught to me by my parents, by my Brownie and Girl Scout leaders, by the librarian at the "Colored public library," and certainly by my African American teachers. That narrative said that there was no truth in the dominant narrative. Indeed, if I committed to being an excellent student, if I cared not only about my own advancement but also remembered to be of service to others, there were no limits to where I could go.

The folk who "grew me up" believed in the power of education like the devil believes in sin. Repeatedly they taught me the truth in these words of the great African American educator, Dr. Mary McLeod Bethune, who said, "Knowledge is the prime need of the hour" [Bethune 1953].

4. Feminism and Women's Empowerment

Johnnetta Betsch Cole uses a feminist lens to illuminate issues of Black womanhood, women's rights, and the dilemmas facing Black women in the following speeches. In her 1989 Spelman College Opening Convocation speech, "The Role of Christian Black Women in Today's World," Cole problematizes assumptions about womanhood often tied to Christianity. She urges her audience to reject "false images" of Christian Black women and calls for a more equitable division of labor within families around nurturing and care work. She calls the names of Harriet Tubman, Rosa Parks, Sojourner Truth, Fannie Lou Hamer, and others to underscore her message encouraging Black women to become "troublemakers" when fighting injustice. The 2006 Delta Sigma Theta Sorority Inc. keynote address, "Taking Stock: The Condition of Black Women in Our Nation," was delivered at a jazz luncheon. As a soror of Delta Sigma Theta Sorority Inc., she offers a praise song for her sorority, and discusses the plight of Black women in the United States, arguing that education can improve these conditions. She also emphasizes the need for a curriculum that "addresses Black women's studies" and explores "the lives of Black women in an international context."

In her 2016 speech "Women's Rights and Human Rights in Africa," Cole reflects on how "culture and tradition" are often used as a justification and as a defense for the institutionalized discrimination and oppression of African Americans. At the time this speech was given, she had been director of the Smithsonian's National Museum of African Art for seven years. This speech highlights several advances in women's rights in Africa, including gender

FIGURE 4.1 *Sistren: Black Women Writers at the Inauguration of Sister President Johnnetta B. Cole.* Top row, *left to right*: Louise Meriwether, Pinkie Gordon Lane, Johnnetta Cole, and Paula Giddings. Middle row, *left to right*: Pearl Cleage, Gwendolyn Brooks, and Toni Cade Bambara. Bottom row, *left to right*: Sonia Sanchez, Nikki Giovanni, and Mari Evans. Photo credit: Susan J. Ross, 1988.

parity in primary education and increased participation of women in politics. However, Cole also notes the challenges that women in Africa still face regarding secondary education, health care, sexual violence, and politics. Invoking African proverbs as well as the memories of Mahatma Gandhi and Nelson Mandela, Cole mobilizes her audience to embrace the cause of ending gender inequality and discrimination against women in Africa. In "Doing the Lord's Work: Black Women and Civic Engagement in South Carolina," Cole applauds the women of Reid Chapel for focusing on the pressing problems that women face in South Carolina. She invokes the names of Mary McLeod Bethune, Elie Wiesel, Harriet Tubman, and Martin Luther King Jr., and draws upon biblical language of "laboring for the Lord" to emphasize the importance of service to others. We conclude this chapter with her 2012 keynote address, "Knowledge Is the Prime Need of the Hour," in which she elaborates upon her personal connection to Dr. Mary McLeod Bethune.

The Role of Christian Black Women in Today's World

President's Convocation Address, Spelman College, Atlanta, GA,

January 1989

Spelman Sisters, Faculty, and Staff of the Spelman Family.

It is a tradition for the president of Spelman to deliver the opening convocation address each semester. I hope that we will continue that tradition for what ideas and inspiration you students may receive but, no less importantly, because it means that your president must also wrestle with ideas that are relevant to your realities, indeed to *our* realities.

The topic of this talk was given to me by some sisters at Friendship Baptist Church. Speak, they asked me, on the role of Christian Black women in today's world.

I realized that I couldn't talk about what is required of us today without first exorcizing from our consciousness burdensome demands made on us in the past. I could not describe a true and viable image of Black women today without challenging a set of false images about who we have been and what we should be.

You see, there are lots of folks who will tell you what women should and should not do—and then to deepen the effect by shaking the index finger—we are told that this is what good women do, what Christian women do. But labeling something Christian doesn't necessarily make it Christian or right.

And so, there is no choice, we must name these false images and roles before we call forth new ones. Let me name three roles assigned to Black women, three roles that bend our possibilities and stunt our growth. Christian Black women must be the nurturers of our families and communities. Christian Black women must always serve as the peacemakers. Christian Black women must stand behind their men.

The most consistent image of Black women, indeed all women, is as the nurturer, the caring one, the provider of the soft, loving, emotional side of life. What is false about this image? It is its exclusivity; it is what it demands of men as much as what it requires of women; it is the assumption that this is the only role women are ever capable of doing well. A child scrapes his knee, and we say, "Let mommy kiss it." It's that time of the day when all the members of a family will partake of the foods that nourish our bodies and everyone turns to say, "Hey, Mom, what's for dinner?" No one marvels when a woman feeds, buys, or changes a baby's diapers—as if such nurturing is genetically driven. But when men carry out such basic human tasks, we congratulate them for helping their wives do what are wifely tasks. Or worse, we question whether such a man is a real man. It's Christmas time, and little girl after little girl receives a baby doll for her special present. But we sit uneasily with offering such a gift to our boys. Whenever our boys are given dolls or doll-like creatures, they tend to be dolls of violence: GI Joe, Rambo, Bruce Lee, and Rocky. Yes, the problem with the image of Black women as the nurturers is the implication that Black men are incapable of being caring souls, loving parents, warm human beings.

If we reject this false image, and surely we must, how do we see Christian Black women of today? Simply put, we must surely stand among the nurturers but reject any suggestion that we are the only ones capable of carrying out that role in our families, communities, and, indeed, our world.

If we women seek a world in which each of us is a caring person but not the exclusive one, there are things required of us no less than of other men folk. Men folk must be willing to kiss bruised knees, stay up at night encouraging a daughter to finish a term paper, hug a teenage son when he's not in trouble as well as when he is, put in hours in the kitchen, at the bedside of sick friends and kin, and in voluntary community activities. But we women folk must be prepared to share these tasks, which means giving up the sense of power that is vested in exclusive rights to be the nurturers of the world. Yes, there is a certain power, ultimately unproductive as it may be, there is a certain power in being "in charge" of the "giving" department while others man the part of the store marked "receiving." But there is even more power in co-nurturing!

There is also a new role for society if indeed both men and women are to live and work as full human beings—as intellectual as well as emotional beings, as thinkers and doers no less than as creatures capable of sensing and feeling the pains and joys of others as well as their own. Think how we constrain life if we envision a nation in which family always means a man, a woman, and 2.5 children. If family can also mean other arrangements it opens up so many possibilities, but it also means that there is a great deal that must be done and redone. For example, we need a society in which every adult has the right to a job, that is, to a decent way of making a living—and we mean women and men. We need decent and affordable childcare so that all women are not inevitably and exclusively cast in that role. And, of course, we need an educational system that instructs each of us in new and healthy ways of thinking about and carrying out multiple roles. Imagine a society in which every woman and man is a nurturer!

The second false image I want to describe and transform is this: it is the image of the Christian Black woman as the peacemaker, and the one who socializes or trains our youth for the status quo. Whether the setting is our families, our churches, our communities, or, indeed, our world, there is the notion that women, far more than men, are the lovers and promoters of peace. In our families where there are mothers and fathers, it is the mothers who are expected to settle the fights between the children. When there is dissension among family members, it is to one of the women folk that everyone looks for arbitration and peacemaking. Indeed, among the corporate executives, college professors, and professional colleagues with whom they work, women are expected to be the peacemakers, the mommies. And certainly, in the minds of most of us, there is the association of belligerence and violence and war with men—and then, by default, it is women who become the symbolic "owners" of peace. If there is one thing our world needs to survive, it is surely that every woman and man becomes a serious promoter of peace.

Connected with the idea that the good woman, the Christian woman, is a peacemaker is the notion that the proper role for females is as socializers for the status quo. Thus, we are said to say to our children:

"Just listen and do what the teacher says and don't ask too many questions!"
"Please don't cause any trouble 'downtown' with the white folks; just watch your step and stay out of trouble!"
"You just do your job and leave changing the world to others!"

Is this the kind of peacemaker Christian women are supposed to be? Are we indeed on this earth to accept the way things are and to train our children to perpetuate only that which exists? It seems to me that the answer is a resounding no!

Along with men, Black women of today have the responsibility, more than ever, to work for harmony and peace among individuals and nations. But it must be a harmony built on equality and a peace that also brings justice. There are things so deeply wrong about our nation and our world. And as long as that is the case, then Black women of today must be troublemakers, not peacemakers. We must socialize our children for struggle not for the status quo. We must be discontented, not satisfied.

Martin Luther King was surely speaking to Black women as much as Black men—he was surely speaking to all women and men when he said that we must be dissatisfied and remain dissatisfied until poverty is no more, until racism is no more, until war is no more. We must be dissatisfied until peace with justice rushes in like a mighty ocean. Indeed, Dr. King, we must remain dissatisfied.

And imagine where our world would be today if Harriet Tubman had been satisfied with slavery, and if Rosa Parks had found the back of the bus to her liking. Where would Black education be today if Mary McLeod Bethune had been content with the way things were? If Ida B. Wells had made peace with lynching, and Fannie Lou Hamer had socialized the young around her not to make trouble, where would our nation be today? Thank God for uppity Black women!

The last of the false images that I present for extinction is that of the Christian Black woman as one who "always stands behind her man." In the ongoing debates about and between Black men and women, how often is it being said that the women are taking over? Why are the sisters taking all the jobs from the brothers? Why the sisters are the ones publishing all of the books and therefore they are getting all of the attention in the literary world. Why the sisters, it's said, are forgetting their place and they are taking over from the brothers.

Fundamental to this image of the Black woman is the notion of limited good. This is the idea that there is only so much of the good things in our land—and so each time one group dips in and receives a dipper of goodies, there is that much less for another group. Now, this idea is being promoted in the richest and most technologically advanced country in the world. Shocking as it may sound, in 1989 there are still many, perhaps most in our country, who believe that there is a host of things that no woman can do as well as a man: driving a car, preaching a sermon, serving as the chief executive officer of anything, piloting a plane—and certainly "presidenting" a college. Not only are there the realities of gender inequality within African American communities, there are those who think all of that is all right: that the average salary of Black women remains below that of Black men; that in the Congress of the United States there are only twenty-three Black men and, as for Black women, there is only one. Yes, there is a false image—that of the Black woman who belongs "behind her man."

As we turn to a description of the role of the new Black woman—an individual who is intellectually, physically, and spiritually centered—perhaps the most important thing we can say is this: a woman who stands behind her man will not be able to see where she is going! But when one person stands alongside another, there is an increased strength.

The notion of limited good—that every advance by a Black woman is at the expense of a Black man and therefore should not be—ultimately leads to the notion that you can buy one group's freedom off of another's slavery. The truth is that we must promote the advancement of every sector of our society, because only when there is genuine freedom for all is there freedom for any one of us.

There is also the notion, false to the core, that diversity inevitably involves inequality—that is, that different groups, genders, races, languages, cultures inevitably mean that one is better, higher, smarter, of greater value than the other. But hierarchy isn't inevitable. There can be diversity with equality, and the role of the new Black woman is to struggle for just that combination.

Morehouse College is not the same as Spelman. Long live the difference. But we also say that the advancement of Morehouse should not be at the expense of Spelman, nor the other way around.

There can and must be diversity with equality. And at Spelman, a Black woman's college deeply rooted in the Christian tradition, this is what we strive for.

It is time to bring closure on this talk. Let me suggest, then, that the time is long overdue for the extinction of false images of Christian Black women—and Black men—for mythology about one requires fairy tales about the other.

I want to end with the words of a great Black woman whose very name stands in opposition to false images. These are the words of Sojourner Truth, the great nineteenth-century soldier in the battle for the rights of our people, and of women: "My friends, I am rejoiced that you are glad, but I don't know how you will feel when I get through. I come from another field—the country of the slave. They have got their liberty—so much good luck to have slavery partly destroyed; not entirely" [Truth 1867].

Taking Stock

THE CONDITION OF BLACK WOMEN
IN OUR NATION

Knightdale–Wake Forest Alumnae Tenth Anniversary Celebration Chapter of
Delta Sigma Theta Sorority, Knightdale, NC, May 13, 2006

My Sorors, Sisters and Brothers: Good afternoon!

Of course, it is a joy for me to speak at this Sisterly Serenade jazz luncheon organized by the Knightdale–Wake Forest alumnae chapter of Delta Sigma Theta sorority—my sorority.

From the year 1913 when the Grand Chapter was founded on the campus of Howard University to today, as we gather for this tenth anniversary of the founding of the Knightdale–Wake Forest alumnae chapter—from then until now is both a long time and hardly any time at all.

Birthdays and anniversaries are times for celebrating. But they are also times for taking stock. This afternoon, I want to do some stock taking by looking at the condition of Black women in our nation. And then I want to propose that the single most effective means for changing our condition—for the better—is education.

But who are we talking about when we say Black women? One thing I can tell you: when you have seen one Black woman, you ain't seen us all. We come in every hue—from the highest of yellah to midnight black. We like to act, some of us, as if we are permanently stuck at a very young age—but of course we are all ages.

We are Christian, Muslim, yes some of us embrace Judaism and believe it or not there are Black women who are agnostics and atheists too.

We are heterosexuals and yes, we must name that some Black women are lesbians, some are bisexual, and we need to acknowledge what it means to be transgendered.

Some of us are physically abled and others are disabled.

Some of us live in cities and others in rural areas.

In terms of class—that word we try to avoid—some of us are like we are in this luncheon: we haven't missed a meal; we live in homes where there are not only necessities but luxuries; we may not have the job we want, but we have usually had a job; health care is getting more and more difficult to come by at affordable prices but we usually have access to it; and, importantly, we are educated, indeed the majority of us (all Deltas are) college-educated women.

Oh, but there are other Black women—sisters who are beaten down, sick, abused, and suffering from years of poverty and discrimination. These are women whose race, gender, and class have subjected them to the worst of health care, if any at all; the most drudgery-filled jobs, when any are to be had; only the most basic of schooling, if that. And housing that offers little if any privacy or safety.

What do we understand from these two images of Black women? We understand that among Black women no less than among all women, there are serious differences just as there are striking commonalities. In short, if you have seen one Black woman, you have not seen us all.

Of course, we Black women have come a mighty long way from slavery. And yet, we must acknowledge that African American women have a very long way to go to reach a new era, to arrive at a different kind of world where racial, gender, and economic inequality are no more.

Today, the number of female-headed households continues to grow among Black families. Let it be known that the problem with such households is not that a woman is in charge. The problem is that they are poor households. We have a long way to go!

The rate of teenage pregnancy among Black youth has declined, thank goodness, but we have a long way to go to solve this problem.

When the average yearly earnings of Black and white men and women are compared, despite the rumor that we Black women are profiting from our position as "twofers," the truth is that African American women are still on the bottom of the pay scale. And, we have a long way to go to reach pay equity!

Because of poverty and discrimination, Black women are still twice as likely as white women to die in childbirth.

Now, we must ask the obvious. If we have such a long way to go, how do we get there?

There are those who respond by saying that nothing short of a revolution in our nations will end the poverty, racism, and sexism under which African American women suffer.

There are others who would challenge the picture I have drawn of the status of Black women and offer, instead, the promise that more pulling of the bootstraps will soon have the problem licked for Black women, no less than Black men.

I want to present yet another case. I want to present the case for education as the most consistent and obtainable means for the empowerment of African American women, And, when the least among us is empowered, "Great God Almighty, we will all be free at last!" In calling education a route to empowerment, I want to argue for a particular kind of education. First, an education that acknowledges our conditions. And, second, an education that contributes to changing our conditions.

To know ourselves is to empower ourselves. Today, we must still call for a process of education that acknowledges the conditions of Black women! There are still those who rant and rave over a decision to replace a Euro-male-centric course with one that draws on works by women and people of color. Why is it that from kindergarten through the professional schools, the majority of Black girls and women are not taught about the history and herstory and culture of Black people, and the particular realities of Black women's lives? A people without a knowledge of who they are cannot successfully participate in determining the direction in which they wish to go.

There is something wrong about teaching young Black girls about Abraham Lincoln, but never about Ida B. Wells. This act of miseducation, this silence about Black women as activists, suggests that we always have been, are now, and must always be no more than the recipients of what is done to us or for us.

A curriculum that fully addresses Black women's studies must explore the lives of Black women in an international context. Nanny of Jamaica must become as familiar to us as Sojourner Truth. The struggles and triumphs of sisters in Port-au-Prince, Johannesburg, San Juan, and the West Indian section of London must be clear to us as our hold on the various conditions of Black women in Manhattan, Atlanta, Topeka, Los Angeles, Washington, DC, and Raleigh, Durham.

Again, an education (not schooling), an education about ourselves would empower Black women because it would help us understand the source of our powerlessness. And understanding is always the first step toward change.

We must change the condition of all of us to truly affect the condition of one of us. We can very seriously ask: What is the purpose of education for Black women? Indeed, what is the purpose of education for all of us? There are those who would argue that we African American women should be educated in order to prepare us to be leaders. And when asked what leadership means, the response is that it means gaining political power and economic wealth.

There are others of us who say that, indeed, Black women should be educated for leadership, but leadership is, at its very core, service to others.

Harriet Tubman wasn't a leader because she struggled and fought for her own freedom. Harriet Tubman was a leader because she risked her own freedom a million times so that others could gain theirs.

Dr. Mary McLeod Bethune wasn't a leader because she sacrificed and struggled for her own education. Dr. Mary McLeod Bethune was a leader because she dreamed and planned and worked for the education of others.

Dr. Martin Luther King Jr. once said: "Every woman, like every man, must decide whether she will be walking in the light of creative altruism or the darkness of destructive selfishness. This is the judgment. Life's most persistent and urgent question is: What are you doing for others?" [King 1957]. And Dr. Mary McLeod Bethune issued the righteous call that we must *lift as we climb*.

I bet by now you have figured out that I am talking about the kind of education that women receive at Bennett College. My sisters, and brothers too, we need you to help us make that life transforming kind of education available to more and more women, help us by recruiting students for Bennett. Because we have rolling admissions, we are still looking for women for the class of 2010. So, send us your daughters, sisters, granddaughters, nieces, church members, and colleagues.

And, of course, we will be mighty pleased if you also send them to Bennett College for Women with at least a start on what they need financially to receive a quality education.

It's time now for me to close this luncheon address on the condition of Black women and a pathway—education—to changing our condition, for the better.

As I do, I must lift a praise song about my sorority. For, from 1912 until today and beyond, women of Delta Sigma Theta sorority have understood and practiced the truth that education and service are at the core of liberating Black women—indeed, liberating all people.

Women's Rights and Human Rights in Africa

Gala for the 2016 African Day Celebrations, Theme: African Year of Human Rights with Emphasis on the Rights of Women, Washington, DC, May 27, 2016

Your Excellences, Distinguished Guests, Dear Friends, My Sisters and Brothers All: Good evening! I begin by expressing my profound gratitude to the cochairs of Africa Dar 2016: his excellency, Oman Arouna, ambassador from Benin, and her excellency, Hassana Alidou, ambassador from Niger. On behalf of the African Ambassador's Group, the distinguished cochairs invited me to give this keynote address. What an honor it is to do so!

The honor is both personal and professional, and I feel especially privileged to address the topic of human rights within a focus on women's rights. I have had close and special ties to Africa, its people, and its diaspora since I was a young doctoral student doing anthropological field research in Liberia in the 1960s. It makes my heart sing to look out and see in this audience, women and men who represent the splendor, diversity, and the promise that you represent for the continent and Africa's people worldwide.

Over the seven years that I have served as the director of the Smithsonian's National Museum of African Art, I have come to treasure the wonderful relationships and special friendships that I have with so many of you in the African diplomatic corps. Much of the critical work that we do at the National Museum of African Art is possible because of your generosity and support.

Indeed, some of our exhibitions, educational programs, and outreach activities would simply not be possible without the support we have received from you, sister and brother ambassadors, from your governments, and your nations. And so, not from the top, not from the middle, but from the bottom of my heart, thank you.

At the Smithsonian's National Museum of African Art, I often greet our visitors by saying, "Welcome home!" I then explain that our museum is the only one of the Smithsonian's nineteen museums whose work is centered in the magnificent visual arts of Africa—the birthplace of all humankind. Thus, we are all descendants of Africa, and thus we are all Africans. The sooner that white folks realize this, the better the world will be! For no matter one's race, gender, religion, nationality, class, sexual orientation, age, ability, or disability, if you simply go back far enough, you have come from Africa. This is captured in the African concept of *ubuntu*, which affirms the belief in the universal bond of sharing that connects all of humanity. *Ubuntu* is often expressed in this saying: "I am because you are. You are because I am."

While this address will focus on women's rights in Africa, those rights cannot be divorced from the rights of all underrepresented and marginalized groups.

I do know that some will not agree with this premise. There are some who feel that "culture and tradition" are legitimate grounds for treating "others" differently. I firmly reject that idea for just as it is the case all over the world, every cultural tradition is not a positive one.

In my own case, I grew up in the racially segregated southern United States. Many used the terms "culture and tradition" as a justification and as a defense for the institutionalized discrimination and oppression of African Americans. All too often people cite culture as a reason to treat others differently and inevitably poorly. In the words of Mahatma Gandhi: "No culture can live if it attempts to be exclusive" [Gandhi 1936].

I now turn to focus on the topic of women's rights in Africa. Please keep in mind that many of the challenges surrounding women's rights, as well as other human rights on the continent of Africa, are similar to the challenges found in every country, including the United States.

The African Union [AU] has declared "2016: African year of human rights with a particular focus on the rights of women." This follows 2015, which was the "year of women's empowerment and development towards Africa Agenda 2063." For the AU to make these proclamations demonstrates that there is an acknowledgment of and a commitment to the rights of women and other discriminated groups on the continent.

In the Quran, Islam's sacred book, there is a passage that says, "We have made you into nations and tribes, so that you might come to know one another" [Quran, sura 49, verse 13].

And then there is the golden rule in Christianity: "Do unto others as you would have them do unto you."

A young student once asked the beloved Rabbi Hillel if he could stand on one foot and recite the whole Torah, the sacred book in Judaism. The rabbi answered, and this is what he said: "That which is hateful to you, do not to another. That is the whole Torah. The rest is commentary" [Babylonian Talmud, Shabbat 31a].

It is highly important to acknowledge that in Africa, progress has been made concerning the rights of women. Afrobarometer Research, an African-led series of national public polls, has shown that support for equal rights for women increased to 73 percent in 2012.* The improved treatment of women has mirrored recent economic gains in many African countries. As many of you know, Africa has the fastest growing economies in the world.

One of the biggest advances in women's rights has been in primary education. Primary school education is a key building block for improvements in the lives of women and their families.

Africa is approaching gender parity in the ratio of girls and boys enrolled in primary school. Today, a girl born in Africa has a better chance than at any point in history of finishing primary school, attending secondary school, and going on to a university.

The result is that more women are working outside of the home and in nonagricultural jobs than at any point in African history and herstory. The workforce participation rate of women in sub-Saharan Africa has risen to 65 percent. On the continent, women now own one-third of all businesses.

There has also been increased female participation in politics. In many African countries, more women are serving as parliamentarians and as ministers. There are now even a few women heads of state. In eleven African countries, women hold close to one-third of seats in parliament. In Rwanda, the parliament is over 60 percent female, the highest percentage in the world!

Women now make up 25 percent of AU parliamentarians. The increasing number of female politicians is not only good for women but for society as well. More women in government often leads to more gender-sensitive and inclusive

---

* Based in Ghana, Afrobarometer is a "pan-African, non-partisan survey research network that conducts public attitude surveys on democracy, governance, the economy, and society." For more information, see https://www.afrobarometer.org/ (accessed December 29, 2022).

policies, which can have a direct impact on the daily lives of women, men, children, families, and countries.

Fifty-one of the fifty-three AU member countries have ratified the United Nations 1979 Convention on the Elimination of All Forms of Discrimination against Women, which is often described as the international bill of rights for women.

And yet, there is still much to be done. In response to meaningful gains in women's rights, we can hear some voices saying women should be satisfied with the progress that has been made. Other voices dare to say that too much progress has been made and that a woman's place is in the house.

Here in the United States, you can hear similar voices. My response is that in my country, it is true. A woman's place is in the House, and in the Senate, too! And, one of these days, a woman's place will be in a very large "White House." Research conducted by the World Economic Forum has concluded that at current rates, worldwide, the gender gap will not be closed until the year 2133! The outlook for other marginalized groups is even bleaker.

In most African countries, long-lasting cultural traditions, laws, and governmental policies continue to restrict women and other marginalized groups from fully participating in their societies. To make matters worse, these attitudes and customs are all too often passed down to future generations, perpetuating this vicious cycle.

While major gains have been made in primary education, especially in nonrural areas, both secondary and postsecondary gender gaps remain a major challenge. Though many governments are committed to providing equal education for girls, in practice girls are less likely to attend school, and those who do are more likely to drop out compared with boys. As of 2013, only twelve African countries had achieved parity in secondary education enrollment. For every one hundred boys in a secondary school, there are only eighty-two girls.

As I look out at each of you in the audience, I am reminded that you are here, as I am, because we received an education and, in most cases, a very good one. Indeed, there is no better means to improve the life of an individual and a nation than through education. As an African proverb states: "When you educate a man, you educate an individual. When you educate a woman, you educate a nation."

A good education is the first step to a meaningful job. Yet, women still work predominantly in the home and in agriculture, where women account for 60 to 80 percent of African food production.

On the continent, women still own only 2 percent of the land due to the laws of inheritance. Women in nonagricultural work still only account for roughly 40 percent of the workforce.

African women, like women the world over, work longer hours than men, by some estimates 50 percent longer. And yet, women on average earn 30 percent less than men for doing the same work.

Women still have very little say over household decisions and how their earnings are spent. This trend is especially troubling when one considers that, globally, when a woman controls her earning the benefits to her family can be as high as twenty times greater than when her income is controlled by her husband.

Health care is also a major challenge for women and children in Africa. As an African proverb states: "If you have health, you have hope and you have everything."

In the same manner, poor health and a lack of access to health care can lead to physical and emotional problems not only for women, but also for families, communities, and nations.

An African woman faces a one in thirty-one chance of dying from complications due to pregnancy or childbirth. In the developed world, that number is 1 in 4,300. Sexual violence against women in African is now at epidemic proportions. In some African countries, over half of all women experience sexual assault in their lifetimes.

Some have argued that on the continent, it is in the area of politics that women have made the biggest strides toward gender equality. However, only one in five politicians is a woman. Africa still has the most countries with the least number of female parliamentarians.

To those who in any way doubt that we need to work toward ending gender inequality and discrimination against women, I submit two reasons why this struggle must continue. The first reason is that treating everyone with dignity and respect is simply the right thing to do.

The second reason is that ending gender inequality, like all forms of discrimination, is essential for enabling groups to fully and equally participate in society and in the formal economy, whether as government officials, in the boardroom, or in growing their own businesses. The true economic potential of African economies will not be reached until the cultural and legal barriers that discriminate against women, girls, and other marginalized groups ends. Only then will women have full access to the educational, employment, and financial opportunities that have usually been accorded to men. In short, gender equality is simply smart economics.

While there has been undisputable progress in the struggle for women's equality across the African continent, this is not time to declare victory. There is still so much to be done, from eliminating sexist remarks about who women are and what they can do, to outright entrenched obstacles to qualified women having equal opportunity with qualified men.

The ultimate elimination of gender inequality on the African continent, indeed anywhere in the world, will come about largely as the result of laws that are not simply made, but enforced. And yet, so much change can come as a result of the courage and persistence of individuals. Remember the African saying, "If you think you are too small to make a difference, then you've never slept with a mosquito."

And then, think about what can be accomplished when people unite in the interest of positive social change. As an African proverb put it, "When the spider webs unite, they can even tie up a lion."

When there are blatant and horrific expressions of sexism, such as the rape of women as instruments of war and forced marriage of girls, some may find it tempting to conclude that gender equality is simply not possible on the continent of Africa.

Oh, but My Sisters and Brothers All, let us find inspiration from these simple and powerful words of President Nelson Mandela: "It always seems impossible until it is done."* Let us get on with getting it done.

* While this quote is almost universally attributed to Mandela, there is no actual record of his saying it.

Doing the Lord's Work

BLACK WOMEN AND CIVIC ENGAGEMENT
IN SOUTH CAROLINA

Reid Chapel AME Church Women's Day, Columbia, SC, June 27, 2010

My Sisters and Brothers All: Good morning! And what a great "gettin' up" morning it is as we come together in this ever so special place of worship. Every day that I work at the National Museum of African Art, I look at exquisite works of African art. My sisters, as I look out at you, I see more of God's exquisite works of art. With a heart full of gratitude and admiration, I want to acknowledge the spiritual leader of Reid Chapel, Reverend Dr. Goff. Over the years that Reverend Goff and I were on Kodak's External Advisory Committee, I saw how this man of God consistently spoke out for, fought for, and stood by his community.

Sisters and brothers of Reid Chapel, I hope you appreciate what a visionary leader, what a man of action you have as your pastor.

Now, I turn to the first sister of this house of the Lord to say what a joy it has been to meet you, Marie Goff, and to witness your amazing and grace-filled work as expressed in yesterday's highly successful Women's Empowerment Conference.

Today, here we are, gathered in the church to participate in an annual Women's Day celebration. Thank you Reverend Goff, thank you Mrs. Goff, and thanks to all of my sisters of Reid Chapel for giving me the privilege of delivering the morning message. I am sincerely honored to do so.

Finally, in terms of extending greetings and appreciation, I want to acknowledge my Spelman sisters, my Bennett sisters, and, yes, my Delta sorors, as well. And now, I lift my eyes unto the heavens and ask: "Let the words of my mouth and the meditations of my heart be acceptable in the thy sight, Oh Lord, my strength and my redeemer."

In verses 35–38 of the ninth chapter of Saint Matthew, there is a charge that the women of Reid Chapel are boldly responding to. Yes, say the sisters of this AME church, they will heed the call to labor for the Lord. That is an admirable stance to take my sisters for, indeed, there is no shortage of problems in our world, problems to which God calls us Christians to respond.

What deeply impressed me about this courageous position that Reid women have adopted is that you are turning your attention to the pressing problems that confront women right here in the state of South Carolina and in this city of Columbia—indeed, in the very communities from which Reid Chapel draws its members.

Let me lift up just one of the stunning passages in the booklet we received for yesterday's empowerment conference: "South Carolina ranks in the bottom third of states on women's earnings [40th], educational attainment [37th], and poverty [38th]."

While those statistics capture a disturbing picture about all women in South Carolina, we know that the realities for Black women are worse. As the saying goes, "When white folks have a cold, Black folks have walking pneumonia!" Yesterday, during our empowerment conference, sisters testified about the range of issues they face, such as challenges tied to their physical health, as well as consequences of emotional stress.

And then the sisters responded to the question: "What will the church do about all of this?" The answer must be that we women, with righteous men who are our allies, will attack these problems. Yes, that together we must take on this work!

Another way of saying all of this is to say that while we women folks can and should continue to come unto the Lord's house, and sing and shout, and, yes, get happy, we must also do the work the Lord calls us to do, work that addresses the everyday ills that keep us women—and, yes, our children and men folks too—from living good, healthy, and productive lives.

To put it all yet another way: for us women folks to be on a mission, laboring for the Lord is to say that we must be of service to others. And is this not the most basic responsibility of every Christian?

It is certainly what my parents taught me, it is certainly what I heard over and over again in the church of my childhood, Mt. Olive AME Church in Jacksonville,

Florida. It was often put in these words: "Doing for others is just the rent you must pay for living on this earth."

One of my sheroes, the great educator Dr. Mary McLeod Bethune, had a special way of issuing this charge to her sisters. In her work as founder of the Negro women's club movement, she would speak to gatherings of high society Black women and she would say this: "My sisters, you've got to stop playing so much bridge and start building bridges back into the communities you've come from."

Dr. Bethune would go on to say, "It's fine to climb to the top of your professions. Go on and climb to the top. But, you must remember to lift others as you climb!"

As you may know, another great shero who recently went to glory, Dr. Dorothy Height, took the baton passed to her by Dr. Bethune and used that motto, "Lifting as we climb," as she advanced the work of the National Council of Negro Women.

Of course, the call to do the Lord's work by serving others is a call that is made and responded to by great men as well as great women and by people of all faiths.

Dr. Martin Luther King Jr. put it this way: "Life's most persistent and urgent question is: What are you doing for others?" [King 1957]. And I love these words of Dr. King. He said, "Anybody can be great because everybody can serve. You don't have to know about Plato and Aristotle to serve. You don't have to know Einstein's theory of relativity to serve. You don't have to know the second theory of thermodynamics in physics to serve. You don't have to make your subject and your verb agree to serve. All you need is a heart full of grace and a soul motivated by love" [King 1968].

And the great Jewish humanitarian, Eli Wiesel, has said: "Our lives no longer belong to us alone; they belong to all those who need us desperately" [Wiesel 1986].

My dear sisters, let us ask: "In Christ, what is required of us to effectively do the Lord's work among women?"

Let me lift up three requirements.

First, we must have faith that we really can effectively do for the Lord and, sometimes, when the problems we are tackling seem insurmountable— problems like sexism, domestic violence, low self-esteem—we must truly keep the faith, we must remind ourselves that through and with the Lord, all things are possible.

Yes, we must keep the faith while we do the Lord's work! Let me remind us all what faith is: it is what you have when you must jump from the top of a mountain—and you jump knowing that when you do, you will either sprout wings, or the earth will rise up to meet your feet.

To labor for the Lord among women folks also requires that we acknowledge and respect the fact that if you have seen one Black woman, you haven't seen us all.

In short, there is great diversity among those of us that Dr. W. E. B. Du Bois called "daughters of the darker hue."

We Black women are of diverse colors, ages, faith communities, classes, sexual orientations, physical and mental abilities and disabilities.

And, as a sister said in one of our workshops yesterday, the church—and remember we are the church—must stop being so judgmental if the church really wants to be of service to those in need.

Third, and finally, if we women are to labor for the Lord, we have got to be bold and bodacious. Why we've got to be uppity Black women! Like Harriet Tubman who could say, "I'm the conductor on this underground railroad and I ain't lost a passenger yet!"

If we're going to do the Lord's work, then, my sisters, we've got to be uppity Black women like Ida B. Wells, Anna Julia Cooper, Mary Church Terrell, Septima Clark, Barbara Jordan, Marian Wright Edelman, and Barbara Lee.

Knowledge Is the Prime Need of the Hour

Women in Philanthropy Lunch Keynote Address, United Way of Greater Greensboro, Greensboro, NC, May 24, 2012

My Sisters All! Top of the afternoon to each of you. There is an African proverb that says, "Home is where you are happy." In that sense, Greensboro is home to me, and it is good to be back home. Over the course of the four years that I was at Bennett College for Women, a big robbery took place. The college stole my heart—and I hope Bennett never gives it back.

I want to take just a minute to share with you that in March of 2009, I received a third F-minus in retirement, and I am now serving as the director of the Smithsonian's National Museum of African Art. Located on the mall in Washington, "my" museum is our nation's only museum dedicated to collecting, conserving, exhibiting, and educating about the visual arts of Africa—that continent from which we all descended. Because Africa is the cradle of humankind, that makes us all Africans!

My sisters of United Way of Greater Greensboro, I thank you for giving me the honor and the joy of participating in this *inaugural* Women in Philanthropy luncheon.

What the women of Greensboro created back in 1999 under the graceful and amazing leadership of Bonnie McElveen-Hunter has become a national movement of women in philanthropy, the likes of which this country has never seen.

Under the steady hands of Bonnie and so many other women in local United Ways throughout the country, we're now fifty thousand sisters strong, operating in 120 Women's Leadership Councils nationwide—raising more than $120 million each and every year to advance the common good. At the end of 2009 we surpassed $700 million. That's well on our way, and way ahead of schedule, to reaching a phenomenal benchmark of $1 billion by 2013!

Clearly, that dollar amount is substantial. But, as every one of us knows, it's not the amount of money that ultimately matters, it's what that money can accomplish. What it has accomplished. What we have accomplished with and for communities across our nation.

Let me make this crucial point again. *Our Women's Leadership Councils aren't just about the money.* We're not just about writing checks anymore. We're about volunteering and advocating and mentoring and mobilizing to have an impact.

Serving others is what we must do. That is because doing for others is the rent you must pay for your room here on earth.

So I thank you all for your service. You've helped make a world of difference right here in Greensboro. You've focused your financial resources, your talent, and your valuable time on the three pillars of the United Way's Campaign for the Common Good—health, income, and education. It's what I'd like to turn to now.

Education. Listen to the words of one of my sheroes, Dr. Mary McLeod Bethune—a great African American educator. She once said: "Knowledge is the prime need of the hour" [Bethune 1953].

How true that was in her day, and it is certainly true today.

Mary McLeod Bethune was born in a small log cabin in 1875. She was the daughter of former slaves, the fifteenth of seventeen children. She attended a one-room schoolhouse, where she used education to lift herself up from her poor family's small cotton and rice farm in Mayesville, South Carolina.

With the help of several women mentors, Mary McLeod Bethune earned a scholarship to college and began a career as a teacher. In 1904, not yet thirty years old, she opened her own school in Daytona, Florida, with six students. She built benches and desks out of discarded crates. She crushed elderberries for the juice to make ink for pens. She fashioned pencils out of discarded wood and charcoal. To raise funds, she'd bake and sell sweet potato pies.

Her school grew and, after several mergers, morphed into Bethune–Cookman College. Today, more than a century after its founding, the school is now a university. A close friend of Eleanor Roosevelt, Dr. Bethune served as an educational adviser to President Roosevelt and as a member of his informal Black cabinet.

One of the great blessings of my early life is that I had opportunities to be with Dr. Bethune. Indeed, her life has served as an inspiration to me, and to countless other Black women and educators. I could spend the rest of the afternoon reading from some of her eloquent writings, but I've selected a single sentence.

She said, "The whole world opened up to me when I learned to read."

Reading is a fundamental foundation for life. It is a cornerstone for a child's success in school, and a predictor for life beyond school. Without the ability to read well, opportunities for personal fulfillment and financial success are lost. And the price is borne not only by the individual, but also by society as a whole. Poor readers comprise the highest percent of school dropouts, which in turn suppresses earnings potential and lowers America's competitiveness and productivity.

"The whole world opened up to me when I learned to read."

I was reminded of Dr. Bethune's words when I came across some statistics recently that I can only describe as shocking. By age four, children of affluent families have heard forty-five million words. Children of working-class families have heard twenty-six million words. Children born in poverty have heard just fourteen million words. Of course, children hear words in conversation and from reading.

This thirty-one-million-word gap between rich and poor kindergarten students puts so many students at risk. Students with smaller vocabularies and poor comprehension skills are less able to understand both their teachers and their lessons.

When parents read aloud to their children, they fire their imaginations. They encourage creative thinking that can soar far beyond today's all too ubiquitous online and on-screen videos and visuals. When parents don't read to their children, they deny not only the children but also themselves.

Dr. Ruth Love, a former superintendent of the public schools in Chicago and Oakland, has said, "If we could get our parents to read to their preschool children fifteen minutes a day, we could revolutionize the schools" [Hechinger 1981]. I believe that!

What's needed is a comprehensive commitment to increase early grade literacy. As part of the Women in Philanthropy's commitment to the United Way's Campaign for the Common Good, we are declaring open season on poor early grade reading skills.

I can sum up the magnitude of the problem with one statistic—one out of every three 4th graders in the US scores below basic in reading proficiency. That's one third of fourth graders! And the numbers, not surprisingly, are even worse for low-income students. A total of 83 percent of fourth graders from low-income families cannot read at a proficient level.

These numbers, by the way, come from a special report from the Annie E. Casey Foundation entitled *Early Warning! Why Reading by the End of Third Grade Matters* [2010].

Reading proficiency is a fundamental determinant of a child's educational development. The inability to read proficiently by the end of the third grade has destructive consequences. It makes a child far more likely to slip behind in her or his schoolwork and, as the years go on, greatly increases the likelihood that that child will drop out of school. This, naturally, has a damaging effect on a child's ability into adulthood to find a good job, earn a decent wage, support a family, and become a productive member of society.

The child suffers. The children suffer.

The child's community suffers. We all suffer.

Right here in this room, there are colleagues from some agencies who are fighting the valiant fight against some of the ugly statistics I've reported here today. Let me share with you just a few of the bright spots in Greensboro that give me hope and warm my heart.

"Julia" has two sons, ages three and seven, and came to the Family Literacy Program at Reading Connections so she could learn how to help them succeed in school. When she started the program in September, her oldest son in first grade was barely reading at a prekindergarten level. He has now made almost a year's worth of progress in his reading level, and his teachers say it is because Julia is reading with him every night. Julia herself has improved her own reading from a fifth-grade to a seventh-grade level. She says, "For me this program is so important because it has helped me communicate better with my children by sharing quality family time together. For me personally it was a very important change because now I have a desire to learn and know more just like when I was in school."

And then there's Angela, who was a shy, reserved Hispanic third grader when she began her Great Leaps reading tutorial sessions at Archer Elementary School in 2009. A program of Communities in Schools of Greater Greensboro, Great Leaps has helped Angela distinguish herself by placing in the highest percentile on a recent school-wide reading test. Angela frequently reads to her younger brother, a pre-K student at Archer, and is using her newfound skills to teach English to her mother.

One more inspiring Greensboro story. When "Terrance" was just three years old, his mother went to the Thriving at Three coordinator at Claremont Courts because she was concerned about his speech. Doris James, the coordinator, observed Terrance and his mother and realized there was no reading in their household. So Doris took lots of books for Terrance's mom to read to him. In January, Terrance had his speech evaluated by a speech pathologist who noted one area of his speech that needed work, but everything else was off the charts and, cognitively, Terrance is on the money. All because his mother started to read to him.

Today our children need us more than ever. I am outraged, as I hope you will be too, by the unacceptably low level of early childhood reading. The stakes are high. The time to act is now. Together, we can narrow the achievement gap. We can help open the doors to our children's dreams. Propel them to new heights. Put fresh opportunities within their reach.

First children learn to read, and then they read to learn. I believe with all my heart that helping children learn to read better is, quite simply, our moral imperative. And so, I hope you will join with me to make this a personal issue for each and every one of you—one that supplements our vital work in advancing the public good. Our *herstoric* journey begins now.

5. Race and Racism

Johnnetta Betsch Cole's incisive and compelling speeches on race and racism span a nearly forty-year period. Her 1981 lecture "Under the Sun" discusses how racism and sexism were on the rise with the emergence of the New Right. From Ku Klux Klan marches to antibusing legislation, from the murders of Black people to anti-abortion legislation, she goes into extensive detail about the state of race and gender relations in the country at that moment. It is significant that many of the issues she discussed are timeless and unceasing, as we are still confronting them today. Ultimately, she emphasizes the need for activism to counter the fact that "racism and sexism are after all grounded in the political economy of our country."

In her 2008 speech "The Black Community in the New Millennium: Assessing Our Progress and Crafting Our Future," delivered at the Harvard University Black Law Students Association Annual Spring Conference, Cole discussed the most pressing issues facing the Black community at the time, focusing on the themes of work, health, education, housing, the criminal justice system, and Black women. She invoked the names of Charles Ogletree, Lorraine Hansberry, President Barack Obama, and W. E. B. Du Bois, as well as biblical scripture and Old Negro spirituals to offer suggestions for how Black lawyers could help solve the problems facing the Black community.

In her 2013 speech "Service of Remembrance and Celebration for Nelson Rolihlahla Mandela," Cole uses storytelling as a way to share lessons that she had learned from Mandela's life, such as the importance of forgiveness and

FIGURE 5.1 Press conference with Coretta Scott King, circa 1990.
Courtesy Spelman College Archive.

taking action to challenge varied forms of oppression. Two years later, she delivered her speech "A Tribute to the Life and Work of Dr. Martin Luther King Jr."
at Yale University. In this speech she lifts up Dr. King's work and applauds his
impact on the anti-war and anti-poverty movements of the 1960s. She raises the
important question, "What lessons should we learn from the way that Dr. Martin Luther King came to connect the civil rights movement with war and poverty?" Cole also reflects on the Yale roots of the Poor People's Campaign and
highlights the important role of Spelman College and Yale University alumna,
Marian Wright Edelman. She concludes the speech with a classic story that she
often told about the old lady and the bird, which teaches us about the importance
of taking responsibility and ownership over our actions.

Finally, in her 2019 speech to the Congressional Black Caucus, Cole contemplates the history of "The 400th Anniversary of the Arrival of the First Enslaved Africans: A Remembrance." She astutely points out that it was "slavery
that built the foundation of America's economic might." She focuses on the resistance and resilience of enslaved Africans in the United States, shown through
their struggles to gain literacy, hold onto African cultures, and contribute to

what we now call American culture. Nonetheless, Cole also highlights the persistence of racial inequality that continues to plague African Americans, noting in her remarks that Blacks were three times more likely to be killed by police than whites. In her usual style, she calls the names of African American heroes and sheroes like Martin Luther King Jr., Dorothy Height, Rosa Parks, and James Baldwin.

Under the Sun

Lecture, University of Massachusetts Amherst, August 1981

Well, in a fairly short period of time, I wanted to present three points. First, to document that racism and sexism are, in fact, on the rise in our society. Second, I'd like to suggest what seems to be the source or the sources of this intensified assault on Third World folk and on women. And finally, I want to suggest something about what should be done.

Racism and sexism on the rise again. . . . Well, first of all, let me be clear about what I'm talking about. I'm talking about an intensification in racism and sexism, taking a couple of forms. That is, we're going to have, and do have now, more of a denial of access to resources, denial of rights, basic human kinds of rights, because of folks' gender and because of their race. But I'm also talking about the rise in those vicious expressions. Those really, truly barbaric expressions of both racism and sexism. In other words, I'm talking about an increase in the brutal and violent form, and an increase in those forms of racism and sexism, to take off from Roberta Flack's song and that fine, fine film. That form that, in fact, is killing us all softly. It's incredible that a matter of months ago, a nineteen-year-old Black youth was lynched in Mobile, Alabama. I find it incredible that, in 1981, women who choose to control and to make decisions about their own bodies are literally attacked at abortion centers.

I don't think that it's just sort of ordinary, that at a time like this the Ku Klux Klan marches with full support of increasing numbers of people in our country.

A teenager, killed on the football field in Boston, Massachusetts. In Salt Lake City, two Black men were killed as they dared to jog with two white women. In June, two Black teenagers were killed as they went to buy hot dogs in the neighborhood store.

Nineteen eighty-one, we're talking about the full public expression of the most hideous symbol of racism in this country, the Ku Klux Klan. I mean, it's not some kind of obscene nightmare that I'm having. It is the reality that there are cross burnings and the distribution of planned literature in Decatur, Alabama; Middletown, Ohio; Columbus, Georgia; Barnegat, New Jersey; Okolona, Mississippi; Castro Valley, California; Muncie, Indiana; and Hartford, Connecticut. In April of 1980, the Klan wounded four Black women in Chattanooga, Tennessee. Five Communist Party workers, killed by a clan in North Carolina. And, of course, the killers were freed. There are Klan special force youth camps at this moment in San Diego, San Bernardino, and Los Angeles, California.

These youth camps and special forces camps that are openly, the Klan says, dedicated to ridding the world of "Jews and niggers" are also in Peoria; in Chicago, Illinois; in Jeffersonville, Indiana, and Oklahoma City; in Denver and Hillsborough, Colorado; [and] in Birmingham, Tuscumbia, Tuscaloosa, and Decatur, Alabama. And unless, of course, we start to think that this is some isolated expression of far out reactionary racism, remember that a Klansman, Tom Metzger in San Diego, California, received over 32,000 votes to win the Democratic nomination for Congress. Racism, in other words, in its most violent and vicious form, is on the rise again. But there's also an increase in that other form of racism too.

That form that creates, in a sense, the living dead. The Senate of this country has already passed an antibusing amendment. Things, in fact, are worsening for Black folk. One out of every four Black families has an income in this country now under $5,000 a year. Compared with one out of every thirteen white families. The income gap, then, between Blacks and whites has widened since 1977 by 14 percent. Throughout the 1970s, unemployment among Blacks was always twice that of whites. Never lower than 8 percent of the Black population. Always well over 30 percent for Black teenagers.

Today in Detroit, Michigan, there are some areas where Black unemployment overall is 55 percent. And, of course, you don't really need me to tell you that racism ain't good for your health. In this country now, a Black baby is twice as likely to die in the first year of life as a white child. Twice as likely to have a mother with no prenatal care. Twice as likely to have a mother who dies in childbirth. Twice as likely to have no regular source of health care. Twice as likely to be malnourished. And, of course, when the police, disease, unsanitary housing, and unemployment don't do us in, unfortunately I have to tell you that because of the societal ills, Black folk are increasingly taking their own lives.

What of gender inequality, is sexism on the rise? Obviously, is the answer. Both in terms of violent attacks on women, as well as in terms of that more subtle form of denial of access to resources. It's certainly an irony that the great defenders of life, the anti-abortionists, have their own clan-like activities attacking the workers, attacking the clients in the abortion center.

The incidence of rape in our country is phenomenally high, with every indication that it will continue to rise. As in the case with racism, it seems to me that there are many legal forms of sexism that are also on the rise in our country. And, of course, racism inevitably joins with sexism to produce certain realities. Women are at the bottom of the economic ladder. While 52 percent of all Black women work, the median income for Black women is only 94 percent of that of white women, 73 percent of that of Black men, and only 54 percent of that of white men.

The general assault though on women and on children has been brutal and now, finally, with the passage of [President Ronald] Reagan's bills, promises to be unbearable. With full passage of the Reagan budget then, Victor Perlo has suggested that in the years 1981 to 1986, the Reagan budget will save rich individuals $100 billion. It will cost the rest of us $200 billion. It is estimated that Reagan's budget will cut over $496 million in federal support for dependent children. This then, is what Reaganomics means for us.

It's a legal attack. That's what you get when you now have Strom Thurmond— the most hated symbol of southern racism—heading the Senate Judiciary Committee, attempting to turn back all of the civil rights legislation. If we can see these increases in the legal attacks on women and Third World folk, if we can see the increase in the violent attacks against women and Third World folk, then we have to ask the question, where is it coming from? Don't look all around you, look to the right, because that's where it's coming from. A very powerful combination and alliance of the old and the new. An alliance of those rather traditional hate groups, combined with a much more sophisticated and very carefully clothed, legitimate reactionary set of forces. Forces that, in fact, are both in government and in the corporate structure. I want to share with you by reading an analysis that is presented in a pamphlet called *The New Right versus Women's Right*. Because it puts it much more succinctly than I could. It is quite correct to entitle this wave of *reactionaryism* as the New Right. They differ from the old right of twenty-five years ago in that the old right directed itself toward the businessman, promoted isolationism, and was prompted by East Coast money entrance. The New Right appeals to the working class, promotes aggressive international expansionism, and is promoted heavily by new industries. Its leadership, although it borrows heavily from the old right, is primarily young, energetic men, who offer so-called new blood, new strategies, including single issue campaigns. The right-wingers are now quite well organized at the grassroots level. They are well received by many people who have honest fears about their own futures. One weakness that the core of the New Right has yet to overcome, is that they are still battling over exactly who will lead in the future.

The moderate Reaganites control the Republican Party, but it is the extremists that control most of those political action committees. The development that we must be alerted to is, of course, the extent to which big business decides to throw its weight into the camp of the right. If the corporations agree that the extreme right-wing faction is not only capable of taking power, but also best represents money interests, then it is conceivable that the people's victories fought so hard for in the past could be reversed. What we have then is a combination of the old and the new, presented in very sophisticated clothing, with enormous technological backing and with the ability to appeal to the real fears of the North American people. The cutting edge, of course, of this particular movement—although registered as a political lobbyist of the so-called Moral Majority—is Jerry Falwell, who is probably the second most watched human being on North American television next to Johnny Carson.

His basic message is that of right-wing fundamentalism. He in fact tells us that he has a divine mandate to go right into the halls of Congress and fight for those laws that will save America.

The New Right may be crude in its beliefs but it is most sophisticated in its techniques. It plays upon the fourteen million North American people who claim that they are Christians. And perhaps one of the most important things of all for us to understand, is that these fourteen million Americans of every possible Christian denomination, are often Black folk who say that they have been born again. There are 128 million listeners to right-wing religious radio shows. That is the New Right's captive audience. The platform is one of pro-segregated schools, pro-prayer in the schools, pro-born-again Christianity, pro cooperation with South Africa, with the fascists of Germany, and with all right-wing Latin American dictatorships. Wow.

What do you get to be against? Don't worry, you can be anti-abortion, anti-gay, anti-evolutionary theory, anti-women working outside of the home. In short, I'm really arguing that although the New Right is fairly sophisticated in how this stuff is put out there, it really is the same old reactionary goal of racism, sexism, and classism. Now, it is important to understand the relationship I think between the New Right and the new administration. It's a very simple relationship. They're in cahoots. Okay? Reagan, in other words, and a good deal of the Reagan administration is supported by the New Right. We're talking about a president of the United States whose candidacy was endorsed by the Ku Klux Klan.

It seems fairly clear to me that it is only a matter of a short period of time before affirmative action loses whatever federal teeth it had. What I think happens or is happening, is we're finding an alliance of conservative and reactionary forces in the new administration, creating, then, a climate in our country that both permits and encourages both the vicious and the more subtle forms of racism and of sexism.

When we realize the possibility that the Family Protection Act could be passed, then you realize the real danger of the New Right. Let me give you a summary of the Family Protection Act. This legislation claims that it will counteract disruptive federal intervention into family life. That it will encourage restoration of family unity, parental authority, and a climate of traditional morality. You see, I think it's important to understand those claims of the Family Protection Act, because it allows us to sense how exactly the genuine fears of North American people are being played upon. It would certainly establish tax deductions for households where there is an elderly or handicapped family member. It offers incentives for adoption. It then enjoins the government from strengthening laws against child and spouse abuse. It requires the federal clinics to notify parents within twenty-four hours if an unwed minor is issued contraceptives.

It forbids federal funding programs that—are you ready?—inculcate values or modes of behavior that contradict the demonstrated beliefs and values of the community. It also forbids federal funding to those programs that tend to denigrate or diminish traditionally understood role differences between the sexes. Public schools that require teachers to join a union will be eligible for federal funds. It stipulates, and I'm reading by the way now from what I think was a very fantastic article in the *Village Voice*, that discusses this within the context of the general assault on the communities. This new Family Protection Act stipulates that no federal funds may be made available to any public or private individual, group, foundation, commission, corporation, association, or other entity that presents homosexuality, male or female, as an alternative lifestyle. Or that suggests that it can be an acceptable lifestyle. This is what the New Right has in store for us.

I don't think that we can excuse, explain the rise in racism and sexism and the New Right, as somehow the strange machinations of a few crooks. Because racism and sexism are after all grounded in the political economy of our country. Today, just as they have always been used, they are a double-edged sword. One edge brings profits to a small group, a small ruling class, and it does so in large measure by creating dual labor markets. In other words, racism and sexism really do pay. They pay the bosses very well. The other edge, of course, manages to keep both workers and potential workers divided from each other so that they not only compete for the crumbs while a small group devours the entire loaf, but in fact they compete for what few jobs there are, by saying that Black be divided from white, let men be divided from women. So to buttress, then, dual labor markets, segregated housing, inadequate health care, to permit unemployment, lack of day-care centers, etcetera, we get a flourishing ideology about both Third World folk and about women.

In a pamphlet put out by the New Right—which of course has as an objective to destroy the right of women to choose abortions—Dr. Grady tells us that abortion is one of many issues. The whole picture includes drug abuse, alienation of youth, disrespect for authority, religious decline, decay of the family structure, destruction of traditional education, revolution on the campus, racial strife, undermining of law enforcement in the judicial system, increase in homosexuality and perversion, inflation, repudiation of our currency, registration and confiscation of firearms, no win wars, destruction of national pride and prestige, deliberate loss of US military superiority, economic strength, planned and fabricated shortages of fuel and food, leading to rationing and increasing controls of the American people: to fight abortion without understanding and fighting the total conspiracy is to ensure certain and total defeat.

What this passage tells us and what I think we really have to understand, is that the new fascist, racist, sexist reactionary groups, you see, are not simply about putting gays and Black folk and Jews and women in their place. In fact, it really is about a kind of society, and a kind of power. It is about who will control. Jerry Falwell, the most important individual in the New Right's direct mail campaign business, puts it quite simply. He says, "The goal of the New Right is about coming to power in America." Now, let me try to say in a very few moments what I think has to be something about our response. First of all, it seems to me that there has been, in fact, a substantial response both on the part of women and Third World people to the increase in sexism and racism.

The Stevie Wonder rally in Washington, DC, is only a national representation of what I'm talking about. What happened in Springfield, Massachusetts, when I know a number of young women that I work with as students, went to make sure that that pro-life amendment didn't get inserted into the Massachusetts constitution. That is what I call organized resistance by women, and by

Third World folk. And, of course, there are massive demonstrations going on all over this country in response to the cutbacks that the Reagan budget brings. I think that resistance has to remain very, very clear in our own minds. Because once we let it out, then assuming that there is none, we also assume that we have no responsibility to create some.

The problem though, of course, is that in fighting the New Right, what we really say, if my comments are correct, if my evidence is clear, is that we're fighting more now than the right. That the right has been legitimized and that it comes now in the form of very vicious and open expressions of racism, and sexism, of homophobia. And that it continues, of course, in those forms that have always killed us often. I think that there is a very concrete response that the academy has to make to this kind of an increase. Inevitably, of course, when it comes to that part of the talk where you say, "What is to be done?" it seems to me, first of all, that the academy has a responsibility to present more of an analysis, in fact of what racism and sexism are, or where they come from. Seems clear to me that we can't even begin to talk about eliminating something until we know its source.

I will also suggest that in addition to our responsibility to make the issues of racism and sexism an integral part of our curriculum, we've got to increasingly put the two together. As some folk know because you're sitting in that class this semester, we tried to do a course on race and gender in the anthropology department. I cannot stress enough that I think it is essential that we demand that the issues of racism and sexism be looked at simultaneously. Because when we do that, it in fact forces a sharp, critical, and, in my opinion, a correct analysis that in fact is much more difficult to come to the head when we isolate one from the other.

If there's a problem, you should talk about it. You should have a course about it. And, best of all, I've even gotten really radical and said you should have a course that talks about two problems. I don't want to belittle that though. I don't want to belittle it because I think both in terms of the kind of work that I hope to do over the coming years and the responsibility that we all have, that we can't remain somehow within the comforts of women's studies and the stepping program, and Afro-American studies, that we really do have the responsibility to raise these issues in the broadest curriculum. But I also want to suggest that there's always a place for activism. There's always a place for activism, which hopefully is based on an understanding of the sources of both racism and sexism. And, in terms of my comments this afternoon, that will also help us to understand the relationship between those and the rise of the New Right. I think activism takes all sorts of forms. It certainly takes the form of folks in the streets marching.

But I think around the issues of racism and sexism, it also takes the form of you raising your hand in a classroom and calling it because that's what it was. I think it takes the form of approaching professors and classmates too and discussing the expressions of those things. I think it takes the form of phone calls and telegrams and committees. But I also think it takes the form of an absolute commitment to struggle against the issues of racism and sexism. Because it is that commitment that I think, first of all, will begin to break down some of the barriers that now exist between those who say they have a primary commitment to struggling against racism, and those who say they have a primary commitment to struggling against sexism. If there is one thing which the New Right shows us, which is very definitively in our interests, it is that they see a relationship between racism and sexism. That they hook them up. And if we, therefore, can only come to understand not only that distorted sense, in which they see abortion and desegregation of schools is all leading to the ultimate demise of this country.

But it is our responsibility to, in fact, understand the genuine sense in which they have an economic base that is fed by a given ideology. And unless dealt with will, of course, be bad news for us all.

The Black Community in the New Millennium

ASSESSING OUR PROGRESS AND
CRAFTING OUR FUTURE

Harvard Black Law Students Association's Twenty-Fifth Annual Spring Conference, Boston, MA, February 23, 2008

My Sisters and Brothers All: Good evening! And what a special evening it is for me. It is special because you have given me the opportunity to address you, a group of women and men who are—to use our shero Lorraine Hansberry's words—"young, gifted, and Black." Old folks in Jacksonville, Florida, would say, "Looking out at this room full of promise, y'all be a sight for sore eyes."

Using an expression that is associated with your generation, I want to give a "shout out" to brother Professor Charles Ogletree. Years and years from now when the history and herstory of this era in American life is told, there will be many pages about the work of Charles Ogletree, a scholar-activist closely associated with one of the most prestigious universities in the world who never forgot who he is and whose he is! Thank you, Brother Tree, for all that you continue to do in the interest of social justice.

The three sister cochairs for this spring conference—Adora Asonye, Sarah Belton, and Calida Motley—asked me to discuss what I see as the most pressing issues facing our Black community and to identify the mechanisms I think will help to solve or alleviate these pressing problems. And the sister cochairs asked that I offer some thoughts on the role that lawyers and legal workers might play in addressing these issues.

My Sisters and Brothers All, let me begin by saying this: If you really understand the brutality of slavery, the relentless barbarism of the Jim Crow era, the persistent way that racism, sexism, and classism continue to attack our people, then the fact that we are here is a mighty victory. Yes, it is a victory, to borrow Dr. Maya Angelou's words—"and still we rise!"

How might we summarize the present condition of Black America? Let me suggest that our story is a tale of two realities. There are some Black folks, who, to use an old expression, are living high on the hog. The lifestyles of these sisters and brothers are a barometer of how far some of our folks have come from the days when our foremothers and forefathers captured their sorrow in song and looked to a place called heaven for relief from their suffering on earth. "Nobody knows the trouble I've seen; nobody knows but Jesus."

Of course, a truly stunning indication of how far we have come is that today, an African American man, a graduate of this very law school is *the* Democratic Party's leading candidate for the presidency of the United States of America. What must be called a movement as much as a campaign is spreading one of the most precious and powerful emotions that any people can experience. It is called *hope*. Hope for a better day. And among all of the positive aspects of "the Obama movement" is that he has ignited the interest of young people. Young people of every race, gender, sexual orientation, religion, class, and physical ability and disability are inspired to believe in the electoral process and they are ready to "sign up" to help to change America.

I must be a truth teller about the state of Black America, knowing that, as our great sister poet Gwendolyn Brooks once said: "Truth tellers are not always palatable. There is a preference for candy bars" [Brooks 1988].

At the same time that there is a small group of African Americans who are doing well economically, the masses of Black folk are still struggling to make a way out of no way. I am talking about the number of our people here in the richest country in the world who are living below the poverty line. In 2006, 24.3 percent of African Americans lived below that wretched line. Many of the children living in poverty in America are the children of African American families headed by single women.

And then there are Black families who thought they finally had a piece of the pie who are having it snatched away and gobbled up in the jaws of a subprime lending beast preying on our folk.

Let us take a quick look at the state of most Black Americans in the major arenas of life.

Work. Work is not only a necessity for making a living, but also an important source of pride and dignity. When we ask who is working and who is not working in America, it is still the case that Black folks are twice as unemployed as white folks.

Health. Life expectancy for Black folks continues to be less than white folks. And when we look at health disparities between the two people, our folks are far more subject to hypertension, diabetes, obesity, and all the other diseases and ailments that lead to early deaths.

And what about the modern plague called AIDS? We African Americans are about 13 percent of the US population but we account for almost half (49 percent) of the people in the United States who have HIV and AIDS.

Housing. While some Black folks live in gated communities with manicured lawns and more rooms than you "can shake a stick at," poor Black folks remain concentrated in inner-city housing where privacy is limited, basic services like decent grocery stores do not exist, and overall conditions are conducive to the despicable behavior of drug dealers and pimps and the level of desperation that leads women into prostitution.

Education. As the good Dr. W. E. B. Du Bois said many years ago, the freedom to learn is a fundamental right. Yet too many Black young folks are denied access to this right. As Professor Linda Darling-Hammond says: "many students in the United States, especially low-income students and students of color do not receive even the minimum education needed to become literate and join the labor market" [Darling-Hammond 2014].

In the 1960s, when the first desegregation plans were crafted, public school enrollment was still about 80 percent white. At that time, desegregation meant bringing Black students into formerly all-white schools. Today, fewer than three out of every five public school students are white.

As you know there is a growing gap between where Black and Brown students are and where white students are in terms of academic achievement and graduation rates. When we look at the huge discrepancy between the allocations to schools in predominantly white suburbs and those in the inner city where poor Black folks live, we see that it is not because our children cannot learn. It is because the conditions for allowing them to learn do not exist.

A word about higher education institutions. As you know, while the overall percentage of Black folks attending a college or university has increased over time, there are deeply disturbing trends such as the number of college-age Black men who are not in university dormitories but are locked away in America's jails and prisons. As of June 2006, 4.8 percent of Black men were in jail or prison compared with 0.7 percent of white men.

Just a word about our historically Black colleges and universities (HBCUs). While the 103 public and private HBCUs are only 3 percent of American colleges and universities, they account for a quarter of all Black college graduates.

There are many facts about these institutions that are worth referencing. Let me offer just two. Three-quarters of all Black folks with a PhD did their undergraduate work at an HBCU. The reason it is common parlance to say that these institutions do so much with so little is that when you combine the endowments of all 103 of our Black colleges and universities, you get close to $2 billion. And here, at just one university called Harvard, the endowment is $35 billion and rising.

The criminal justice system. When will this nation of ours wake up to the reality that there are gross inequities in how Black and Brown vs. white folks are treated by the criminal justice system. At this very moment, one in four Black men are in some way entangled in the criminal justice system. And it is Black women who are the fastest growing group who are being incarcerated.

Black women. What can be said about the condition of Black women in America? The first thing that must be said is that in America, race matters . . . but gender matters, too. Of course, there are some African American sisters who are doing well in various fields, but those few must be contrasted with the large numbers of Black women who are trapped in poverty that is not always but is often associated with being single parents. And don't let anyone tell you that violence against women is a white folks thing. Indeed, Black women experience violence at higher rates than white women, and Black girls are mandated to juvenile detention at higher rates than white girls and Latinas.

And don't let anyone tell you that calling us Black women out of our names is simply an expression of free speech when gangsta rappers do it but it's reprehensible when others do it. Coming out of anybody's mouth, the offensive language, glorification of violence, and profound misogyny of gangsta rap is an affront to the humanity of every woman and every man as well.

A few words about political representation: there is no story that is as exciting and hopeful in terms of where we are politically as what is going on with the brother senator from Illinois, Barack Obama. Whispers of "can the brother possibly make it to the White House" have been quieted by the shouts of joy as he addresses important issues, delivers inspiring messages, and tallies up votes and delegates. Whether you are for Clinton or Obama or McCain, this is clear:

you have got to feel mighty proud to see one of "our own" leading a movement that dares to suggest that if the American people want change, then we are the ones we have been waiting for.

With no intention of detracting from the extraordinary significance of the movement that brother Senator Obama is leading, we need to remember that it will take more than one African American presidential candidate or president to wipe away the widespread ways in which in our political system we are still underrepresented. There is so much work to be done to get legislative and judicial branches of federal and state government to pass and enforce laws that would provide Black citizens with the opportunities that white citizens have.

I have given quite a litany of some of what is ailing Black America. And I have shared some revealing data from the Pew survey. Now I had better exercise the Noah principle. *The Noah principle?* Years ago, after I gave a speech that offered a litany of what was not right in our communities, in the Q&A, a brother raised his hand and said: "my sister I heard you but you need to start practicing the Noah principle." I responded that I grew up in an AME church in Jacksonville, Florida, and I certainly knew about Noah, but what, I asked, is the Noah principle? The brother said, "The Noah principle is that there will be no more credit for predicting the rain, it's time to build the ark!"

There are activists and advocates all across America who are working on particular planks that will help to build "the ark." But rather than focusing on those projects and actions, I want to turn the spotlight on you, my sisters and brothers, acknowledging that you are in a unique position to be change agents; and I want to lift up what each of you has a responsibility to do.

Please do not think that I am going to badger you to work for little, to sacrifice material comforts, and take a vow of poverty in the name of our struggling sisters and brothers. You see, I believe that it is possible to do good and do well at the same time.

With your Harvard law degrees, you will be in positions to have a substantial impact in government, in corporate headquarters, and in the not-for-profit world. Because you will have a Harvard law degree, you will have access to places of power where you can make a good living yourself *and* you can develop policies and practices that will help African American communities, and indeed the "larger" community, to live a better life.

I must lift up the charge that W. E. B. Du Bois made when he said that those of us who are the talented tenth among Black Americans have the responsibility to be of assistance to the rest of our people.

My shero, the great educator, Dr. Mary McLeod Bethune said that folks like you, dear sisters and brothers here in Harvard's law school, folks like you should go on and climb to the top. But, she said, "you must lift others as you climb!"

If the words of Du Bois and McLeod do not move you, then be guided by these words from the Bible: in the book of Luke, chapter 12, verse 48, it says: "From everyone to whom much has been given, much will be required." The next verse doesn't get quoted as much. But here is what it says: "and from the one to whom much has been entrusted, even more will be demanded."

So, my sisters and brothers, go on and have a lucrative law practice. But you can also provide free legal counsel through a community-based program. My sisters, you can use your law school training in or outside of a law practice, but you also can offer legal assistance to women in a shelter who are the victims of domestic violence; and you can surely provide sisterly compassion and comfort to women in a rape crisis center.

My Sisters and Brothers All: no one expects you to fix all that is broken in our public schools, but you can surely become a buddy and a mentor to at least one African American girl or boy. And if you do so, you may well turn that girl or boy away from failing and toward excelling in school because you are tutoring that youngster in math; or taking your young mentee to a science museum; or, most of all, because your words and actions show that you care.

Here at Harvard, you are being prepared to be leaders. I remind you that at the core of leadership is service to others. Dr. Martin Luther King Jr. put it this way: "Everybody can be great because anybody can serve. You don't have to have a college degree to serve. You don't have to make your subject and your verb agree to serve. You don't have to know about Plato and Aristotle to serve. You don't have to know Einstein's theory of relativity to serve. You don't have to know the second theory of thermodynamics in physics to serve. You only need a heart full of grace. A soul motivated by love."*

And so, My Sisters and Brothers All: I know you will do well. I beg you to also do good. Our people are counting on you.

* This quote is from Dr. King's sermon "The Drum Major Instinct," delivered on February 4, 1968, at Ebenezer Baptist Church in Atlanta, GA.

Service of Remembrance and Celebration
for Nelson Rolihlahla Mandela

St. John's Church, Catholic Diocese of Washington, DC, December 15, 2013

Bishop Mariann, other members of the clergy, My Sisters and Brothers All: It is an honor and a joy to participate in this service of remembrance and celebration for President Nelson Mandela, one of the greatest leaders of all times, a Xhosa man of South Africa whose determined struggle against the horrific system of apartheid left an indelible mark on the worldwide struggle against racism and all forms of inequality, an extraordinary human being whose profound humanity was something to behold.

Since President Mandela went to glory, I have been recounting the story of the one and only time that I was privileged to be with Madiba. Across the continent of Africa, a good story, a story that has an important lesson, can be and indeed is told again and again. So, once again, here is my story.

During the time that I was serving as the president of Spelman College, Nelson Mandela was invited to Atlanta, Georgia. Among the events during that visit of Nelson and Winnie Mandela was a ceremony in the Martin Luther King Chapel at Morehouse College. During that ceremony, Mr. Mandela was to receive honorary degrees from the historically Black colleges and universities in the United Negro College Fund.

I was given the responsibility to figure out how in the world we were going to do this. For surely, we did not expect Mr. Mandela to stand still while we placed forty-one hoods on him.

The decision was made to make a quilt with the emblems of each of the colleges and universities. On July 5, 1990, in a profoundly moving ceremony we celebrated Madiba's release from prison and his continuing efforts for freedom and democracy in South Africa.

As I presented the quilt to Nelson Mandela, I referenced the fact that during the period of enslavement in the United States, quilts made by Black women provided warmth from the chill of the night, and they offered a few hours of comfort before sunrise when men, women, and children would begin another day of brutal and unpaid labor.

At the end of the ceremony, as Nelson and Winnie Mandela were about to leave, I said to Mr. Mandela that we would send the quilt to him in South Africa. He quickly responded that that would not be necessary because he and Winnie Mandela would take the quilt with them.

A few years after that very special ceremony, I visited the Mandela home in Soweto, a place visited by people from all over the world. Imagine how I felt when I saw in that home the quilt we had presented to Nelson Mandela.

While this is my treasured story, it speaks to connections between the struggle in South Africa against apartheid and the struggle in the United States against legal segregation and now the struggle that we continue to wage against racism.

During the anti-apartheid struggle there was a saying: "We can't free Johannesburg until you free Mississippi, and we can't free Mississippi until we free Johannesburg."

What will be the lasting impact of President Mandela in our country and around the world? Madiba personifies attributes and actions that are truly admirable and that may seem to be beyond the reach of us ordinary folks.

Ah, but I truly believe that what Nelson Mandela's life and work really says to us is that he managed to do what each of us is capable of doing.

Each of us can "keep the faith" and carry on through circumstances that seem totally unbearable. For as Madiba once said: "The greatest glory in living lies not in never falling but in rising every time we fall."

Each of us has the capacity to forgive. When we think of how Nelson Mandela walked out of prison, put aside what must have been bitterness and hatred, and went on to lead a process of reconciliation in South Africa, we wonder if we could have done that. The truth is that each of us has the capacity to forgive and to reconcile with our enemies. For as Madiba said: "Forgiveness liberates the soul. It removes fear. That is why it is such a powerful weapon."

Each of us can do something, day after day in the interest of challenging racism, sexism, heterosexism, and all of the other isms that haunt our world.

Madiba once said this: "No one is born hating another person because of the colour of his skin, or his background, or his religion. People must learn to hate, and if they can learn to hate, they can be taught to love, for love comes more naturally to the human heart than its opposite."

And each of us can remain in the struggle against all other forms of injustice. Nelson Mandela never ceased to be engaged in those struggles. Let us remember Madiba's words: "It always seems impossible until it is done."*

I close now by joining with each of you in asking God to give us the wisdom and the determination to do in our own way—no matter how small that might be—to do in our own way what his servant, Nelson Mandela, did so effectively and with such amazing grace.

* While this quote is almost universally attributed to Mandela, there is no actual record of his saying it.

A Tribute to the Life and Work of Dr. Martin Luther King Jr.

"No Work Is Insignificant: Moving Forward through Service,

Scholarship, and Solidarity," conference at Yale University,

New Haven, CT, January 18, 2015

My Sisters and Brothers All: Good evening! And a special greeting to the Martin Luther King Committee and the Afro-American Cultural Center here at Yale. I want to acknowledge the important work that you do that reflects the philosophy and the action of Dr. Martin Luther King Jr., the man Nina Simone called the Dark Prince of Peace.

I also want to express my gratitude for the invitation to speak with you about the extraordinary life and legacy of the Rev. Dr. King, a disciple of Gandhi, who was not only a mighty force in the transformation of America, but whose short yet purpose-driven life inspired movements around the world for peace with justice.

On the eve of Martin Luther King Day, and with the recent release of the movie, *Selma*, this is a very special time for us to think about and discuss the breadth and depth of what Dr. King was engaged in and accomplished in the all-too-few years that he lived.

Dr. King visited your campus several times during his brief life, and thus there will always be ties that bind this great university to who the great drum major for justice was and what he stood for.

I also feel a special tie to Dr. King even though I never had the privilege of meeting him. However, I was an active participant in the civil rights and anti-war movements of the 1960s.

And I will always be grateful for the honor and the joy of knowing Coretta Scott King, an amazing and grace-filled woman whose contributions to the struggle for ending all systems of inequality remain underappreciated.

Most Americans, as well as people around the world, are well versed in Dr. King's lifelong work as a civil rights leader who valiantly engaged in and indeed was a leader for racial equality in our nation. Indeed, he was truly an iconic figure who helped alter the course of our nation's history. And while Dr. King's contributions to the civil rights movement are enormous and cannot be understated, this evening I want to focus on Dr. King's life and legacy in relation to his work and impact on the anti-war and anti-poverty movements of the 1960s—and to ask what lessons might be learned with respect to the current state of our nation and our world.

Dr. King's positions on the war in Vietnam and the struggle to eradicate poverty evolved over time as he came to see links between the civil rights struggle, poverty, and a protracted war. Later in his life he argued that the struggles for an end to racism, poverty, and war were inexorably linked and had to be addressed concurrently. However, many in and outside of the civil rights movement criticized Dr. King for his position.

I firmly believe that were he able to speak with us right here, right now, Dr. King would say that of course we have made substantial progress since the days of legal segregation. And were he alive today, I believe that he would applaud the progress that has been made in struggles that he did not address during his lifetime: the struggle for the rights of women, for the rights of lesbians, gay, bisexual, and transgender people. And he would certainly stand in solid opposition to all forms of discrimination based on religion, nationality, age, and on physical and mental ability.

But I think Dr. King would also speak up and speak out against the ways in which poverty, as well as our long, costly, and many would argue unnecessary wars are still sapping our ability to realize his dream, which in reality is the unrealized American dream.

In his commencement speech at my alma mater, Oberlin College, in June 1965, Dr. King said this:

> Anyone who feels that the problems of mankind can be solved through violence is sleeping through a revolution. I said this over and over again, and I believe it more than ever today. We know about violence. It's been

the inseparable twin of Western materialism, the hallmark of its grandeur. I am convinced that violence ends up creating many more social problems than it solves. In international relations, we must come to see this. We must find some alternative to war and bloodshed. It is no longer a choice between violence and non-violence. It is either non-violence or nonexistence. It is not enough to say we must not wage war. We must love peace and sacrifice for it. We must fix our vision not merely on the negative expulsion of war, but upon the positive affirmation of peace.

Dr. King's insight into the connections and interdependence of racism, poverty, and militarism ring as true today as they did fifty years ago. In 1967, the poverty rate in our country was 22 to 23 percent. While the War on Poverty initially did have some tangible results, from 1973 to 2013 the poverty rate has remained statistically unchanged at roughly 15 percent. The war in Vietnam cost the United States $140 billion, worth around $950 billion in 2015 dollars. The Iraq War has cost the United States over $2 trillion and could end up costing $6 trillion.

When Dr. King spoke out against the Vietnam War, many in our country still supported the conflict and even those who did not urged him to focus solely on the civil rights movement. He was widely criticized for his position.

While US involvement in the Vietnam War had been steadily increasing from the early 1960s, there were three facts that encouraged Dr. King to delay in speaking out against that war. The first is that he was trying to develop a good working relationship with President Lyndon Johnson in the interest of passing the civil rights bill. He no doubt thought that criticizing President Johnson's Vietnam policy could adversely affect upcoming civil rights and voting rights legislation that he had fought so long and hard to achieve.

Second, there was push back from within the civil rights community in response to Dr. King's efforts to address America's increasing involvement in a war in Southeast Asia. Many civil rights leaders felt that discussing that conflict would take attention away from the civil rights movement. And many also felt that the two movements were separate movements and should not be conflated.

A third reason that Dr. King delayed in addressing the Vietnam War is that his opposition to the war evolved over time. He began by making a connection between the war, racism, and poverty; and then, over time, he reached a point where he could no longer remain silent on the Vietnam War.

While Dr. King had discussed the topic in private, his first public statement on the war in Vietnam was made in 1965 at an event at Howard University.

In that speech he called for a negotiated settlement to the war as he argued that US involvement in Vietnam had "accomplished nothing." It was during that same period that Dr. King spoke out strongly about what he saw as a connection between military spending abroad and a lack of domestic spending on programs to address poverty and equal opportunity for all Americans.

While testifying before a congressional subcommittee on budget priorities in 1966, Dr. King called for a "rebalancing" of America's fiscal priorities away from spending on a war in Southeast Asia and toward programs designed to reduce poverty in the United States, and one day to actually end it in the richest nation in the world.

In February 1967, in Chicago, Martin Luther King Jr. led an anti-war march for the first time. Listen to these words that Dr. King spoke at that march: "The bombs in Vietnam explode at home—they destroy the dream and possibility for a decent America" [King 1967a]. With those few words, he directly and forcibly connected war, poverty, and racism.

It was a month later, in April 1967, that Dr. King gave a speech in which he clearly articulated his objection to the Vietnam War, and he also made a clear case for the connection between racism, poverty, and the war. Dr. King entitled that speech "Beyond Vietnam: A Time to Break the Silence" [King 1967e].

That extraordinarily important speech was given at the Riverside Church in New York City. That ever so important speech was drafted in large part by theologian and civil rights activist Dr. Vincent Harding. Here is a passage from that speech.

> Over the past two years, as I have moved to break the betrayal of my own silences and to speak from the burnings of my own heart, as I have called for radical departures from the destruction of Vietnam, many persons have questioned me about the wisdom of my path. At the heart of their concerns this query has often loomed large and loud: Why are you speaking about the war, Dr. King? Why are you joining the voices of dissent? Peace and civil rights don't mix, they say. Aren't you hurting the cause of your people, they ask? And when I hear them, though I often understand the source of their concern, I am nevertheless greatly saddened, for such questions mean that the inquirers have not really known me, my commitment or my calling. Indeed, their questions suggest that they do not know the world in which they live.

Dr. King would go on to explain his reasoning for making the connection between the war in Vietnam and the struggles at home as budgets and a lack of political will took their toll on domestic programs for the poor:

There is at the outset a very obvious and almost facile connection between the war in Vietnam and the struggle, I and others, have been waging in America. A few years ago there was a shining moment in that struggle. It seemed as if there was a real promise of hope for the poor— both Black and white—through the Poverty Program. Then came the build-up in Vietnam, and I watched the program broken and eviscerated as if it were some idle political plaything of a society gone mad on war, and I knew that America would never invest the necessary funds or energies in rehabilitation of its poor so long as Vietnam continued to draw men and skills and money like some demonic, destructive suction tube. So, I was increasingly compelled to see the war as an enemy of the poor and to attack it as such.

This speech was widely criticized, by politicians, people within the civil rights movement, and the press. The *Washington Post* said the speech "diminished his usefulness to his cause, his country, his people." The NAACP, failing to see the links that Dr. King had outlined so eloquently, stated that it was improper for him to link the civil rights struggle to opposition to the war. President Johnson disinvited Dr. King to the White House and effectively severed their relationship.

Later in the month of April 1967, Dr. King participated in an anti-war march from Central Park to the United Nations that drew ten thousand people. He was joined by Harry Belafonte and the renowned pediatrician and activist Dr. Benjamin Spock. As you no doubt know, Dr. Spock was a New Haven native and a Yale graduate. Dr. King would continue his activism with Dr. Spock as the two worked on "Vietnam Summer," a project geared toward impacting the upcoming 1968 elections through peace activism.

Concurrent with Dr. King's increasing outspokenness to the war in Vietnam, he began to speak more forcefully and frequently about the need for a "new phase" in the civil rights movement to address the economic plight of poor Americans. While the civil rights movement had won the desegregation of public accommodations and broad new voting rights for Black citizens, Dr. King argued that these victories had not addressed the central and underlying problem of systemic and widespread poverty. Martin Luther King Jr. was certainly not naive about this matter. Indeed, he knew that attacking poverty would be a much more difficult struggle than earlier civil rights campaigns had been.

In June 1967, in a speech at Victory Baptist Church in Los Angeles, Dr. King said, "We aren't merely struggling to integrate a lunch counter now. We're struggling to get some money to be able to buy a hamburger or a steak when we get to the counter. It didn't cost the nation one penny to integrate lunch counters. It didn't cost the nation one penny to guarantee the right to vote. The problems that we are facing today will cost the nation billions of dollars" [King 1967b].

While this new strategy was designed to address poverty in the Black community, it was multiracial in its approach and reached out to Latino, Native American, and poor white communities. Once again, Dr. King's broad, multi-faceted approach to addressing civil rights was met with resistance, with many of the movement's leaders calling his focus on economic justice too ambiguous with unattainable demands and goals. Dr. King was undeterred.

The genesis of the Poor People's Campaign that Dr. King and the Southern Christian Leadership Conference started had strong Yale roots. Marian Wright Edelman, a Spelman College and Yale Law School alumna who was working as a young lawyer for the NAACP in Mississippi, was called upon to give Robert Kennedy a tour of poor, rural Mississippi. Appalled by what he saw in terms of conditions of the poor, Senator Kennedy urged her to talk to Dr. King about the possibility of bringing to the nation's capital a protest against the conditions of poor people. Marian Wright Edelman suggested the idea of the Poor People's Campaign to Dr. King. The goal was to assemble "a multiracial army of the poor" that would march on Washington to engage in nonviolent civil disobedience at the Capitol until Congress created an "economic bill of rights" for poor Americans.

In early 1968, Rev. Dr. Martin Luther King Jr. and other civil rights leaders made plans for a Poor People's Campaign in Washington. They planned to demand that President Lyndon Johnson and Congress help the poor to get jobs, health care, and decent homes. But weeks before the march was to take place, Dr. King was assassinated. Coretta Scott King and a cadre of Black ministers, including Rev. Ralph Abernathy and Rev. Jesse Jackson, decided they would pick up where Dr. King had left off, and the Poor People's march would go on. And indeed, that march took place on May 12, 1968. As many as fifty thousand people ended up marching; and Resurrection City was erected at the foot of the Lincoln Memorial.

Participants in the Poor People's march and campaign who were still traumatized by the assassination of Dr. King were traumatized again when Robert Kennedy was killed. The demonstrators were discouraged and disheartened, and many declared the Poor People's march a failure. But many others held on to the position that the march and the ensuing weeks brought before the American people the plight of the poor in the richest nation in the world. Rev. Joseph Lowery, who cofounded the Southern Christian Leadership Conference with Dr. King, captured the relationship between the civil rights movement and the Poor People's Campaign with these words: "It's one thing to have the right to check into the Hiltons and the Marriotts, it's another thing to have the means to check out."

In a blog posted on January 16, 2015, Max Ehrenfreund [2015] posed this question: "What if Martin Luther King, Jr. hadn't been killed?" He then repeated a point made by the African American journalist Eugene Robinson, who noted that toward the end of his life Dr. King was talking as much about class and the economy as about race. Robinson offered the following words by Dr. King as evidence for his point: "Now our struggle is for genuine equality, which means economic equality. For we know that it isn't enough to integrate lunch counters. What does it profit a man to be able to eat at an integrated lunch counter if he doesn't earn enough money to buy a hamburger and a cup of coffee?"

Max Ehrenfreund went on to say this:

Blacks and whites eat at the same establishments these days, but in other ways, King's warning has proven accurate. Persistent economic inequality has arguably undermined some of the most important achievements of the civil rights movement. Legally, our schools are integrated, but in practice, research suggests they're becoming more segregated. White and Black children in kindergarten and younger are much more likely to be separated from each other than whites and Blacks in the population at large, which is largely because Black families still can't afford to live in the neighborhoods with the best schools.

And why segregation between neighborhoods has been steadily decreasing, there are still many places like Ferguson, Mo. where the economic ramifications of decades of racially biased business practices and government policies keep low-income Blacks from finding a way out.

It's often said on Martin Luther King Day that the civil rights movement still has unfinished business, but somehow, the events of the past year seem to have made that fact especially clear.

It is time now to ask the inevitable question. Namely, what lessons should we learn from the way that Dr. Martin Luther King came to connect the civil rights movement with war and poverty?

First, we must surely learn and relearn the responsibility each of us has to speak the truth as we see it. It is so easy to remain silent about complex and unpopular issues. I think about how complex is the matter of police actions that take the lives of young Black men. I think about how important it is to speak up about this matter but to not let the plight of Black women go unnoticed.

Hear Dr. King's words: "The ultimate measure of a man [and let us also say a woman] is not where he stands in moments of comfort and convenience, but where he stands at times of challenge and controversy" [King 1963b].

A second lesson we learn from Dr. King's position on the civil rights movement, war, and poverty is that various struggles are in fact tied together. How clearly he made that point in a passage written from a Birmingham jail: "Injustice anywhere is a threat to justice everywhere. We are caught in an inescapable network of mutuality, tied in a single garment of destiny. Whatever affects one directly, affects all indirectly" [King 1963a].

Third and finally, from all that Dr. King said and did about the connections between the civil rights movement, war, and poverty, we must learn the importance, indeed the necessity for us to continue to struggle for peace, with justice. Dr. King's charge back in the 1960s remains a clarion call today: He said: "If you can't fly then run. If you can't run then walk, if you can't walk then crawl, but whatever you do you have to keep moving forward."

Yes, the struggle for peace with justice and equality for all must move forward! I want to end this talk by telling a story that clearly says who is responsible for continuing this struggle. It is a story that was a favorite of the great civil rights leader, Fannie Lou Hamer. She loved to tell this story as a way to emphasize who is responsible for doing the work that had to be done. Listen carefully to the last line, for it will say who is responsible for continuing the struggle for peace with equality and justice for all.

One day some boys decided to play hooky from school. As they set out to find a little trouble to engage in, they came across a bird, and proceeded to mess with that bird. Bored with doing that, they looked around for something else to do. The ringleader said, "I have an idea. Let's go up the road to where that old lady lives and I will ask her a question that she will not be able to answer." One of the boys said to the leader: "What's the question?" The leader responded: "I am going to put this bird behind my back, and I will ask the old lady if the bird is dead or alive. If she answers that the bird is dead, I will release my hands and the bird will fly away. But if she says the bird is alive, I will crush it."

Convinced that the old lady would never be able answer the question correctly, the boys did their high fives, their bumps, and then they headed out to find the old lady. When they found her, the ringleader said in a disrespectful tone: "Yo, old lady, are you going to answer my question?" With the warmth and humanity that characterizes so many of our elders, the old lady said: "Why my son, I will try." The ringleader, confident that the old lady would never be able to give the correct answer, posed his question: "This bird that I have behind my back, is it dead or alive?" The old lady took her time in pondering the question until, with confidence that what she would say was true, she responded: "The bird, why it's in your hands."

My Sisters and Brothers All: that is also the answer to the question, "Who is responsible for continuing the struggle that Dr. Martin Luther King so valiantly led for peace with justice and equality for all?" It's in your hands! And in mine!

The 400th Anniversary of the Arrival of the First Enslaved Africans

A REMEMBRANCE

Congressional Black Caucus, Washington, DC, September 10, 2019

Here in Emancipation Hall, a sacred place, it is a privilege for me to address members of the Congress of the United States and special guests. We are here to commemorate a particular date, an event in the history of all Americans.

It was in August of 1619 that some twenty negroes landed in Virginia. This date is indelibly associated with the beginning of the four-hundred-year trans-atlantic slave trade. For centuries, African women, men, and children were kidnapped, placed in shackles, and marched onto ships that waited to take this human cargo across the Atlantic Ocean. One African writer wrote this of such crossings: "The shrieks of the women and the grounds of the dying rendered the whole scene almost inconceivable" [Equiano 1789].

The African women, men, and children who managed to survive the horrific conditions on slave ships were offloaded and placed on auction blocks, where they were sold to the highest bidder. Thus, they began a life of enslavement, working on plantations wherein overseers with an overseer's whip across a Black man's back asked that he picked more cotton and a faster rate. And that the right of a slave owner included that women work alongside men, cook, clean, and serve as nannies to his children. And that women do what he said they must do. In the darkness of night. Slavery was a tremendous economic boom for America. Indeed, it was slavery that built the foundation of America's economic might.

Let us not forget that so much else happened during enslavement. So much else happened that speaks to the capacity of a people to make a way out of no way. It is the resistance to enslavement and the resilience of an enslaved people that we must recognize and honor on this occasion. For example, it was illegal for a slave to read and write, but many found a way to acquire those skills. Some, like Frederick Douglass, used their literacy in the interest of others. Enslaved people were forbidden to speak their native languages. They weren't allowed to practice their religions and play the music of their native lands. And yet, they found a way. A way to hold onto much of their African culture. To blend it with patterns, ideas, and practices they encountered. Thus was born much of the flavor and substance in the music, dance, food, and style that is known throughout the world as uniquely American.

The day finally came when enslavement was morally impoverished *and* morally abolished. Not without the help of white abolitionists such as Elizabeth Chandler. However, the struggles of African American people were far from over. Our hearts and our bodies were broken again as the promises of reconstruction gave way to a period of terror that involved the lynching of 4,743 Black people between 1882 and 1968. We endured church bombings, harassment, police beatings, and animal attacks. Like the brutalities inflicted on so many in the civil rights movement, including honorable Congressman John Lewis and others, who marched across the Pettus bridge in 1965. There were major victories, with the passing of the Voting Rights Act of 1964 and the Civil Rights Act of 1965, and yet African Americans are still second-class citizens.

Black Americans are three times as likely as white Americans to be killed by police. Even though they are twice as likely to be unarmed. Black men are more than six times as likely as white men to be incarcerated in our nation's state and federal prisons and the incarceration rate of Black women is twice that. Today, Black American families earned just $57 and $0.30 to every $100 in income earned by white families. For many health conditions, Black Americans bear a disproportionate burden. And the resegregation of schools in our country is happening at an alarming rate. Why are there such stark differences in the life experiences of Black and white Americans? The answer is found in how enslavement and the use of racial discrimination that followed have affected each and every institution in our nation.

And yet, our resilience and our patriotism lead us African Americans—in the words of the Declaration of Independence—"all men [and yes, all women, too] will be acknowledged as created equal." Now surely, we will always remember the sterling leadership of great heroes like Dr. Martin Luther King Jr., Dr. Dorothy Irene Height, and Miss Rosa Parks. We remember their sterling leadership and the struggles of civil rights, women's rights, and human rights. And yet, every victory in these struggles required their persistence and sacrifice of ordinary people young and old. Women and men, children and allies of all races, religions, and backgrounds. And so, we come to the question. What must each of us, you and I, and all Americans of goodwill, do to move our country toward a more perfect union?

As we continue to perfect our democracy, carrying on the struggles of previous generations, we must own our nation's history of enslavement and racial discrimination. As the African American writer James Baldwin has said, "not everything that is faced can be changed, but nothing can be changed that is not faced" [Baldwin 1962].

Owning our history allows us to break free from its shadow. It empowers every American of goodwill to have the courage to challenge everyday expressions of bigotry and hatred. To be a nonviolent activist against systemic inequality. Such inequality not only affects African Americans, but countless other Americans, because of their gender. Their gender identity, their sexual orientation, class, age, religion, place of origin, or disability. The Congress of our country has a particular responsibility to enact laws that will bring us closer to the day. That day that Dr. Martin Luther King dreamed of. That day when every African American, every American will say, because it will be true, "Free at last, free at last, great God Almighty, we are free at last."

6. Art and Museum Life

After spending nearly forty-five years of her life as a college professor, author, and two-time college president, Johnnetta Betsch Cole made the bold step of shifting her career in a completely new direction when she became the director of the National Museum of African Art in 2009.

Although art and museums were a new area for her, it was also a homecoming of sorts. As she mentions in these speeches, her mother had an "eye for art," and exposed her children to great works of African American artists despite limited access to museums due to segregation. The first speech in this chapter, "Do Your Dreams Scare You?," is a 2012 high school commencement speech delivered at the Duke Ellington School of the Arts. In this speech Cole offers insightful advice for those pursuing a career in the arts, and she also highlights the importance of the arts for society. Next is her 2008 speech "The Treatment of Gender in Opening Exhibitions," delivered at the National Museum of African American History and Culture. This speech provides a framework that lays the foundation of thinking about gender in exhibitions. Here, she offers a feminist analysis that examines how gender is treated in opening exhibitions at museums. She argues, "We must portray African American men as well as African American women as gendered beings and we must capture ways in which their racial experiences have been shaped by gender." Furthermore, Cole uses this framework to specifically analyze the *Slavery and Freedom* exhibit at the National Museum of African American History and Culture.

FIGURE 6.1 Cole during her tenure as director of the Smithsonian Institute's National Museum of African Art, with Senegalese sculptor Ousmane Sow's *Toussaint Louverture et la vieille esclave* (Toussaint Louverture and the elderly slave), 1989. Photo credit: Jessica Suwaroff.

The next speech, "Diversity in American Art Museums," is the 2015 keynote address at the American Alliance of Museums Annual Meetings. In this speech she claims that museums can and must be of social value to society. She urges museum professionals to work toward greater diversity in staff, exhibitions, educational programs, and visitors. Her vision of diversity and inclusion in the museum space includes attention to race, gender, sexual orientation, gender identity, disability, and generation.

The final speech in this chapter is her 2012 speech "Great Art at Historically Black Colleges and Universities: To Whom Does It Belong?" delivered at Clark Atlanta University. This speech brings attention to the thousands of works of African American art housed at HBCUs like Hampton, Clark Atlanta, Fisk, Lincoln, and Howard universities. Interrogating crucial questions of "ownership" of these art collections, Cole thoughtfully poses the question, "does any HBCU have the right to sell the legacy of future generations to pay today's light bills?" Here she draws an important distinction between what may be *legal* and what is *ethical*. Finally, she urges her audience to attend to the proper care and use of Black art at HBCUs.

In summary, we start with an inspirational commencement speech for young graduates of the Duke Ellington School for the Arts. Cole's subsequent speech focuses on gender in museum life, and her third speech moves toward a broader vision of diversity and inclusion in the art world. That is followed by a focus on Black art and HBCUs in the fourth speech. So, what can we take away from these speeches on art and museum life? Ultimately, they illustrate the depth and breadth of Cole's contribution to a broad range of fields, disciplines, communities, and institutions.

Do Your Dreams Scare You?

Thirty-Seventh Commencement Exercises, Duke Ellington School of the Arts,

Ellington Theater, Washington, DC, June 8, 2012

My Sisters and Brothers All: Good evening! And what a great "gettin' up" evening it is as we come to celebrate the graduation of 103 highly talented, artistically gifted young women and men.

I want to begin by greeting the head of this ever so special Duke Ellington School of the Arts, Rory Pullens. And to you, my colleagues, the academic and arts faculty, I greet you and acknowledge the central role you play in the education of Ellington students.

To all the staff, I want you to know that I know that when you carry out your various responsibilities, you contribute substantially to fulfilling the mission of the Duke Ellington School of the Arts.

Now I turn to greet and applaud for all of her mighty work for this school, my sister friend, the cofounder of the Ellington school, Peggy Cooper Cafritz.*

There are surely some Ellington alumnae here, and I want to greet you. And a very warm and hearty greeting to an alumna of Ellington who interned with me at the National Museum of African Art, Shalonda Hardy.

---

* Peggy Cooper Cafritz (1947–2018) was an American art collector and educator. She co-founded the Duke Ellington School of the Arts in 1974.

A special hello to all of the friends of this extraordinary institution.

And I definitely want to acknowledge my husband, James Staton, who is enjoying his first visit to the Duke Ellington School of the Arts, one of the jewels in the district.

This is the season of graduations. But there is something special and different about this graduation and about each of you. And that is, that you have chosen a high school that focuses on the arts. Now, I can imagine that when you made it clear that you would be going to Ellington as an important step toward a career in the arts, lots of folks responded by asking if you realize that you could end up as a starving artist. Others urged you to choose a safer or more lucrative career, like law or business.

I applaud your choice, and I congratulate you on following your passion and developing your talent. After the solid academic instruction and excellent artistic training that you have received at Ellington, you are well prepared for the next leg of your life journey. And for many of you, that will mean continuing your formal education in a college or university.

If one of the arts is your passion—and surely that is the case, for why else would you be graduating from Ellington—then I urge you to stick with your passion. The arts are so vital in our lives.

Listen to how that point is made by the National Standards for Arts Education: "The arts have been an inseparable part of the human journey. Indeed, we depend on the arts to carry us toward the fullness of our humanity. We value the arts for themselves, and because we do, we believe knowing and practicing them is fundamental to the healthy development of our children's minds and spirits. That is why in any civilization—ours included—the arts are inseparable from the very meaning of the term 'education.' We know from long experience that no one can claim to be truly educated who lacks basic knowledge and skills in the arts."

As Charles Segers, the CEO of Ovation, puts it, "The strength of every democracy is measured by its commitment to the arts."

One of my sheroes, the late congresswoman from Texas, Barbara Jordan, once described a very important role that the arts can play in our lives. She said, "The arts are not a frill. The arts are a response to our individuality and our nature, and help to shape our identity. What is there that can transcend deep difference and stubborn divisions? The arts. They have a wonderful universality. Art has the potential to unify. It can speak in many languages without a translator. The arts do not discriminate. The arts can lift us up" [Jordan 1993].

I love the way someone put it, "Art is the only way to run away without leaving home."*

I find it particularly important to listen to top business folks on the question of the arts, particularly the critical role they see the arts playing in preparing individuals for work in the twenty-first-century global marketplace.

The cofounder of Microsoft, Paul Allen, has said this: "In my own philanthropy and business endeavors, I have seen the critical role the arts play in stimulating creativity and in developing vital communities. . . . The arts have a crucial impact on our economy and are an important catalyst for learning, discovery, and achievement in our country."

Annette Byrd of the GlaxoSmithKline pharmaceutical company says quite clearly that in her professional world, "We need people who think with the creative sides of their brains—people who have played in a band, who have painted. . . . [When you have practiced the arts] it enhances symbiotic thinking capabilities, [it encourages] not always thinking in the same paradigm, [it encourages] learning how to kick-start a new idea, or how to get a job done better, less expensively."

As you know, some misguided folks think that the arts are nice but not a necessity. But as Maria Shriver (an award-winning journalist and author) has put it, "Art is fundamental, unique to each of us. . . . Even in difficult economic times—especially in difficult economic times—the arts are essential" [Shriver 2010].

And as President Barack Obama put it, "The future belongs to young people with an education and the imagination to create" [Obama 2009b].

And so, dear graduates, having followed your passion for one or more of the arts, now what is your dream? When you close your eyes, do you dream of being on Broadway, or is your dream to win the Pulitzer Prize in Literature? Is it your dream to become a visual artist who is as respected and beloved as Elizabeth Catlett and Romare Bearden? Or perhaps your dream is to win an Oscar, or two. Or is it that you dream of winning a Grammy or two?

I hope that among you, there is somebody who dreams that one day, she will have my job as the director of the Smithsonian's National Museum of African Art.

My young sisters and brothers, the most important thing that I can say to you about your dreams is captured in words spoken by President Ellen Johnson Sirleaf, the first woman to serve as the president of one of the fifty-five African countries, and a winner of the Nobel Peace Prize. President Johnson Sirleaf has said: "If your dreams do not scare you, they are not big enough" [Sirleaf 2011].

* This quote has been attributed to Twyla Tharp, an American dancer, choreographer, and author.

Now hear me, when your dreams are big enough to scare you, they can come true! But obviously, there are some things that are required of you to help to make those big ole scary but ever so wonderful and significant dreams come true.

First, and ever so importantly, *you must believe that your big dreams can come true*. To put it another way, you must have *faith*. Now let me tell you in symbolic terms what I mean by faith. Imagine that you are standing on the top of a mountain, and you must jump from that mountain top. If you have faith, then you will jump, because you believe that when you do so, one of two things will happen. Either you will sprout wings, or the earth will rise up to meet your feet.

I fully respect the religious diversity that exists in our country and our world—and indeed it is important for us to respect an individual's right not to have religious beliefs. But I feel comfortable in saying this to you, my young sisters and brothers, you need to believe in someone or something that is bigger, and wiser than you are. And as we used to say in the civil rights movement of the 1960s: "You've got to Keep the Faith!"

Here is a second requirement if you are indeed to make those big, scary dreams of yours come true. *You must believe in collaboration and teamwork and remain connected to others*. Of course, you must continue to develop your artistic talents, and I trust you will never cease to be a student, that is, someone who is engaged in discovery and learning. But I can assure you that few things are ever accomplished by a single individual. There really is something that is good and effective about teamwork.

Do you know why a flock of birds fly in a group?

They do so because they are lifted 17 percent higher if they are in a group than if they fly alone. So, while you continue to develop as an individual, you will end up flying higher when you are connected to others.

The third requirement for making your humongous dreams come true is that you *never lose your integrity*. In your quest to be that great star on Broadway or the lead choreographer of the Alvin Ailey dance company, or a twenty-first-century kind of Duke Ellington, I beg you to never engage in any behavior that requires you to lose your integrity. Some of the soundest advice my mother ever gave me was when she said: "There are many things that you can lose and manage to find. But once you lose your integrity it is close to impossible to get it back."

Engaging in behavior that is unethical or immoral, or indeed illegal, might bring you fame in the world of the arts; and such behavior could fill your pockets with lots of money. Ah, but my young sisters and brothers, I hope there is nothing in the world that you want so badly that you are willing to sell your soul to have it.

Now let me talk about something else that will be required of you in order for your wildest, biggest and truly scary dreams to come true. Today, in this rapidly moving, technologically sophisticated and diverse world of ours, it is increasingly the case that doing well will require that you have knowledge about and respect for people who are quite different from you.

If you remain connected to the world of the arts, you are bound to encounter and, indeed, work with people of diverse backgrounds and attributes . . . people of different races, genders, sexual orientations, classes, ages, nationalities, religions, and different abilities and disabilities. And so, while it is of the utmost importance that you feel comfortable with and proud of who you are, you must also respect people who are from a range of other communities.

There is a Chinese saying that captures this point: "One flower never makes a spring." That is to say, it is in the array of flowers in bloom that we experience the true meaning of a spring.

Hear this Native American saying: "With all things and all beings I must be kin."

Listen to this truth that is expressed in the words of Cesar Chavez, the great Chicano organizer: "Preservation of one's own culture does not require contempt or disrespect for other cultures" [United Farm Workers n.d.].

In the Quran, the holy book of Islam, it says: "We were made into different tribes so that we might know and love each other" [Quran, sura 49, verse 13].

A beloved rabbi was once asked, "Rabbi Hillel, can you stand on one foot and say everything that is in the Torah?"

The rabbi said "Yes, I can."

And so, he stood on one foot and said: "You must treat each person as you wish to be treated. That is the whole Torah. The rest is commentary" [Babylonian Talmud, Shabbat 31a].

And of course, in the holy book of Christianity, it says quite clearly, "We must do unto others as we would have them to do unto us."

It will not surprise you if I say that *in order to have your truly big dreams come true you have got to work really hard*. Even if you are incredibly gifted as a dancer, visual artist, musician, actor, or writer, you will never reach your full potential unless you really work at moving your talent to the next level.

And, dear graduates, remember that racism and sexism are still very alive in our country and around the world. And that means that the advice that my mother gave me is still relevant advice for me to give you. My mom said to me: "You are a Black woman, and that means you are going to have to work twice as hard to get half as far!"

And so, you must set your sights on goals that are way out there, and then work ever so hard to reach them. I am reminded of the advice that Zora Neale

Hurston, a Black anthropologist, said her mother gave to her and her siblings: "Jump for the sun. And if you miss it, at least you will have gotten off the ground."

The very last requirement for making your big dreams come true is that *you have got to be of service to others*.

No matter what profession you have, I truly believe that you must be responsive to these words of Dr. Martin Luther King: "Life's most persistent and urgent question is: What are you doing for others?" [King 1957].

When I was growing up in Jacksonville, Florida, my parents put it this way: "Doing for others is just the rent you must pay for your room on earth."

And so, while you are becoming the big star that I think each of you is capable of becoming, and yes, even after you are a famous artist, musician, actor, dancer, or writer, I believe that you must continue to give some of your time to being of service to women, men, and children who need you—to work in a shelter for the homeless, to comfort women in a place of refuge from domestic violence, to tutor youngsters in an after-school program.

I say this because as Elie Wiesel, a great Jewish humanitarian, has said: "Our lives no longer belong to us alone; they belong to all those who need us desperately" [Wiesel 1986].

Or in the words of the National Council of Negro Women: "We must lift others as we climb."

It is time now for me to bring closure on your graduation address. I will do so by saying once again, urging you to continue your love affair with the arts. And as you do so, to dream those big, mighty, humongous dreams—the kind that are so big that they scare you. And then, dear graduates of the class of 2012, do what must be done to have your dreams come true.

The Treatment of Gender
in Opening Exhibitions

National Museum of African American History and Culture, Washington, DC, December 17, 2008

My Sisters and Brothers All: I am grateful for this opportunity to offer some comments that can launch our discussion of the treatment of gender in the opening exhibitions.

Rather than taking on the responsibility to critique how gender issues are or are not "discussed" or portrayed in the opening exhibitions—a task that properly belongs to all of us—I think I can be most helpful if I do the following:

First, I want to offer a few basic comments about how gender is viewed and lived out in African American communities and beyond—after all those who come to the National Museum of African American History and Culture will be African Americans, Americans of many other communities, and people from around the world.

Second, I want to look at one particular gallery through gender lenses to illustrate how much more textured, complex, and truthful such an exhibition is when gender is neither ignored nor downplayed. The gallery I've chosen is *Slavery and Freedom* in Area 1.

As I turn not to some basic comments about gender, I ask that you listen to these points with the same attitude that you take to your church on Sunday morning, or your mosque on Friday evenings, or synagogue on Shabbat. Do not expect to hear something new. The purpose is to offer what you already know.

The first, and in many ways, the most fundamental point is this—that for many African Americans, dare I say most African Americans, if I asked which attribute in their identity matters most to them, the answer would be that *race matters*, to use the title of Cornel West's book [West 1993].

Of course, Black women know they are women and Black men know they are men; poor Black folks live the consequences of their socioeconomic plight and Black folks in the LGBT community are conscious of how homophobia and heterosexism order their lives. But, until recently, we could say that the majority of Black folks see race as the primary determinant in their lives.

This, I am convinced, is the result of the tenacity, the brutality, the ubiquity of racism.

Take myself as an example: growing up in the segregated South, it was not until I was a grown woman that I began to see a problem identified only in terms of my "race."

A closely related point is that it is far easier for most Black folks to see the danger in privileging gender over race than to acknowledge that it is problematic to privilege race over gender.

As you know, the privileging of gender over race is what the suffragettes did as they stood in opposition to abolitionists. Interesting how the Elizabeth Cady Stanton versus Frederick Douglass "debate" of the nineteenth century was replayed when Hillary Rodham Clinton supporters argued that *all women* had an obligation to support Clinton over Obama. Did you notice how Barack Obama was referred to as the Black or African American or biracial candidate, as if he has no gender?

And Hillary Rodham Clinton was "the woman" candidate, as if she has no "race."

One of the consequences of denying one's multiple identities is that we can then deny how one can be the victim of one basis of oppression and then turn and victimize others on another basis.

Black folks clearly experience racism, and some of us then turn and practice heterosexism. White women clearly experience sexism and can then turn and practice racism.

It is not only instructive but essential for all of us human beings to acknowledge and deal with our multiple identities *and* bases of privilege. I do so when I acknowledge and deal with my heterosexual privilege, my class privilege, my privilege based on being a Christian, and my privilege as an "able-bodied" person.

It is interesting and instructive to note who it is among Black folks who challenge notions of the primacy of race in their self-identification. As I said earlier, the presence of racism feeds a focus on race in the lives of many Black folks, especially of older generations. And the perpetrators of racism can be easily identified as white folks.

Matters get far more complicated with questions of gender within the African American community. For expressions of gender inequality come not only from "the larger community," but from within the African American community. Think of the most brutal issues associated with sexism and gender inequality—rape, domestic violence, misogyny—and you see that discussing such issues is considered as airing our dirty laundry in front of white folks.

There is the obvious point that for many African American men, and some African American women, any call for a gender analysis is seen as a "woman's thing," more specifically a white women's thing that is designed to bring discord between Black women and Black men.

And then there is the ultimate punch that says, "Any Black woman who raises the gender issue must be a lesbian."

Let me make the basic but seldom acknowledged point that men—Black men—are as influenced by their gender as women are.

What this says in terms of our museum project is that we must portray African American men as well as African American women as gendered beings and we must capture ways in which their racial experiences have been shaped by gender.

An obvious point that cannot be overstated is that African American history, until very recently, has been portrayed, and yes, exhibited, as just that: his-story, with only fleeting recognition of her-story. When African American history is presented largely as a male narrative, it not only denied the presence of Black women, it distorts what are in fact the realities of Black men.

Twenty years ago, we didn't have the scholarship required to accurately present in the written or spoken word, nor in exhibitions, a "balanced" view of African American history and herstory, nor of how African American women no less than men discover poetry in their lives, create graphic and plastic arts that are both beautiful and functional.

But even with Black feminist scholarship to draw on, looking around at the institutions in African American life tends to feed the ole notion that men are simply better at doing certain things than women. That's why Black men are disproportionately the leaders in our civil rights organizations, our elected officials, our pastors, our college and university presidents, and CEOs in corporate America.

Now, I want to turn to the subject of one of our opening exhibitions, *Slavery and Freedom*, and assert how the adding of gender lenses brings more texture, complexity, and truth to that incredibly oppressive system.

I fully appreciate that it is quite a challenge to present highly complex realities within the confines of what we traditionally call a museum. But we must try to do so, for it is only then that a museum meets the challenge of reflecting lived lives and inspiring folks to participate in the creation of freer and more fulfilled lives.

Every girl and every woman who comes into "our" museum will bring her gendered self with her. And so will every boy and every man.

We must strive to make sure that each individual leaves not only with a greater understanding of how gender has mattered in the history and culture of a people called African Americans. Each person should see how gender is a fundamental matter in what shaped every people, indeed every life.

I do not think we will accomplish this mission by doing exhibitions "as usual" and then adding on a special exhibition on African American women. No! We must tell herstory along with history; we must ask why Shirley Chisholm's run for the presidency of the United States is not as remembered as Jesse Jackson's and Al Sharpton's; we must ask why young women can and do participate in performing misogynist rap music; we must ask our young people why they know of the heroes of the civil rights movement but not the sheroes like Septima Clark, Ella Baker, and Ruby Doris Smith-Robinson; we must challenge all who come to our museum to think about how and why the world of sports is so strongly gendered; we must present Frederick Douglass not only as a great abolitionist but as an amazing feminist.

Finally, let our museum of African American history and culture illustrate that in the long march from slavery to freedom we all have the responsibility to act in response to these questions: Freedom for whom? Freedom from what? Freedom at what price?

Diversity in American Art Museums

Keynote Address, 2015 American Alliance of Museums Annual Meeting, Georgia World Congress Center, Atlanta, GA, April 27, 2015

Drawing on my roots in a southern Black church and my involvement in the civil rights movement, I greet each of you as My Sisters and Brothers All. Good morning! And if I draw once again on my roots in a southern Black church, I would say it's a great "gettin' up" morning!

I want to thank sister chair Kaywin Feldman and brother president Ford Bell and the organizers of this year's AAM conference for giving me the honor of offering this keynote address as we gather in a city that is often described as the cradle of the civil rights movement—a movement that called for, struggled for, and indeed brought about monumental changes in our nation and inspired other movements for freedom and justice in America and around the world. We are in this city called Atlanta, a city that is the birthplace of Dr. Martin Luther King Jr.—the man Nina Simone called the Dark Prince of Peace.

We are in a city called Atlanta that is the home of major institutions that address issues of social justice: the Martin Luther King National Historic Site, the Carter Center, and the National Center for Civil and Human Rights.

Because we are in such a city, the theme for this 2015 AAM annual meeting is especially appropriate. "The Social Value of Museums: Inspiring Change."

Over the course of the next few days that we are together, there will be many responses to this theme.

What I have chosen to do in this keynote address is to make the case that our museums can and must be of social value by not only inspiring but creating change around one of the most critical issues of our time—the issue of diversity. For us in the world of museums that means inspiring and creating far greater diversity in our workforces, our exhibitions, our educational programs, and among our visitors.

I want to turn to our colleagues who are here from museums around the world to say this: as I speak about the need for greater diversity in the US museum, please know that I know that your realities may be quite different. I only hope that some of the points I will make will be helpful to you.

I also want to acknowledge the other slant in this talk and that is, that I am drawing most heavily on the question of diversity in art museums. And to my colleagues, who work in zoological parks and aquariums, while I will not make specific references to your organizations, please know that I know that you too are wrestling with questions of diversity.

Colleagues all, I believe that we cannot fully carry out the visions and the missions of our museums, and indeed our museum cannot continue to be of social value if we do not do what is required to have more diversity in who works in our museums, in the work we present in our museums, in the audiences we welcome to our museums, and in the philanthropic and board leadership in our museums.

One of my sheroes, the late Dr. Maya Angelou, issued a call to all women and men who are parents when she said: "It is time for parents to teach young people early on that in diversity there is beauty and there is strength" [The Root Staff 2014]. In our museums, we have the possibility to teach that same important message.

When we look back at the history of American museums, we see that they were products of and reflections of the political, economic, and social times. Back in the day, museums were run by and largely catered to middle-aged and middle-income and upper-class white folks. And the collections, exhibitions, and educational programs reflected what one of my colleagues, Dr. Beverly Guy-Sheftall at Spelman College, calls the three Ws: they were largely focused on *Western* places and ideas, the overwhelming majority of the staff and the visitors were *white* folks, and the exhibitions were largely *womanless*.

Let me briefly reference my own experience with museums "back in the day." Like all African Americans who grew up in the pre–civil rights days of legal segregation in the South, as a youngster I went to colored schools, used the colored "public" library, only drank from colored water fountains, and could only sit in the back of the bus. There were no art galleries or museums where I or any Black people could visit. But how fortunate I was to have a mother who had a passion for visual arts. As we say in the art world, "She had the eye!" And she had the will and the means to adorn our home with reproductions of art works that, ironically, I would not have seen in museums had I been permitted to visit them. For in our home were reproductions of masterworks of African American artists, and books on the art of Henry Tanner, Romare Bearden, Elizabeth Catlett, Jacob Lawrence, Lois Mailou Jones, Charles White, Augusta Savage, and Aaron Douglass.

Today, with legalized segregation a thing of the past, I can go to any museum whose entrance fee—if there is one—I can afford. And yet, too often I will not find much in those museums that reflects the history, herstory, culture, and art of who I am, and underrepresented people of our country and the world.

Today, from a legal standpoint, every American museum must honor EEO [equal employment opportunity] guidelines. In addition, it is the right thing to do to have diversity in our museums' staff, boards, programs, and audiences. It is also the smart thing to do if we want our museums to be vibrant twenty-first-century places that reflect the diversity of our nation and the world.

A comprehensive look at diversity in our museums would include an assessment of the presence and the absence of the range of underrepresented groups. That is people whose primary identity is based on their race, ethnicity, gender, sexual orientation, age, religion, nationality, class, and physical abilities and disabilities. I have used the term "primary identity," because each of us has multiple identities.

Let me return to the point that embracing, encouraging, and sustaining a diverse workforce in our museums is the right thing to do. That is, there should be an equal opportunity for all qualified people to not only enter the workforce at our museums, but to be welcomed there and supported to advance there.

There is a second reason for having and sustaining a diverse workforce. Namely, it is the smart thing to do. There is a business case for diversity. It says if businesses are to compete effectively in this global economy, they must have within their company employees of diverse backgrounds who will bring different and innovative ideas to the table. It is also my experience that being with people of diverse backgrounds can be and often is intellectually exciting!

This business case for diversity in American companies, and in our museums, rests heavily on demographic realities. Over the past few decades there have been massive demographic and social shifts. According to US Census data, currently 35 percent of all US residents are "minorities." Demographers have stated that this trend will not only continue but will accelerate well into the next several decades. In the next thirty years, the United States will become a majority minority country with white folks no longer in the majority.

The future of American philanthropy, like the future of everything else in the country, will be shaped by increasing racial and ethnic diversity. According to the Minnesota Council on Foundations, "Who donates and what they give will be profoundly impacted, and public policy will become more representative of minority communities."

As Arnold Lehman, the retiring director of the Brooklyn Museum puts it: "For our museums, diversity is a 'critical issue' and 'the most important book any museum director should read is the US Census.'"

What is the state of workforce diversity in our American museums? Today, the professional staff at most American museums do not mirror the diversity of American people. Currently only 20 percent of art museum staff in all positions are people of color. When we look at the number of people of color in senior positions, the situation becomes even starker. In the 241 museums of the Association of Art Museum Directors, fewer than 5 percent have people of color in senior management positions.

Tony Hirschel, director of the Smart Museum of Art at the University of Chicago, who led an AAMD task force on diversifying membership, has said this: "Few museums would say that their staffs are as diverse as they should be." Which begs the question that he has also asked: "How can we create a new stream of professionals that is more diverse?"

Of course, once a museum is successful in recruiting a diverse staff the question is: What kind of environment, atmosphere, and culture will these diverse colleagues encounter? I cannot stress enough the importance of an inclusive culture that says in countless ways, all colleagues from all backgrounds are welcome at this museum table! In addition to asking about racial and ethnic diversity among museum staff, we must also ask who visits our museums? While people of color make up over one-third of the American population, according to a National Endowment for Arts report [cited in Levitt 2015], they make up only 9 percent of museum visitors.

Brother President Ford Bell makes this point: "The big challenge is going to be how museums deal with the increasingly diverse American public, which could be 30 percent or more Hispanic by 2050. If you go to a museum, and don't see anyone who looks like you, from visitors to staff, and the boards are not reflecting the community, you may be less likely to come back, or even to go in the first place."

Marketing studies affirm the rather obvious fact that African Americans are more likely to attend events that are characterized as "Black themed" and events where Black people are well represented among performers. Studies of Latino attitudes toward museums show similar results. A report by the Smithsonian's National Museum of American History found second-generation Latinos surveyed had "very strong expectations that museums should include diverse staff, bilingual interpretation, Latino perspectives and some Latino themed content."

In Houston, our colleague, the late Peter Marzio of the Museum of Fine Arts started a Latin American department in response to the city's rapidly expanding Latino community. Peter also added several permanent Asian art galleries in response to Houston's growing and diverse Asian community. And he did not start these exhibitions and programs in some vacuum but rather by engaging the local community and seeing what they wanted. This has resulted in very strong local support, donations, and engagement. As an example, the Korean community donated over $2 million for a permanent art collection.

I turn now to the situation of those of us who are described in a Native American saying as holding up half of the sky . . . us women folk. Where do we stand in terms of women on museum staff?

Among the museums in the Association of Art Museum Directors, women make up slightly less than 50 percent of the directors. However, of the 243 members of the Association of Art Museum Directors, there are only five African American women! It is also important to note that the larger a museum's budget the less likely it is that the director is a woman.

From the National Museum of Women in the Arts in Washington, DC, here are these facts:

Fifty-one percent of visual artists today are women.
Over the past fifteen years, only 28 percent of the museum's solo exhibitions spotlighted women in eight selected museums.
Only twenty-seven women are represented in the current edition of H. W. Janson's survey, *History of Art* [Janson 1986], up from zero in the 1980s.

And I can't resist sharing this fact: less than 3 percent of the artists in the modern section of the Metropolitan Museum of Art are women, but 83 percent of the nudes are women!

Women lag behind men in directorships held at museums with budgets over $15 million. We women folks hold only 245 of all art museum directorships and women earn seventy-one cents for every dollar earned by male directors.

Calvert Investments discovered that companies whose commitment to diversity was viewed as "robust" were not only at a financial advantage but were also better positioned to generate long-term shareholder value. In addition, advocacy groups like Catalyst, a nonprofit organization that promotes inclusive workplaces for women, found that Fortune 500 companies with higher percentages of women board members significantly outperformed companies with fewer female members. This is the business case for why promoting diversity and inclusion makes good financial sense!

And let us note that women have more philanthropic clout than ever before, consistently outgiving their male counterparts.

I also want to make an observation in terms of American museums and LGBTQ communities. Whatever the number of lesbian, gay, bisexual, and transgender individuals there are among museum professionals—such statistics are not available—it is clear that American museums have paid grossly insufficient attention to art works done by and about individuals of these communities.

The exhibition at the Smithsonian's National Portrait Gallery, *Hide/Seek: Difference and Desire in American Portraiture*, was the first museum exhibition to focus on themes of gender and sexuality in modern American portraiture. As you may recall, there was a major controversy around that exhibition when the Smithsonian removed a 1987 video about the suffering caused by AIDS. At the Smithsonian, we continue to talk about what we have learned from that controversy.

We must also address the question of how inclusive our museums are in terms of exhibitions by and about differently abled people. And we must ask ourselves to what extent our museums welcome disabled professional staff, and the extent to which our museums accommodate and welcome people with disabilities.

Finally, in terms of underrepresented groups I pose this question: How are our museums doing in terms of igniting the interest of the folks that I respectfully, yet playfully, call the young 'uns? As you know, millennials are quite different from yesterday's museumgoers in how they see the world, how they engage with technology and how they pursue their interests. It is not being overly dramatic to say that unless we make changes in our museums that will speak to the patterns and interests of young people, when the middle age to older folks who are now our core visitors go on off to glory, our museum galleries will be places in which there is a dwindling number of visitors. We all know that our museums must become more technologically savvy if we are to court the millennials whose electronic devices have become extensions of their bodies.

Not only is reaching out to the millennial generation important for cultivating healthy visitorship, but it is critical for preparing the next generation of donors and trustees. While the baby-boomer generation has been the main source of charitable giving and philanthropic leadership for decades, the realities and habits of the millennial generation are not the same as the current aging generation. From a recent *Trends Watch* report compiled by the Center for the Future of Museums [2015] and a recent *New York Times* article, "Wooing a New Generation of Museum Patrons" [Gelles 2014], we learn this: "While charitable giving in the United States has remained stable for the last forty years, there is reason for concern. Boomers today control 70 percent of the nation's disposable income. Millennials don't yet have nearly as much cash on hand. And those who do are increasingly drawn to social, rather than artistic, causes."

The fiscal reality of the millennial generation is not the same as the reality of older generations. Tax laws are changing, and wealth is becoming increasingly concentrated, which will in turn affect the philanthropic habits and the focus on giving of the younger generation. Also, there may just be fewer wealthy patrons and donors, making donor relations and cultivation a more critical and targeted effort.

Colleagues, My Sisters and Brothers All: when we pause to confront the need for far greater diversity in our museums, in many ways we are at the proverbial fork in the road. And we cannot do as Yogi Bera said you should do at the fork of the road: namely, take it. We have to decide if we will take the fork that represents continuing to have our museums reflect the histories and herstories, the cultures, art, and science of only some of the many people who make up our nation and our world. Or do we take the other fork, that requires inspiring and creating change?

If your museum is large or small, old or young, famous or not yet famous, the need for seeking and sustaining diversity in your museums and in mine has never been greater. If we are to be relevant in this ever-changing world, to stay artistically and financially viable, all of our museums must boldly, indeed bodaciously, commit to rethinking about what takes place in our museums, to whom our museums belong, and who the colleagues are who have the privilege of telling important stories through the power of science, history, culture, and art.

As members of AAM, you my colleagues are aware of efforts in this organization to address issues of diversity in our museums. There are also programs initiated by other museum organizations, like AAMD, and by foundations like Ford and Mellon, to encourage far greater involvement of underrepresented groups in every facet of American museums.

There is no city that is a more appropriate place for us to commit to the task of bringing greater diversity to who works in American museums, and to the work that our museums do. And there is no time that is more appropriate for us to carry out this commitment than right now! So, let us heed the counsel of Atlanta's son, Dr. Martin Luther King Jr., in terms of how we are to get this critical work done. He said: "If you can't fly, then run. If you can't run then walk, if you can't walk then crawl, but whatever you do you have to keep moving forward."

My Sisters and Brothers All: I want to bring closure to this talk by telling you a story that was a favorite of a great civil rights worker, Fannie Lou Hamer. She loved to tell this story at the end of her talk to stress who was responsible for doing the work she had said must be done.

The last line of this story will say who is responsible for doing the work that will make our museums far more representative of the diversity of our nation and our world.

A group of boys decided to play hooky from school. To entertain themselves they decided to mess with a bird that one of the boys had caught. But they were soon bored with messing with that bird. One of the boys asked: Now what can we do? The ringleader said: I know what we can do, we can find the old lady who lives up the road and ask her a question about this bird that she will never be able to answer. I will hold this bird behind my back and say, old lady, old lady this bird that I have behind my back, is it dead or is it alive? If she says the bird is dead, I will release the bird so that it can fly away. But if, to my question, she says that the bird is alive, I will crush it.

Convinced that the old lady would never be able to answer the question about the bird, they gave each other high fives and bumps before starting out to find her. When they did, the ringleader in a tone that characterizes some but certainly not all of our young people said: Yo old lady, are you gonna answer my question? The old lady with the warmth and gentleness that characterizes so many of our elders said: My son, I will try.

Holding the bird behind his back, the ringleader said: Old lady, this bird that I hold behind my back, is it dead or is it alive? Like so many of the elders in the southern community that I grew up in, the old lady took her sweet time before giving an answer. The bird, you want me to tell you about the bird. Well, let me see, where is this bird? [The answer the old lady finally gave is the answer to the question: Who is responsible for inspiring and creating greater diversity in our museums?]

The old lady said: Well, my son, I'll tell you about the bird, why it's in your hands!

My Sisters and Brothers All, that is the answer: the responsibility for bringing far greater diversity into each and every one of our museums is in your hands, and in mine.

Great Art at Historically Black Colleges and Universities

TO WHOM DOES IT BELONG?

Keynote Address for Seventieth Anniversary Celebration of Clark Atlanta's Historic Art Collection, Clark Atlanta University, Atlanta, GA, May 6, 2012

My Sisters and Brothers All: Good afternoon! It is a joy for me to come home to the Atlanta University Center, the largest contiguous consortium of African Americans in higher education in our nation. It was here, in the Atlanta University Center, that I had the privilege of serving as the president of Spelman College for ten memorable years.

While any day in the Atlanta University Center would be a special day for me, this day is extraordinarily significant as we gather to commemorate the seventieth anniversary of the founding of Clark Atlanta University's historic art collection, the sixtieth anniversary of the unveiling of the "Art of the Negro" murals, and we mark the publication of a magnificent book: *In the Eye of the Muses: Selections from the Clark Atlanta University Art Collection* [Clark Atlanta University, Tina Maria Dunkley, and Jerry Cullum 2012].

I am deeply grateful to my colleague and sister friend, Tina Dunkley, for this opportunity to be a part of such an historic and *herstoric* celebration. However, it is a bit unnerving for me to offer this keynote address in the presence of two giants in the field of African American art, Dr. David Driskell and Dr. Richard Long. I am also aware that in this gathering are distinguished scholars of African and African American art, and renowned visual artists of the African diaspora.

And so, as I offer this keynote address, I will simply have to follow the advice of the great chief justice of the Supreme Court, Thurgood Marshall, who said: "You've got to do the best you can with what you've got!"*

To this highly important occasion, I have brought with me my past experiences, my values, my concerns, and, yes, my hopes and dreams. Especially relevant for this occasion are these experiences: growing up in a family where my mother, who "had the eye," adorned our home with Black art; going off to Fisk University as a fifteen-year-old early entrance student where I was surrounded by works of art by master painters, sculptors, and muralists; putting on the agenda when I was the president of Spelman College the need for a fine art gallery in the Camille Olivia Hanks Cosby Academic Center; and during my presidency at Bennett College for Women, the opening of that institution's first art gallery; and now, as the director of the Smithsonian's National Museum of African Art, having the responsibility of stewardship of priceless traditional and contemporary works of African art.

From the folks in Jacksonville, Florida, who "grew me up," I learned that "you've got to take care of your own." From the discipline of anthropology that has provided a set of lenses through which I see my own culture and that of others, I have witnessed the powerful role that art can and does play in the life of a people. From you, my colleagues in the field of art history and museum administration, I receive constant affirmations of the basic fact that masterfully crafted works of art are priceless and irreplaceable. And from women and men with whom I have journeyed in the academy, I am reminded of the value of developing and implementing a pedagogy for integrating collections at colleges and universities into the academic curriculum so that artifacts can be used to teach across academic disciplines.

It is from these experiences, lessons, and values that I pose this basic question: To whom does the great art of our HBCUs belong? Before I respond to that question, let us look at one or two works of great art by African American artists in the collections of some of our historically Black colleges and universities. The images you will see are barely enough to be considered a sample of the thousands of great works of African American art that are being exhibited, are on loan, or in storage at our HBCUs. I have not included works of African art, Native American art, and European art in the collections of these HBCUs.

---

* A version of this quote has been attributed to Theodore Roosevelt, who attributed it to Squire Billy Widener.

Hampton University, founded in 1868, which has the oldest African American museum, currently has a permanent collection of 1,500 objects and is considered one of the largest and strongest collections of African American art in the world. At Hampton, there are also other collections: American Indian, Asian, and Pacific Islands.

Clark Atlanta's permanent collection consists of 640 works in three categories: contemporary American, African American, and African art. One can safely say that the Clark Atlanta University collection is rivaled only by the collections at Hampton and Howard universities.

Let me return now to the fundamental question: To whom do the great works of art at HBCUs belong? The technically correct answer is that a collection of art, like the buildings and grounds of an HBCU, belong to that institution. However, like all other colleges and universities, HBCUs hold their art collections in trust for present and future generations of students, faculty, and staff. It is a fiduciary responsibility tied to the nature and mission of the institution.

I think a case could be made that these great works of art are also held in trust for the public—with a particular responsibility to the African American public who have a special historical and ongoing connection to HBCUs. And I further suggest that our HBCUs should feel a special sense of responsibility to hold these great art collections in trust for practicing artists, art historians, and other scholars across our nation and the world.

In recent years, there have been contested discussions and lawsuits over the "ownership" of university and college art collections. In January 2009, trustees at Brandeis University voted to "transition" the Rose Art Museum that has one of the most important collections in New England, into a teaching center and gallery, and to conduct "an orderly sale or other disposition" of its works to raise money. Two supporters of the Rose Art Museum went to court to stop the trustees from carrying out their plan. The settlement was such that Brandeis said it has "no aim, plan, design, strategy or intention to sell any artwork donated to or purchased by" Brandeis for the museum, and the Rose Museum will remain "a university art museum open to the public" [Kennedy 2011].

This month, when the legendary collection of the Barnes Foundation is opened in its new Philadelphia location (from the Lower Merion Township where it was housed) I doubt it will put to rest all of the arguments, legal battles, and discussions about one of the world's finest holdings of impressionist, post-impressionist, and early modern paintings, African sculpture, metalwork, and more. Much more ink will be spilled, and debates will be added to the already existing theatrical production, books, and articles about this collection that

Dr. Albert Barnes left to Lincoln University. It is indeed a strange saga that involved Dr. Barnes bequeathing to Lincoln University his collection—worth billions of dollars—without even informing that historically Black university that he was doing so. As the saga of the Barnes collection continued, at a certain point the then president of Lincoln, Richard Glanton, suggested that Barnes should sell the famous Matisse painting *Joy of Life* to pay off Lincoln's debts.

There is also the saga surrounding the magnificent collection Georgia O'Keefe willed to Fisk University. It consists of ninety-seven modernist paintings first collected by her husband, Alfred Stieglitz, along with four of her own works of art. More than a decade ago, it was proposed that the collection should be sold to bail out Fisk from its financial troubles. Last month, the Tennessee Supreme Court upheld a lower court decision that allows Fisk to sell a 50 percent stake in the 101-piece art collection that O'Keefe said should never be sold or broken up.

The Tennessee Supreme Court decision permits Fisk to sell a 50 percent stake in the 101-piece collection for $30 million. The sale is to the Crystal Bridges Museum in Bentonville, Arkansas—a museum founded by Walmart heir Alice Walton. The terms of the sale will allow Crystal Bridges to display the collection two out of every four years, along with the right of first refusal should the rest of the ownership of the collection ever come up for sale. Alice Walton also pledged $1 million to upgrade Fisk University's display facilities.

President Hazel O'Leary, who has been in a bitter dispute about the O'Keefe collection with a group of alumnae at Fisk as well as professional art organizations, expressed her pleasure over the Tennessee Supreme Court's decision: "We're feeling pretty happy up here" [Burke 2012].

When the Tennessee Appeals Court made a ruling on November 29, 2011, in favor of Fisk, Dan Moore, the president of the Association of Museum Directors, said in a statement that it would be foolish for the association to stand in opposition to a legal decision. It is my view that because something is legal does not make it ethical.

I am pleased to say that in an official statement, the Association of Art Museum Directors took a strong stance on the ruling by the Appellate Court of Tennessee. Here is that statement:

> AAMD is extremely concerned by the ruling of the Appellate Court of Tennessee that allows Fisk University to pursue an agreement to sell a half share of its Stieglitz collection to fund operations. As AAMD has stated consistently, such an action would violate a core professional standard of AAMD and of the museum field, which prohibit the use of funds

from the sale of works of art for purposes other than building an institution's collection. Using funds from the sale of works of art for general expenses undermines the institution's public trust, service to its community, and the relationship between museums and their supporters.

AAMD believes that art collections owned by colleges and universities are an irreplaceable component of academic and community life and that they should not be treated as disposable financial assets. Art museums and galleries—standing alone or operated as part of a college or university—fundamentally compromise the field's core principles and negatively impact the entire art museum community when they sell art to support operations. [Rosenbaum 2011]

Just as our HBCUs, many of which were founded in the 1860s, have a long and very special relationship with African American communities, there are also very special ties that bind African American communities to the spectacular collections of African, African American, and African diasporic art at our HBCUs. Our HBCUs began because Black people could not go to white colleges and universities. And HBCUs collected great Black art because white people wouldn't collect or exhibit art by African Americans. I do not think it is hyperbole for me to say that efforts to sell, destroy, and neglect the great art at HBCUs is to symbolically sell, destroy, and neglect our heritage.

However, as the former president of our two historically Black colleges for women, I am not insensitive to the financial plight of many of our HBCUs. But does any HBCU have the right to sell the legacy of future generations to pay today's light bills? My answer is that any one of our colleges or universities may well find a way to legally do so. But, again, because an act is legal does not necessarily make it ethical.

I turn now to suggest ways that the proper care and use of the great Black art at our HBCUs could help to address some of the pressing pedagogical and fiscal challenges that confront so many of our higher education institutions.

During this year's Porter Colloquium at Howard University, Tina Dunkley presented a brilliant paper that she entitled "Beyond Market Value: Utilizing Art Collections to Distinguish the Collegiate Experience at HBCUs." Hear her major point: "In this epoch of recurring fiascos over the sale of these unappreciated and underutilized historic treasures at HBCUs, the static character of our art collections has to change for them not to be rendered expendable in the potentiality of an institution's insolvency."

Dunkley then presents four ways in which benefits can be reaped from using the great art at our HBCUs as powerful pedagogical tools.

The imagery and narratives of Africans and African Americans in these collections can help to balance the ubiquitous presence of European imagery presented by the media.

By integrating a great art collection into the academic curriculum, we can encourage in our students the development of critical thinking and visual literacy.

Art collections at our HBCUs can be effective promotional tools in an institution's recruitment.

The last benefit that Dunkley points out is this:

Because art imparts cultural and historical information across disciplines, it can "heighten the collegiate experience with a potential increase in the return of alumni giving."

As a former college president and now the director of an African art museum, it seems to me that the great art at our HBCUs can and should be integrated into carefully constructed and executed fundraising strategies. For example, we need to take advantage of the reality that many potential major donors have an interest in the arts and are often collectors of visual arts. What I am suggesting will not bring the "quick fix" of millions of dollars that can come from selling our legacy that is captured in the great Black art at our HBCUs, but what I am suggesting can be, over time, an effective component of a fundraising campaign.

There is a long and close association between the art and the artists of Africa and the African diaspora. This is reflected in how the art collections at several of our HBCUs include quality traditional and contemporary African art. Of course, the influence of African art on the works of African American artists is reflected in the works of so many of our master artists. We see it in bold ways in the works of Hale Woodruff, John Biggers, Lois Mailu Jones, and David Driskell; in the works of artists like Jeff Donaldson of the AfriCOBRA movement, and in the works of great contemporary artists such as Radcliffe Bailey and Renée Stout. We must note that there are contemporary African artists who consciously draw from the works of artists in the African diaspora. These connections between the art and artists of the African continent and the African diaspora might be the basis for well thought out efforts to interest wealthy Africans, some African governments, and American corporations that do business in Africa in supporting our HBCUs.

The final point that I must make circles back to the question of who owns the great art at our HBCUs. If you share my view that in a moral and ethical sense that great art of HBCUs belong to future generations, then we might say that these magnificent collections belong to eternity, we must take command of our ability to conserve this legacy.

We do have the power to save our great art. Of course, one of the ways that this can be done is through partnerships between an HBCU and other cultural and philanthropic institutions. A sterling case in point is the partnership between Talladega College, the High Museum, and the Atlanta Art Conservation Center that has saved the Woodruff murals at Talladega.

What has happened at Texas Southern University [TSU] is a sterling example of the power of a small group of committed people to put the brakes on what could have been the ongoing destruction of a legacy. Among the truly significant contributions that John Biggers made to the world of art was the project he carried out of having each of his art students paint a mural as a part of the requirement for graduation. Last September, two murals painted by Harvey Johnson when he was a student forty years ago were destroyed when workers used white paint to cover them. Johnson went on to become a professor and retired in 2007 after thirty-four years of teaching at TSU. The president of TSU, Dr. John Rudley, said the murals, which were in the Hannah Hall administration building, had become eyesores, and he said, "When I bring dignitaries to campus, I can't have them seeing that kind of thing. All art isn't good art."

Johnson's mural made President Rudley uncomfortable. Let's be clear: art is not made to make people comfortable.

Professor Alvia Wardlaw, art history professor and university museum director at TSU, was devastated by this destruction of Johnson's murals. But rather than only mourning that irreplaceable loss, she began to organize efforts that have culminated in amazing results. The same president who ordered the destruction of Professor Johnson's murals has now committed $50,000 to restore murals at TSU and $60,000 for a major publication. Our shero, Alvia Wardlaw, has also secured additional funding for these projects from the Brown Foundation. Dr. Richard Long has said: "People create their own future to an extent."

What has happened at Texas Southern University is proof of what anthropologist Margaret Mead said: "Never doubt the ability of a small group of committed citizens to change the world. That is the only way it ever happens."

In his essay in the book *To Conserve a Legacy: American Art from Historically Black Colleges and Universities*, Richard Powell issues a charge to all of us when he said that our great works of art at HBCUs require "conservation not just in the natural sense of preserving and saving old objects. No, what these works need is a perceptual overhaul: reappraisals of their intrinsic value and reinvestments in their collective cultural worth" [Powell 1999, 139].

I want to bring closure to this talk by telling a story that Fannie Lou Hamer would tell at the end of one of her talks in order to say quite clearly who was responsible for doing the work she had laid out. The last line of the story will say who has the responsibility to help to conserve the legacy that is wrapped up in the great art at our historically Black colleges and universities. The last line in this story is a call for self and institutional agency.

It is the story of some young boys who decided one day to fool an old lady by asking her a question that they thought she would be incapable of answering. The ringleader would take a bird that they had caught, and placing it behind his back, he would pose a question to the old lady:

> "Old lady, old lady, this bird that I have behind my back, is it dead or is it alive?"
>
> If the old lady said that the bird was dead, then he would release his hands and the bird would fly away. But if, to the question, she said that the bird was alive, he would crush it.
>
> They found the old lady and asked if she would respond to a question. She would try, she said.
>
> And so, the ringleader put the bird behind his back and said: "Old lady, old lady, this bird that I have behind my back, is it dead or is it alive?"
>
> With simple but powerful wisdom she said: "The answer is in your hands!"

7. The Fierce Urgency of Diversity, Equity, and Inclusion

This chapter showcases the range of Johnnetta Betsch Cole's work in inspiring change around diversity, equity, and inclusion in academia, philanthropy, museums, and even corporate America. The first two speeches in this chapter both make a "compelling case" for diversity and inclusion, but the first is applied to the corporate world and the second is applied to higher education. In her 2010 speech "The Compelling Case for Diversity, Equity, and Inclusion," delivered at Goldman Sachs, she outlines the moral and business case for diversity and inclusion in order for a company to compete successfully in the global economy. In other words, not only is ensuring a diverse workforce the right, just, and legal thing to do, it can also foster innovation, enhance productivity, and attract consumers who want to see themselves in the companies from which they are buying goods and services. She contends that "The goal is to move beyond tolerating diversity to respecting it, celebrating it, treasuring it, and then using diversity in the interest of a company's business objectives."

In her 2011 speech "Exploring Our Differences," delivered at The Ohio State University, Cole argues that "excellence in education is only possible if there is diversity." Drawing upon her training as a cultural anthropologist, she argues how the "power of empathy" can help people to understand the stories and experiences of those different from themselves. In "Lessons from the Life and Work of Dr. Martin Luther King Jr.," she ponders Dr. King's global vision of a "beloved community." She then focuses on Coretta Scott King's activism to champion the rights of women and people within the LGBT community.

FIGURE 7.1 In Chautauqua, NY, speaking on the significance of diversity, equity, and inclusion. Photo by Brian Hayes for the *Chatauquan Daily*.

Finally, in her 2015 speech "Moving beyond Barriers: Transforming International Education through Inclusive Excellence," at the Third Annual Diversity Abroad Conference in New Orleans, Louisiana, Cole meditates on education globally as she contemplates her study abroad experiences in France, affirming study abroad as an important component of one's college experience. She points out, "But as mind opening as my experiences were at Fisk, Oberlin, and Northwestern, it was the time I spent in Tours, France—living outside of my own culture and my own country—that most surely set me on a path that I continue to travel. It is a path on which I encounter other people and their cultures and, in the process, I continue to learn about my own culture and, indeed, about myself." This speech outlines the benefits of study abroad, the need for more diverse students to take advantage of study abroad opportunities, and the impediments that often prevent students from studying abroad.

What is significant about these speeches is that they take on diversity, equity, and inclusion—a timeless social issue that has become even more popular in the wake of anti-Black violence that has occurred in recent years (e.g., the murders of George Floyd, Ahmaud Arbery, Breonna Taylor). The fact that these speeches are given to completely different audiences—corporate America, a university setting, and an international education conference—once again shows the range of her expertise and the breadth of her impact and contributions.

The Compelling Case for Diversity, Equity, and Inclusion

Goldman Sachs Reception, Goldman Sachs, Washington, DC, June 14, 2010

Good late afternoon to each of you. And to Joyce Brayboy, a special thanks for giving me this opportunity to be a part of Goldman Sachs' first America's Diversity Week, as it takes place here in the Washington office.

When Joyce described the purpose of this meeting, I quickly consented to be here, knowing that it would give me yet another chance to talk about why diversity and inclusion in the workplace is so important and a vital "best practice" for successful global companies.

As I prepared my remarks for this particular talk, I chuckled to myself as I recalled that this is not the first time that I will address this subject, and it will not be the last.

Of course, as I prepared to spend this time with you, I also went to Goldman Sachs' web page and found this well-crafted statement on your approach to diversity: "For us to be successful, our men and women must reflect the diversity of the communities and cultures in which we operate. That means we must attract, retain, and motivate people from many backgrounds and perspectives. Being diverse is not optional; it is what we must be" [Goldman Sachs n.d.].

Let me turn now to what I see as the compelling case for Goldman Sachs and all global companies to increase the diversity in their workplaces *and* to increase an inclusive environment that allows the companies to retain a diverse workforce.

When you think about it, you realize that it would be rare to find a workplace where there is absolutely no diversity among the employees, particularly in terms of gender and age. But is the workplace one where the women are concentrated in what we used to call the "secretarial pool," and people of color are in large numbers in the mail room but rarely found in the executive suites, individuals of the LGBT community are in the workplace but are hesitant to "bring their whole selves to work," and few if any accommodations are made for people who are differently abled?

The goal must be more than having a diverse workforce. The goal must be to also create an environment in the workplace that values all employees, that moves beyond simply counting heads—so many African Americans, so many women, so many gay people—to making sure that there is an atmosphere where every head counts!

The goal is to move beyond tolerating diversity to respecting it, celebrating it, treasuring it, and then using diversity in the interest of a company's business objectives.

Let me play the professor and ask and answer my own question: Why is there such a compelling case today for diversity and inclusion if a company wants to compete successfully in the global economy?

The answer, in very clear and simple terms is this: because there is a *moral case* for doing so but, more importantly to companies that want to succeed, there is a *business case* for doing so.

In terms of the *moral case*, it is simply the correct thing to do to provide an equal opportunity for employment to qualified people of all cultures, backgrounds, orientations, and circumstances who wish to work in a company.

And we should note that for US-based global companies, there is also a *legal imperative* because, quite simply, it is against the law to discriminate against applicants based on their race, gender, and other attributes that are not barriers to successful employment.

But the most compelling case for diversity and inclusion among corporations is what is called the *business case*. Others call it the economic imperative. Still others say to promote diversity and inclusion at a company, why it is just the smart thing to do. What is this business case in quick and straightforward terms?

First, in order for a company to compete in the global economy, it must move beyond the same old ideas of doing the same old things that produce the same old results. When associates who come from different backgrounds and circumstances are brought into a company, they bring with them new and different ideas from which the most innovative and profitable ones can be chosen. In short, innovation is a necessity for successful competition in today's global economy.

A second point in terms of the business case for diversity and inclusion is this: customers and clients want to see themselves reflected in the company from which they are buying goods and services. And that means they want to see individuals from their communities in the boardroom, in the executive suites, among the middle managers, among the suppliers, and indeed throughout the enterprise. The demographics in our country are such that when we talk about customers and clients, we must understand that the term minority is rapidly ceasing to have meaning when applied to people of color. And the ideas that women, 50 percent plus of a population, are a minority never made sense. What does make sense is the Native American saying: "Women hold up half the sky!"

The third and final reason I want to reference as to why smart corporate leaders advance the case for diversity and inclusion is that they know that a work environment where everyone is respected and treated fairly encourages productivity. By contrast, a work environment where there is suspicion of, or actual expressions of, bigotry and discrimination sets up an unhealthy work environment that negatively affects productivity.

I am anxious for us to have some interchange on the points I have made, so let me bring closure to my remarks by telling you another story. This was a favorite story of one of my sheroes, the great civil rights worker, Fannie Lou Hamer. She loved to tell this story at the end of a talk to emphasize who had the responsibility to do the work she had described. I tell this story so that you will hear, in the last line, whose responsibility it is to bring greater diversity into the workforce at Goldman Sachs, while simultaneously creating a welcoming environment for all associates.

It is the story of some young boys who decided one day to fool an old lady by asking her a question that they thought she would be incapable of answering. The ringleader would take a bird that they had caught and, placing it behind his back, he would pose a question to the old lady:

"Old lady, old lady, this bird that I have behind my back, is it dead or is it alive?"

If the old lady said that the bird was dead, then he would release his hands and the bird would fly away. But if, to the question, she said that the bird was alive, he would crush it.

They found the old lady and asked if she would respond to a question. She would try, she said.

And so, the ringleader put the bird behind his back and said: "Old lady, old lady, this bird that I have behind my back, is it dead or is it alive?"

With simple but powerful wisdom she said: "The answer is in your hands!"

Exploring Our Differences

Seventeenth Annual National Conference on Diversity, Race, and Learning,

The Ohio State University, Columbus, OH, May 3, 2011

President E. Gordon Gee, my colleagues of the faculty and staff, members of the Columbus community and beyond, and dear students—who are the reason that OSU exists—Good afternoon! And thank you for this opportunity to share with you what I consider to be the compelling case for diversity and inclusion in American higher education, and to do so as you convene for the seventeenth Annual National Conference on Diversity, Race, and Learning.

It is not out of arrogance that I claim to have "found the note," but out of a deep conviction that learning to explore our differences *and* our commonalities, to celebrate them, and to grow from them is one of the most important tasks that we humans must carry out at this moment in time.

Today, in my role as the director of the Smithsonian's National Museum of African Art, I have a way of lifting up the duality of our diversity and commonalities. At the opening of an exhibition, at one of our educational programs, indeed whenever I am to speak for our museum, this is what I say: "Welcome home! Yes, this is your home in the sense that you are in a place that collects, conserves, and educates about the visual arts that come from Africa—the only place on earth from which we all have descended. Africa is the cradle of humankind. And, the sooner that white folks admit that they are Africans, too."

Let me ask: What is the state of our nation in terms of "the race question" and, more broadly, diversity and inclusion?

An insight can be gained by recalling words written by W. E. B. Du Bois, one of our nation's great African American intellectuals and activists. He said, "The problem of the twentieth century is the problem of the color line" [Du Bois 1903].

Now here we are in the twenty-first century and, as a nation, we still have not successfully dealt with the color line. And there are so many other lines that continue to divide us: lines based on gender, class, religion, nationality, sexual orientation, age, and physical and mental abilities and disabilities.

From many quarters in our country—and our world—we continue to hear these messages: All people of color are in the category of "other" in relationship to white Americans; the proper place for women is in the house; heterosexuality is the only "normal" way to bond; and the poor are that way either because they prefer it to being "normal" middle- and upper-class folks, or their plight is, for a host of other reasons, their fault.

Such a climate requires that all of us dedicate ourselves to analyzing and understanding negative reactions to difference. Yes, our nation has for the first time placed in the White House a Black president and his family. But because President Obama is there does not mean that we are now in a post-racial society. President Obama's election certainly does tell us that race as a barrier to the highest office in the land has been challenged. But in my view it does not mean that racism has ended.

When we turn specifically to "the academy," we see that there is an enormously destructive myth in the world of education. Namely, that excellence in education is impossible if there is diversity. I am convinced that excellence in education is only possible if there is diversity, and I want to make two points in this regard.

The first is that excellence in education requires the incorporation of diverse perspectives and cultures in our curricula. To be well educated, students here at the Ohio State University and in all of our higher education institutions need to confront, explore, and critique Shakespeare and T. S. Eliot. But they should do no less with the works of Chinua Achebe, Maxine Hong Kingston, and Sandra Cisneros. They need to read Joy Bargo, and Paula Gunn Allen on Native American women's realities, the works of Audre Lorde and Adrienne Rich, and students need to wrestle with the powerful words of Gwendolyn Brooks and Toni Morrison.

My second point is this: excellence in education also requires that the very participants in the great process of teaching and learning are of different backgrounds and conditions and that higher education institutions create an inclusive environment that is critical for retaining diverse students and faculty. With respect to the need to diversify our faculties, we know that even on the most progressive of campuses it is difficult to instantly bring about a more multicultural, multiracial, multi-ethnic composition. I hope that we also know that taking a business-as-usual procedure will never bring people of color in meaningful numbers to our predominantly white faculties.

And so, we must be creative, we must demand of our white faculty that they struggle to bring folk of color to their campuses. But they must also struggle to raise their own consciousnesses and engage in the kind of study and human empathy that will permit them to teach and treat students of color in fair and humane ways.

As an anthropologist and as a "practicing" human being, I am convinced of the power of empathy. I think that with enormous hard work, men can come to empathize with the realities of women; gringos with the realities of Hispanics; and white Americans with the realities of Black Americans. One of my sheroes, Audre Lorde, frequently said if Black professors can learn to teach Shakespeare, white professors can learn to teach James Baldwin. While they do, we must still have as one of our most urgent priorities the creation of communities of diversity and this means increasing the number of faculty of color as well as students of color on our campuses.

In terms of college and university staff, let me say clearly and strongly, I see staff as critical partners in the great project called education.

For it is you, my colleagues of the Ohio State University staff, who can or cannot help to provide an environment for learning and growth outside of the classroom.

And that is why the staff of a college or university needs to reflect the composition, the behavior, and the values we hope our students will embrace.

The absence of diversity among staff makes a statement about the world our students must be prepared to live in that is neither accurate nor desirable.

Of course, the academy does not exist in a vacuum.

In the so-called real world, there is so much negativity about "difference."

And because various forms of bigotry and discrimination are so widespread and tenacious, many come to believe that it is "just human nature" to dislike people who are different from the way you are, and to create systems of inequality based on those differences.

No! Bigotry is not "just human nature," and it is not passed on genetically! Bigotry is learned and, because it is learned, it can be unlearned, and indeed we could just stop teaching it.

I am not naive enough to think that we can rid the world of bigotry by declaring a moratorium on teaching it. How well I know that bigotry and discrimination are about power and privilege, and those with it do not easily decide to just give it up.

As the great abolitionist and feminist, Frederick Douglass put it, "Power concedes nothing without a demand. It never did and it never will" [BlackPast 2007].

Here in the United States, power and privilege based on race and gender stand out, and so, as an African American woman, I know what it is like not to have white skin privilege and not to have male privilege. But it is ever so important to acknowledge and deal with the reality that there is some power and privilege that I do have. I clearly have some power and privilege as someone who is upper-middle class, heterosexual, a Christian, and physically able.

This reality, that each of us has some form of power and privilege, flows from the fact that each of us has multiple identities. And it is so important for us to be aware of those identities and to guard against efforts to characterize us in singular terms.

Let me share one haunting and most unfortunate reality about this stuff that we call bigotry and discrimination. It is this: being the victim of one form of bigotry or discrimination does not make someone immune to victimizing others. For example, some white women who have been victims of sexism practice racism. Some Black people who have known the bitter sting of racism are homophobic, and practice heterosexism. Some people who are Jewish and have been victims of anti-Semitism can harbor feelings and can carry out actions that stem from Islamophobia.

"How does this relate to your world?" you might ask.

In considering individual and institutional barriers to recruiting and retaining a diverse academic community, I want to pose two fundamental questions and, indeed, I want to offer responses to my own questions.

The first question is, "Why bother?" Why put in your time and your effort to not only increase the diversity on your campus but to build the kind of inclusive culture that makes diverse folks want to remain at Ohio State? There is a moral reason to do so and a "business" imperative.

A *moral imperative* means that it is simply the right thing to do to make sure that qualified people of underrepresented groups have an equal opportunity to be employed as staff, to join the ranks of the faculty, and to matriculate here at Ohio State and to enter and advance in a business.

And, just as the leadership in corporation go on to say that there is a business case for diversity, I say that there is *pedagogical case for diversity* because, when it is absent, you cannot be successful with the task of teaching and learning that prepares students to live effectively in what is an increasingly diverse world.

Corporation leaders say they need a diverse workforce because the presence of different perspectives can lead to new and highly innovative ideas to flourish. And thus, the corporation develops a competitive advantage.

In the case of academic institutions like Ohio State University, I assume you are convinced, as I am, that quality teaching and learning flows far more easily when the participants in the process bring to the discussion different ideas, different experiences, and different "truths."

My second question is, "What do you mean when you refer to increasing underrepresented groups on campus?" Do you mean racial and ethnic "minorities" that are fast on the way to being numerical majorities? And what about women? If you increase the number of white women—on the faculty, staff, board of trustees, and students—isn't that "good enough" and you won't have to do special outreach to women of color?

What about underrepresented groups who are lesbians, gays, bisexuals, and transgender people? Or is that a taboo topic?

And individuals from various communities of disabled folks? Do you shy away from increasing the number of faculty, students, staff, and board members who are differently abled because you know there are financial costs to address the conditions required for their involvement in the full life of this community?

And then there is the "unspoken word" among us: class. And to "be inclusive about being inclusive," what about addressing the underrepresentation of various religious groups? And what about age?

Based on the points I have just made about ongoing challenges to human diversity, challenges that take the form of bigotry and discrimination, what can I ask of you? What must I ask of you? There are indeed some very concrete things that I want to ask you to do, but please know that I will not ask anything of you that I do not continue to ask of myself.

First, learn how you learned your prejudices. That is, interrogate yourself about your particular journey around questions of diversity and inclusion. And, as parents, if that is something you are or want to become, please contribute to changing the world by refusing to teach bigotry to your children.

Second, I ask that each of you get in touch with your multiple identities. And, once you do so, then you must never let others relate to you in terms of only one of your attributes. And please do not relate to anyone in terms of a single attribute.

I also urge you to honestly examine your own power and privilege. For if you are to avoid using your power and privilege in ways that exploit and oppress others, then you must be in touch with what power and privilege you have, the basis of it, and how it can be used in positive ways.

And finally, I ask each of you that you take personal responsibility for helping to transform this institution into a more diverse place with a spirit and reality of inclusion. That means in concrete terms making sure that the curriculum moves from the three Ws, i.e., a curriculum that is highly Western, white, and womanless.

That means not only recruiting a diverse class of students every year but creating the kind of inclusive culture that will help students of color, students of the LGBT community, students who are differently abled, students of many underrepresented groups—all students to feel truly welcome and sought after.

Lessons from the Life and Work
of Dr. Martin Luther King Jr.

Office of Diversity, Inclusion, and Multicultural Education, George Mason University, Fairfax, VA, February 25, 2014

President, faculty, staff, students, alumni, and friends of George Mason University: Good evening! Please accept my heartfelt appreciation for this opportunity to share some of my thoughts with you on the occasion of your annual Black Heritage Month.

When you read the title I chose for this topic, you may well have asked yourself: "Is Dr. Cole confused about which month we are in? Does she think we are still in January when we annually celebrate the life and work of Dr. Martin Luther King Jr.?"

Let me assure you that like any of us human beings, I can certainly get confused but, on this occasion, that is not the case.

I am fully aware that the overarching theme for this year is within and across identity groups, and I fully intend to address that topic. However, I have purposefully chosen to launch this address by lifting up the life and work of one of the most respected and beloved leaders in our nation and the world period. From Dr. Martin Luther King Jr., we can learn a fundamental lesson. Namely, that we not only have the responsibility to acknowledge and respect who we are in terms of our identity groups, but to move toward that day when no one will be judged by their membership in any identity group. That is to say, Dr. King taught us that no one should ever be judged by the color of their skin; by the economic circumstances they were born into; by their gender; by their sexual orientation or identity; by their religious beliefs or the absence of any religious belief; by their nationality; or by their physical or mental abilities or disabilities.

Yes, Martin Luther King deeply believed that every woman, man, and child should be judged by the content of their character. That is such a basic lesson that Dr. King believed and lived by. Oh, but think how different our world would be if in every community, and in every country, that basic lesson was *taught*, and *learned*, and *practiced*.

A second fundamental lesson that Dr. King taught us is this: The oppressive and destructive attitude we call bigotry is not carried on the chromosomes! It is learned. And indeed, because we learn to be bigots, we can unlearn those horrific attitudes.

And here is the most important and encouraging part of this lesson. Because bigotry is learned, we could stop teaching it!

Yes, Dr. King truly believed that we human beings learn to hate and, if we learn to hate, we can unlearn that horrific behavior. Listen to these simple but powerful words of Dr. King: "I have decided to stick with love. Hate is too great a burden to bear."*

But Dr. King was not naive about how we could rid the world of bigotry. He did not assume that we could get rid of bigotry by declaring a moratorium on teaching it. He knew, as surely we know, that bigotry and discrimination are about power and privilege. And it is not easy for folks who have power and privilege to decide to just give it up.

We have to offer to those who have it a more rewarding alternative. And, for Dr. King, that alternative was what he called "the Beloved Community."

Here is Dr. King's view of the Beloved Community, as explained in a document from the King Center in Atlanta.

For Dr. King, The Beloved Community was not a lofty utopian goal to be confused with the rapturous image of the Peaceable Kingdom, in which lions and lambs coexist in idyllic harmony. Rather, The Beloved Community was for him a realistic, achievable goal that could be attained by a critical mass of people committed to and trained in the philosophy and methods of nonviolence.

Dr. King's Beloved Community is a global vision, in which all people can share in the wealth of the earth. In the Beloved Community, poverty,

* This is a paraphrase from the 1967 speech "Where Do We Go from Here?" (King 1967d).

hunger and homelessness will not be tolerated because international standards of human decency will not allow it. Racism and all forms of discrimination, bigotry and prejudice will be replaced by an all-inclusive spirit of sisterhood and *brotherhood*.

In the Beloved Community international disputes will be resolved by peaceful conflict-resolution and reconciliation of adversaries, instead of military power. Love and trust will triumph over fear and hatred. Peace with justice will prevail over war and military conflict. [The King Center n.d.]

Clearly, when Dr. Martin Luther King Jr. was in the civil rights struggle, his focus was on the rights of African Americans. Indeed, he was the leader of a nonviolent movement that focused on ending legalized racial discrimination in America.

However, Dr. King was certainly conscious of the plight of groups other than African Americans, and among his most remembered words are these: "Injustice anywhere is a threat to justice everywhere" [King 1963a].

I honestly believe that if Dr. King were living today, he would call upon us to work, in a nonviolent way, for the end to all expressions of bigotry, to all legal and practiced forms of discrimination.

I want to turn now to views expressed by Coretta Scott King, the wife of Dr. Martin Luther King and, in her own right, a shero. Yes, I said shero. Indeed, I insist that for every hero in this world there is at least one shero.

It is very instructive to note that my shero, Coretta Scott King, as she remained an activist after Dr. King had gone to glory, spoke out not only for the rights of African Americans, but she was also a vocal and committed champion for the rights of women, and the rights of sisters and brothers in the LGBT community. Listen to these words, spoken by Coretta Scott King.

"Freedom and justice cannot be parceled out in pieces to suit political convenience. I don't believe you can stand for freedom for one group of people and deny it to others." [King 1994]

"Homophobia is like racism and anti-Semitism and other forms of bigotry in that it seeks to dehumanize a large group of people, to deny their humanity, their dignity and personhood." [King 1998]

"Gay and lesbian people have families, and their families should have legal protection, whether by marriage or civil union. A constitutional amendment banning same-sex marriages is a form of gay bashing and it would do nothing at all to protect traditional marriages." [King 1998]

"I believe very strongly that all forms of bigotry and discrimination are equally wrong and should be opposed by right thinking Americans everywhere. Freedom from discrimination based on sexual orientation is surely a fundamental human right in any great democracy, as much as freedom from racial, religious, gender, or ethnic discrimination." [King 1998]

Were Dr. King among us today, I believe that he would align himself with the views expressed in the words I have just shared from speeches given by Coretta Scott King. Why Dr. King might even say about what his wife was saying: Amen! And A-women too!

In short, the great lesson that the legacy of Martin Luther King and Coretta Scott King call upon us to work toward is quite simply this: That we must do our part to move ourselves, our communities, our nation, and our world toward that day when difference won't make any more difference!

Perhaps the first step in joining that righteous struggle is to simply believe that everyone, yes, everyone, must be "invited to the table"—and indeed to bring their whole selves to that table. And if the table is not big enough for everyone, then we must set about building a bigger table.

I want to turn now to a more specific focus on identity groups.

As an African American woman, I know what it is like not to have white skin privilege and not to have male privilege. But it is ever so important that I acknowledge and deal with the reality that there is some power and privilege that I do have.

I clearly have some power and privilege as someone who is upper-middle-class, heterosexual, a Christian, and physically able.

This reality, that each of us has some form of power and privilege, flows from the fact that each of us has multiple identities. And it is ever so important for us to be aware of those identities and to guard against efforts to characterize us in singular terms.

On February 16, around the world countless people who believe in freedom for everyone celebrated Audre Lorde's eightieth birthday. And I bet you from up in glory she may well be reminding us of these words that she spoke: "If I didn't define myself for myself, I would be crunched into other people's fantasies for me and eaten alive" [BlackPast 2012].

Let me share another reality about this stuff that we call bigotry and discrimination. It is this: unfortunately, being the victim of one form of bigotry or discrimination does not immune one from victimizing others.

For example, some white women who have been the victims of sexism practice racism. Some Black people who have known the bitter sting of racism are homophobic, and practice heterosexism. Some people who are Jewish and have been the victims of anti-Semitism can harbor feelings and carry out actions that stem from Islamophobia.

It does not require the smarts of a rocket scientist to make the observations I have just made about each of us having some power and privilege, each of us having multiple identities, and each of us having the potential to victimize others. And I honestly believe that it also does not take the smarts of a rocket scientist to identify some very basic steps that each of you can do in the interest of making your university and your community more inclusive. Please know that I will not ask anything of you that I do not continue to ask of myself.

First, learn how you learned your prejudices. That is, interrogate yourself about your particular journey around questions of diversity and inclusion.

Can you remember when you first learned derogatory words about other people? Who taught you those words?

And what about positive experiences? Can you remember your first interactions with someone of different identity groups than yours? What was that like? What did those experiences teach you?

To you who are students, when that day comes when you are parents—if that is something you wish to become, and that you will become—what will you teach your children about other people? Stop for a moment and realize what extraordinary power you will have: you will be your children's very first teachers. You will be able to teach them to be bigots and to practice some form of discrimination. Or you will be able to contribute to changing the world by refusing to teach your children how to be prejudiced toward people who do not share their identity groups.

Regardless of what position you hold at George Mason University—student, faculty, staff, administrator—you can speak up and call out folks who tell racist, sexist, and homophobic jokes. They are not funny, and these so-called jokes hurt, and hurt deeply whoever they are about.

Something else that each of us can and should do in terms of continuing on our respective journeys to not only understand but to embrace and celebrate diversity is this. We can take the time to truly understand the issues involved with highly charged topics such as immigration, and the number of Black and Latino men—and yes women too—who are entangled in our nation's criminal justice system.

Second, I ask that each of you get in touch with your multiple identities. And once you do so, then you must never let others relate to you in terms of only one of your attributes.

During the era when I grew up in the segregated South, I was far more conscious of my "race" than my gender. But into my adulthood, as I developed a consciousness of myself as a woman, it became difficult for me to prioritize one of these attributes over the other. I owe much of my understanding of my multiple identities to what I was exposed to and then participated in during the years that I was a professor.

In the 1960s, I was a leader in the movement for Black Studies, helping to found one of the first Black Studies programs in the United States. But the day came when I began to ask the question: "Where are the women in Black Studies?" As I became deeply involved in efforts to establish women's studies in colleges and universities, I then found myself asking the question: "Where are the Black folks and other folks of color in women's studies?"

And then came a real day of reckoning when at Hunter College, where Audre Lorde and I were both professors, she helped me to ask the question: "Where were people of LGBT communities, older women, differently abled folks, biracial folks—where were all of those folks in women's studies and in Black Studies?"

I can tell you this, once I came to embrace my multiple identities, I have not only refused to ignore any of them, I also made the commitment to do my best to acknowledge the multiple identities of others.

And, finally, I urge each of you to honestly examine your own power and privilege. For if you are to avoid using your power and privilege in ways that exploit and oppress others, then you must be in touch with what power and privilege you have, the basis of it, and how it can be used in positive ways.

In this great country of ours, when we think about issues of prejudice and discrimination, it is easy to immediately think about issues of race and gender. I am certainly aware of when I am the victim of white skin privilege and when I am the victim of male privilege. What I continue to work on is being aware of when I have power and privilege. For example, in this country of mine, it is easy to ignore the fact that I have privilege and power as a Christian. And if I do not remain conscious of this fact, I could easily fall into expressions of anti-Semitism and Islamophobia.

I certainly have power and privilege as an able-bodied person. One of my close colleagues and friends, Deb Dagit, who is an activist in support of the rights of differently abled people, has taught me this: The privilege and power of being fully abled can immediately disappear with an accident or a certain kind of illness.

In asking those three things of each of you, I have asked you to engage in what might be called simple acts in the interest of a huge cause—that is simple actions that can contribute to the ongoing effort to make our world a place of peace and justice for all.

Now I want to move toward closure by sharing with you some inspiring words that come from the heads and the hearts of women and men of diverse communities.

From a Native American people, the Sioux, we hear these words: "With all beings and all things we shall be relatives."

Here are words that value gender equality that in various versions are said by different peoples: "Women hold up half the sky."

There is a Chinese saying that speaks to the beauty of human diversity with these words: "One flower never makes a spring."

Cesar Chavez, the exemplary Chicano leader, once said: "Our ambitions must be broad enough to include the aspirations and needs of others—for their sakes and for our own" [United Farm Workers n.d.].

The beloved Rabbi Hillel was asked if he could stand on one foot and say everything that is in the Torah. He responded that he could, and this is what he said: "What is hateful to you, do not to your fellow men [and women]. That is the whole Torah. All the rest is commentary" [Babylonian Talmud, Shabbat 31a].

There is a passage in the Quran that says this: "We are made into nations and tribes that we may know and love each other" [Quran, sura 49, verse 13].

Audre Lorde, perhaps the most celebrated Black feminist, lesbian, professor, mother, warrior poet of this era said these profound words: "It is not our differences but our silence about our differences that harms us" [Lorde 1980].

I offer these words of Helen Keller, an amazing social activist who was deaf and blind from the age of ten months: "Each of us is blind and deaf until our eyes are opened to our fellow men and women, until our ears hear the voices of humanity" [Keller 1903].

And yes, the last words I want to offer you are those of Dr. Martin Luther King—perhaps his most often quoted words: "I have a dream that my four little children will one day live in a nation where they will not be judged by the color of their skin but by the content of their character" [NPR 2023].

Moving beyond Barriers

TRANSFORMING INTERNATIONAL
EDUCATION THROUGH INCLUSIVE
EXCELLENCE

Third Annual Diversity Abroad Conference, New Orleans, LA, March 22, 2015

Friends, colleagues, students—My Sisters and Brothers All: Good evening! When my dear brother-friend, Julius Coles, asked me to participate in the second annual Diversity Abroad conference, I was not able to do so. I am genuinely pleased to be able to join you for this third annual conference, and to offer some thoughts on the value of studying abroad for all students, and the importance of increasing the number of students from underrepresented groups who engage in this very special form of education in international settings.

So, here I am once again taking on the topic of diversity. I certainly do not have *the* definitive answer as to how more students of color and students from other diverse communities can be encouraged to study abroad. No one person does. But answers will come from people coming together as we have here to exchange ideas, present best practices, propose new ways of doing things, and, importantly, by honestly looking at and critiquing the way things are currently done in study abroad programs.

Many moons ago when I was a graduate student at Northwestern University, I had an opportunity to go to Tours, France, where I and Erik Hansen, a student from Denmark, lived with a French family. The immediate reason for me to do this was to gain enough competency in French to pass a language requirement for a PhD in anthropology.

That mission was accomplished! But an even more important mission was accomplished. Namely, that by being open to listening and learning about French culture—going to the market with madam, going in search of snails and learning how to prepare *des escargots*, listening to conversations at the dinner table, and a host of other everyday experiences—by being open to listening and learning about French culture, I came to see the world of the French *and* my own world in clearer and often in very different ways.

I was born and grew up in Jacksonville, Florida, during those wretched days of legal segregation. My parents made every effort to expose me and my sister, and years later my brother, to life beyond the confines of colored schools, the colored "public" library, colored movie houses, etc., But it was not until I left Jacksonville, Florida, at the age of fifteen, to attend Fisk University in an early entrance program that my horizon began to significantly broaden.

It was at Fisk that I deepened my passion for African and African American art and began to fully appreciate the power of the visual arts.

When I went on an exchange program to Oberlin College, the lenses through which I saw the world grew larger and larger. It was at Oberlin that I was cast into situations that were vastly different from the ones I had grown up with. Why in Jacksonville, Florida, the notion of interfaith or interdenominational exchange meant a setting where AME, that is African Methodist Episcopal church, interacted with Baptist and Pentecostal folks. But at Oberlin, I was exposed to and came to respect folks who were not only of far more diverse Christian denominations but were of the Jewish, Hindu, Islamic, and Buddhist faiths, and those who were agnostic and atheist.

But as mind opening as my experiences were at Fisk, Oberlin, and Northwestern, it was the time I spent in Tours, France—living outside of my own culture and my own country—that most surely set me on a path that I continue to travel. It is a path on which I encounter other people and their cultures and, in the process, I continue to learn about my own culture and, indeed, about myself.

Years after my own experience in studying abroad, I strongly encouraged one of my sons to live and study in Japan. And as a professor and college administrator, I enthusiastically encouraged students to take advantage of opportunities to live and study outside of the United States.

While I served as the president of our nation's only two historically Black colleges for women—Spelman and Bennett colleges—I actively promoted the study abroad programs at those two institutions. I am proud to say that today, at both of those colleges, there is great appreciation of the value of that form of international education. At Spelman, it was clear that under Professor Margery Ganz's leadership, studying abroad would become a goal for many of that college's students. At Spelman College, the percentage of students studying abroad has reached 40 percent of a graduating class, and they do so in thirty-two different countries.

One way of indicating how strongly I endorse studying abroad as a component of an excellent college or university experience is to say this. If I were given the power to make only one change in American higher education that would substantially improve the quality of education students receive, it would be this. I would make it mandatory that no student graduate from an undergraduate institution without spending at least a semester in a culture and country outside of the one he or she was born and grew up in.

I make this statement because of the extraordinary value there is in studying abroad. While I do not need to convince any of you of this, it will not hurt to do a little preaching to the choir to indicate some of the reasons American students need to study abroad if they are to succeed in this fast-changing world that is defined not only by the role of information and technology in everyday life, but the enormous diversity in who the world's people are.

Perhaps you have heard the joke: "What do you call someone who speaks only one language?"

The answer: you call that person an American.

One of the obvious benefits for students who study abroad in countries that are not English speaking is that they can acquire some degree of proficiency in another language. And, for many young people, such a proficiency will be a great advantage as they work in firms that do business internationally, and indeed as they work in US settings where the first language of increasingly large numbers of their coworkers is Spanish.

Recently I asked a very successful African American woman who is engaged in the world of international business who she was looking for to serve as a nanny for her daughter who had just been born. Without hesitating she said she planned to immediately expose her daughter to another language, and she had chosen a nanny whose first language is Cantonese.

We may well reach a time when most professional careers in the US will require multilingual skills. Studying abroad in a non-English-speaking country is an excellent way to begin to prepare for that possibility.

And then there is the sheer joy of learning enough of another language to be able to enjoy acquaintances and friendships with people who are native speakers of that language.

Commanding another language also opens up the possibility of being able to watch films in that language, of ordering from a menu written in that language, of listening to vocal music in that language, and reading novels and poetry in that language.

In a country and a world where diversity is increasing exponentially, the opportunity to learn about another culture and by extension one's own culture is mighty important. As anthropologists often muse, "It would hardly be the fish who discovered the existence of water."

Misconceptions and stereotypes about one's own culture and the culture that students are living in are often challenged and overcome through the study abroad experiences. Studies have shown that studying abroad helps students realize and better understand their own cultural biases. What better way to help produce well-rounded citizens at home and abroad than through an international study program!

For white students, studying abroad in many parts of the world allows them the very rare opportunity to experience life as an ethnic minority. What a great opportunity for white students to gain a much deeper understanding and sensitivity to what individuals who are different from themselves experience in daily life!

Studying abroad often helps students to better understand themselves and to grow in ways that they would not at home, for living in a different country entails almost daily challenges to pre-held beliefs and thoughts.

In the study I just referred to, 97 percent of respondents reported that studying abroad made them mature faster and 96 percent reported increased confidence as a result of the experience. A total of 95 percent stated that it impacted how they viewed the world. And 90 percent of the students reported that the experience led them to have more diverse friends.

There is considerable anecdotal evidence that studying abroad improves a student's academic success. While there are not many studies on the performance of returning students of color, a study by the University System of Georgia found that African American students who studied abroad were 30 percent more likely to graduate in four years compared to students who did not study abroad [Sweeney 2013]. For other students of color, the four-year graduation rates were 18 percent higher compared to students who did not study abroad.

The experience of international study also has a large impact on a student's future study and employment. In the study I just cited, 87 percent stated that study abroad had a major influence on their future academic study and 64 percent stated it had a direct influence on their decision to attend graduate school. In addition, almost half of the students who studied abroad reported that they went on to work in fields with some connection to the international community.

Indeed, for most students, a study abroad experience is considered a defining moment in their lives. It is something that will stay with them, guide them, and shape them throughout their entire lifetime.

A student who studies abroad will not return as the same person, nor will that student look at the world in the same way. They will have a much richer and fuller view of themselves, their friends and family, and the world around them.

Indeed, the experience of studying abroad can be so transformative that students who return from such an experience are often said to undergo "culture shock" in re-entering their native culture.

When the advantages of studying abroad are so clear, why is it that the profile of students who take advantage of such opportunities continue to be largely white, middle- to upper-income students?

How can we encourage and guarantee far greater diversity among students who take advantage of international educational programs?

Before I respond to my own questions, I should be clear about what I mean when I use the term diversity. While I am focusing on race and ethnicity in this talk, I am aware of the need for us to bring into our discussions about diversity in other attributes such as class, religion, nationality, age, disability, and sexual orientation and identity.

Over the past several decades, we have made substantial progress in increasing the numbers of underrepresented groups on our campuses. However, while we celebrate that progress, we must address the reality that too much of the effort of PWIs [predominantly White institutions] is focused on recruiting diverse students. And too little attention is given to retaining those students by making sure there is a welcoming and inclusive culture on the campus, that there are programs to keep these students from giving in and dropping out, and that every possible effort is made to make sure that there is little difference between the graduation rate of students of color and white students.

In short, on too many campuses, not nearly enough attention is placed on a more holistic approach that stresses support, mentoring, and fostering an inclusive culture so that students from diverse backgrounds can feel welcome and "at home" on a campus where they are clearly in the numerical minority. Only when efforts to guarantee a diverse student body are met with the creation and sustaining of an inclusive culture can we say that we are on the road to providing the kind of educational experience that all students have the right to obtain.

While the gains in underrepresented groups studying abroad have not been as pronounced as the gains in white students in study abroad programs, there have been slight gains nonetheless. From 2005 to 2010, the rate of African American students studying abroad increased from 3.5 percent to 4.8 percent, for Latino students from 10.8 percent to 13 percent [Sweeney 2013]. There was little change for American Indian and Alaska Native students. Overall, minority students represent less than 25 percent of the students who study abroad. Students who study abroad are still overwhelmingly white and from middle, upper-middle, and upper-class families.

Let us be clear that in addition to the challenge of increasing the number of students from diverse backgrounds who study abroad, we must also pay greater attention to the need to increase the total number of all students who have that very special opportunity. Today, fewer than 10 percent of all US college students study abroad at some point during their undergraduate years.

There is also a need for greater diversity in where students study internationally. As the world becomes more and more diverse and multicultural, it is still the case that almost 60 percent of students will study in Europe with 40 percent of students studying in just four countries, the United Kingdom, Italy, Spain, and France.

Despite the growing importance of Asia, Africa, and Latin America in economic and political ways, only 12 percent of students will study in Asia, only 15 percent in Latin America, and less than 5 percent in Africa. These figures are especially disturbing when one considers the fact that for many students one of the strongest incentives for participating in a study abroad program is the chance to connect with their heritage and family roots. For Hispanic American, Asian American, and African American students, the absence of a range of viable study abroad programs in Latin America, Asia, and Africa may well be a deterrent to their going abroad.

I turn now to note reasons why the rich, rewarding, and increasingly important experience of studying abroad is not a part of the education of so many students of color, as well as students from other underrepresented groups.

We all speak of these impediments, and I will summarize them here as the five Fs that lead to students from diverse communities failing to study abroad: family, friends, faculty, finances, and fear.

Many underrepresented students are the first in their family to attend college, and they and their parents and other relatives have had little exposure to the idea of studying abroad. Many of these students, their family members, and friends have never traveled outside of their immediate area, and certainly not to a different country. This can lead students to feel that studying abroad is for other students but not for them.

Parents and family members of students of color, students from low-income families, students who are gay, lesbian, and bisexual, and students who are differently abled may feel that their children face enough bigotry in their own country, and they do not want to risk having them face racism, heterosexism, and ablism many miles away from home.

There is also the fact that for many "minority" and working-class families, participating in a study abroad program is seen as a potential delay in finishing college and, thus, to be avoided.

At a speech at Howard University, First Lady Michelle Obama [2011] described this phenomenon: "I grew up in a blue-collar neighborhood on the south side of Chicago, and the idea of spending time abroad just never registered with me. My brother and I were among the first in our families to go to college. So, trust me, we were way more focused on getting in, getting through, and getting out, than we were with finding opportunities that would broaden our horizons."

There is much that we can learn from this statement by someone who went to Princeton on a scholarship, graduated from Harvard Law School, became a leading corporate attorney, and eventually first lady of the United States.

Students on college and university campuses are not only taught by faculty, but they are also strongly influenced by their professors. If faculty members do not encourage diverse students to study abroad, who will?

There is considerable evidence that when faculty and staff seek out students from various underrepresented groups, raise the possibility of their having a study abroad experience, and stay close to these students to work through the challenges they will encounter, the results can be quite positive.

While any faculty member should be able to encourage and counsel students of color to pursue a study abroad experience, for obvious reasons faculty of color are often more successful in getting students of color to explore and to actually do a study abroad program. Thus, the small number of faculty and staff of color on predominantly white campuses is an impediment to having large numbers of students of color involved in international education experiences.

A major impediment for students of color and students from low-income families studying abroad is the cost of participating in such programs. While at many private universities there has been a concerted and sustained effort to ensure a diverse student body, including one that represents all economic groups, this same effort has not always taken place in study abroad programs. This not only affects students of color, who disproportionately come from lower economic families, but also has a large impact on white students who come from lower-middle-class and lower-class families as well.

It is simply the case that the cost associated with studying abroad—air tickets, visas, passports, housing, and living expenses and spending money—can be prohibitive for lower income students.

Most students of color spend many years learning to navigate in a society where their experiences range from not feeling welcome to blatant expressions of bigotry. For these students, there is understandably a fear of going into an environment where there may well be bigotry and discrimination, *and* it will be an environment where they are not familiar with the cultural clues that trigger such attitudes and behavior *and* the best way to deal with systems of inequality in a "foreign" country.

The same can be said for students of LGBT communities, students with disabilities, nontraditional students in terms of age, and students of certain religious groups. The fear of how they will be treated by both their host country and fellow students who are studying abroad can be very real and traumatic.

One of my sons who studied in Japan says it was one of the greatest experiences of his life and continues to shape who he is as a person and how he sees the world. As a biracial individual, he certainly experienced racism growing up. But he has commented on the fact that while living and studying in Japan, the most overt racism he encountered was from fellow students studying abroad with him in Osaka.

In giving voice to what you and I know are major impediments to greater diversity among American students studying abroad, I am reminded of something that happened some years ago when I gave a speech that listed a host of problems, including racism, sexism, heterosexism, anti-Semitism, Islamophobia, ageism, ablism, war, violence, and poverty.

At the end of my talk, during the Q&A, a man stood up and asked me when I was going to start practicing the Noah principle. "The Noah principle, what is that?" I asked. He responded by saying this: "There will be no more credit for predicting the rain, it is time to start building some arks."

In that spirit, let me suggest these "planks" that can be used in building greater diversity in study abroad programs at American colleges and universities.

First, administrators, faculty, staff, and students at American universities and colleges must look inward and engage in serious *self-examination* of the situation on their campus in terms of diversity and the presence of an inclusive culture. For obvious reasons, a campus that is diverse in its student body, faculty, and staff and has created a culture that welcomes people of diverse attributes will have an easier time encouraging students from underrepresented groups to take on the adventure of studying abroad. In short, the more diverse a campus is, the greater the possibility that diverse students will engage in study abroad programs.

Second, while most colleges and universities have a coordinator or faculty member "in charge of" studying abroad, there is a great advantage in also having a study abroad coordinator who focuses on the recruitment and retention of students from underrepresented groups. This colleague would be charged with "reaching out" to underrepresented groups and organizations, creating goals and metrics in connection with a concerted effort to increase the number of students who applied for and went on to study outside of the United States.

Third, what about the *marketing material* for study abroad programs? Does the material show a diverse "picture" of students? Does the mission statement speak directly to a commitment to involve underrepresented students in study abroad programs?

Fourth, when recruitment and orientation sessions are held to encourage students to consider studying abroad, are the "recruiters" from diverse groups? Or are these "ambassadors" all from similar backgrounds?

Fifth, while studies have shown that longer-duration study abroad experiences produce better results, shorter programs may be helpful in getting students from diverse backgrounds—especially students from economically challenged backgrounds—to consider a study abroad experience. In general, more students are studying abroad for shorter periods of time. In the 1960s, 72 percent of students studied for a full year, while in the 1990s only 20 percent did so.

Sixth, there is an old adage that says we put our money on things we really care about. If having greater diversity among the students who study abroad is something a given college or university really cares about, then it must be willing to raise and allocate funds to support that effort.

Finally, while recruiting diverse students should involve special outreach efforts to those students, colleges and universities would do well to also organize special outreach efforts to parents and families of these students. Positive results should come from bringing these family members to campus where films are shown, students of color who have been abroad give a talk, and good counsel is given on how the study abroad experience for their student can be financed.

It is time now for me to move toward closure of this talk. I want to do so by stressing once again that not a few, not some, but *all* American students need global skills, and studying abroad is an effective and exciting way to obtain those skills. An international educational experience is now one of the most important components of a twenty-first-century education.

As Evan Ryan, assistant Secretary of State for Educational and Cultural affairs, has said: "It is in America's national interest . . . to build and sustain a globally minded and internationally literate workforce" [Schmelzer 2015].

It is also the case that studying abroad cannot only help a student to make a good living, it is bound to help that student to go on to live a good life.

And, finally, I strongly believe that the more students of diverse backgrounds join with those students who have traditionally enjoyed that unique opportunity, the more chance we have of knocking down stereotypes and misunderstandings among people.

President George H. W. Bush put it this way: "International exchanges are not a great tide to sweep away all differences, but they will slowly wear away at the obstacles to peace as surely as water wears away a hard stone" [Bush 1989].

And I conclude with these words from President Barack Obama: "Simple exchanges can break down walls between us, for when people come together and speak to one another and share a common experience, then their common humanity is revealed. We are reminded that we're joined together by our pursuit of a life that's productive and purposeful, and when that happens mistrust begins to fade and our smaller differences no longer overshadow the things that we share. And that's where progress begins" [Obama 2009a].

8. Commencement Addresses

Perhaps there is no better way to end this book than with commencement addresses. Commencement speeches capture a synthesis of the sage wisdom and inspiring advice that Johnnetta Betsch Cole offers to new graduates. In her 1996 speech "A House Divided," at Emory University, she offers lessons learned from anthropology to help graduates as they venture out into the world: "the world's problems are your problems, even if you turn your back on them, they are still yours." In her 2011 speech "Attributes of Twenty-First-Century Women Leaders," at Trinity Washington University, Cole recalls key experiences with inspiring women teachers from her childhood, who taught her vital lessons that she has relied on throughout her life. She also praises the crucial work of women's colleges in educating twenty-first-century leaders. Finally, in her 2014 speech "Courage, It's What Really Matters," at Bennington College, she meditates on bravery. She offers a personal story of her courage in choosing to embark on a new career as a museum director. Finally, she encourages the graduates to exercise courage as they choose their life's work, take risks, speak out against injustice, and serve others.

FIGURE 8.1 Delivering the 2014 commencement address at Wheaton College, Norton, MA, where Cole was presented with an honorary degree. Cole's robe was designed and made by Dr. Barbara Nicholson. Nicholson received a doctorate from Ohio State University and founded the Champagne and Grits Studio and Galleria in Columbus, OH. The clothes Nicholson designs draw heavily on African symbols. Cole's robe has a strip of African cloth down the middle of the robe with the Ghanian adinkra for *sankofa*. Adinkras are symbols that represent concepts or aphorisms. The *sankofa* adinkra says, "Go back and fetch it," which is to say, "Go back and understand the past in order to move forward toward the future." Cole's robe and cap are displayed in the Smithsonian's National Museum of African Art. Source: Wheaton College, Massachusetts.

A House Divided

Emory University, Atlanta, GA, May 14, 1996

Members of the Board of Trustees; Brother President, Bill Chace; my colleagues of the faculty and staff; alumni and friends of Emory University: I greet you ever so warmly on this marvelous celebratory morning.

But I save my warmest and most enthusiastic greetings for those for whom we have gathered today: you, my young sisters and brothers of the mighty class of 1996 and your families and friends. As you graduate from this great university, only sixty-seven days before Atlanta hosts the centennial Olympic Games, may you receive the blessing that is asked for in an old African American song: "Guide my feet while I run this race, for I don't want to run this race in vain."

Because I am a college president, I know better than most folks what it has taken for you to get here today. An extraordinary amount of hard work, discipline, determination, and no doubt some good luck too. But you are here, you made it. You certainly would not have done so without the love, the sacrifice, and the material support of your families. Surely you have thanked your moms and dads and all of your kin folks; but why don't you do it again by standing and applauding all of your loved ones.

I wish that I could give each of you graduates a congratulatory embrace, but since I cannot, please do it for me. Wrap your arms around yourself with a big hug and feel good about what you have accomplished.

A part of the ritual of receiving whatever alphabets you have earned the right to put behind your name—BA, PhD, JD, MD, MBA—a part of the ritual is that you must also receive a little advice, a little last-minute advice before you go.

In a commencement speech at Georgetown University, Bob Hope once said: "To those of you who are about to go into the world and want my advice, here it is: Don't go!" [Hope 1962].

But you don't have a choice and there is no safer thing to do. The world's problems are your problems: even if you turn your back on them, they are still yours. That is why you and the graduates of Spelman College and all of America's colleges and universities must participate in defining and enacting a common agenda for our nation for the coming century.

So, my young sisters and brothers: What kind of world are you about to commence to?

In too many quarters, and in too many ways, it is not a pretty place. And our own place? What of our America? It is clearly such an extraordinary country. And for each of us here, there is surely a sense of mighty good fortune that we live in this nation of ours.

And yet, there is so much work that remains to be done to bring into reality the dream that was so eloquently and powerfully articulated in 1963 by Dr. Martin Luther King Jr.

Today, in some ways even more than when Dr. King shared his dream, ours is a divided house, and a house divided against itself cannot stand!

Abraham Lincoln uttered those words in the context of slavery in June of 1858, as he spoke before the Republican State Convention in Springfield, Illinois. Many of you will recall that these words are also found in the Bible in the gospel according to St. Mark, chapter 3, verse 25: "And if a house be divided against itself, that house cannot stand."

All around us there are spokespersons for a divided society, some more frightening than others. Rather than celebrating the magnificence and the strength of so many different kinds of folks all living under one American roof—there are those who call for "keeping certain people in their places." But the uniqueness and the long-term viability of our nation rests on the powerful idea that there is a place of respect in the American house for each and every one of us.

And just look at us, what a people we Americans are! What a people we are in our full array of human diversity. For we Americans are folks of different races and ethnicities; we are women folks and men folks; we are of different ages, religions, and sexual orientations; and we are differently able.

The problem is that, in this house of ours, we have not yet found the way to teach people how to decently, not to mention lovingly, interact with those who are different. We have not yet proven to the satisfaction of all the power of people engaging across communities to solve problems. We have not yet found the way to demonstrate that groups can preserve their distinctiveness and still work together for the common good. And, we have not sufficiently illustrated the benefits of multiple ways of seeing and doing and being. There is a wonderful Chinese saying that captures this point: "One flower never makes a spring."

These days, My Sisters and Brothers All, we feel the bitter return of racism, anti-Semitism, and ethnic chauvinism, forms of bigotry that we thought we had dismissed: and we are reeling from assaults on affirmative action, as they come one after another in every sector of our society.

Today, in certain quarters, there are renewed attacks on the rights of women. We see and hear and feel repetitive challenges to an important vision that is captured in a Native American saying: "Women hold up half the sky."

And today, there is a swelling of the ranks of the poor that spells a crisis for us all.

Such a climate of intolerance and mean spiritedness demands that we in the academic world rededicate ourselves to analyzing and understanding such violent reactions to difference. Inside and outside of the walls of our colleges and universities, we must recommit ourselves to the fundamental principles of a pluralistic democracy.

In calling for a renewed commitment to inclusiveness, to diversity in our schools, colleges, workplaces, and neighborhoods, on one level we are talking about what is fair and just. But there is an additional impetus for respecting diversity and assuring equity for all. It is the demands of the American economy.

We simply cannot afford the social and economic costs of color-coding our citizenry so that large numbers of African Americans, Native Americans, and people of various Hispanic communities are deprived of the academic skills that are necessary to function in a rapidly changing, technologically complex society. And as the workforce of the coming century is increasingly one of people of color and women, we certainly cannot afford glass ceilings.

On the agenda of those who are successfully involved in the global marketplace, there is no room for old myths and stereotypes about how all Asians are inscrutable, all Mexicans are lazy, and all Africans are insufficiently civilized.

Today, more and more American businesses are coming to grips with a diverse workforce and developing specific marketing for diverse communities at home and abroad. They are doing so not simply as the right thing to do, but because such actions are the economically smart thing to do.

Dear graduates, my message to you must not only identify the problem of a divided house, but it must also at least suggest how we can begin to rebuild the kind of understanding and unity among diverse peoples that will set our nation for success in the coming century and beyond.

As I search for ideas and materials that might be of use as we try to fortify our house, I turn to the very field in which I was trained. I turn to anthropology, the discipline in which I received my degrees many years ago. Let me share with you now some lessons that we can all learn from anthropology, the study of the human condition.

Lesson number one. While the pitting of one group against another is found in culture after culture and nation after nation, we have yet to find a gene that is the cause of it all. No matter how widespread and tenacious we find racism, sexism, and other forms of bigotry, I am here to tell you that this stuff ain't genetic!

We humans learn how to discriminate, and we are taught ugly names to call each other. Since we learn how to pit one group against another, then it is possible to unlearn it. And best of all, we could just stop teaching bigotry!

A second lesson from anthropology is this: While certain groups of people have consistently and over time oppressed other groups, there is no group of people immune to practicing intolerance. Look around our world and you will see that from blatant prejudice to the barbaric victimization of one group by another, such expressions of bigotry are not the sole possession of any particular people. Just look at the Middle East, Bosnia, Ireland, India, Mexico, Haiti, Rwanda, Liberia . . . and yes, our own nation.

The power of human empathy is a third lesson that anthropology can teach us. Empathy, not sympathy. Trust me when I tell you that if men really work at it, they can come to understand many of the realities in women's lives. We gringos really can come to understand the history and the realities of various Latino communities. And surely one does not have to be Jewish to sense the pain and suffering of the victims of the Holocaust.

What is required to engage in human empathy is basic. It is simply to imagine oneself in another's shoes. To imagine oneself without any shoes to wear.

I heard Mayor Bill Campbell* say that he would spend part of a day in a wheelchair, going about the city of Atlanta in order to better understand and improve what it will be like for all of the athletes who will be competing here

---

* William Craig Campbell was mayor of Atlanta, GA, from 1994 to 2002. He was the third African American mayor in the city's history.

during the Paralympics. Every now and then, each of us needs to place ourselves physically or figuratively in a wheelchair.

We need to put ourselves in someone else's skin. As the folks say in the Caribbean, "We need to be in somebody else's yard."

The fourth lesson from anthropology is grounded in the notion that no matter how much one reads and studies about the condition of another people, one's understanding will be incomplete without participating in their way of life. That is why an anthropologist does fieldwork, living among the people he or she wishes to understand.

Well, my sisters and brothers, each of us has the possibility to get at least a taste of the insights, the excitement, the joy of another way of life. It is yours for the taking whenever you venture beyond your habitual paths to try other people's languages, foods, films, literature, music, and art. Some of you have spent substantial time in someone else's space by participating in study abroad programs, or perhaps by working in the Atlanta Project of the Carter Center, or by doing sustained community service.

Regardless of how you do it, the most powerful insight from a cross-cultural experience is that you come to better understand your own culture, you come to better understand yourself.

The American anthropologist Clyde Kluckhohn captured this when he said: "It would hardly be fish who discovered the existence of water" [Kluckhohn 1949].

Here is the fifth and final lesson that I want to share with you from anthropology as an aid to putting our American house back together: change is possible! No matter how stubbornly people hold on to ideas and ways that have lost their usefulness, or that are destructive to the very social fiber of the society— they can change.

Anthropology teaches us that the key ingredient in bringing about change is *US*. It is the will, the determination, the intelligence of ordinary and sometimes extraordinary women and men who transform the world. Think of how an "ordinary" woman named Rosa Parks did so by her simple but courageous refusal to move to the back of a bus in Montgomery, Alabama. Think of how a man named Ralph McGill used the power of a journalist's pen to help Atlanta move toward being a city for all of its citizens.

And so, my young sisters and brothers all, I ask of you today that you take these simple but ever so powerful lessons of anthropology and begin to participate in the great American construction project of unifying our house.

I would be a lot prouder today if we in the academy had learned and then practiced these lessons, if we had shown the way. Maybe some of you will join us in the academic world and help.

But each of you, no matter what career or further study you are about to engage in, please lend a hand in putting our house back in order.

As I bring closure on your commencement speech, I want to tell you a story. I must have told it a hundred times, but I do not know of a better way to emphasize who must do the work of putting our house back together again.

This story was often told by one of my sheroes, Fannie Lou Hamer. The final line of the story will say once again who has the responsibility and indeed the power to rebuild our American house.

It is the story of some young boys who decided one day to fool an old lady by asking her a question that they thought she would be incapable of answering. The ringleader would take a bird that they had caught and, placing it behind his back, he would pose a question to the old lady:

"Old lady, old lady, this bird that I have behind my back, is it dead or is it alive?"

If the old lady said that the bird was dead, then he would release his hands and bird would fly away. But if to the question she said that the bird was alive, he would crush it.

They found the old lady and asked if she would respond to a question. She would try, she said.

And so, the ringleader put the bird behind his back and said: "Old lady, old lady, this bird that I have behind my back, is it dead or is it alive?"

With simple but powerful wisdom she said: "The answer is in your hands!"

That is the answer, dear graduates of the class of 1996, putting our divided house back together is in your hands, and it is in mine.

Congratulations on your graduation, and Godspeed.

Attributes of Twenty-First-Century
Women Leaders

Trinity Washington University, Washington, DC, May 22, 2011

Sister President Pat McGuire; Sister Chair Laura Phillips and members of the board of trustees; sisters of Notre Dame; my colleagues of the faculty and staff; alumnae, families, and friends of this ever so special university; and, of course, the women and men of the class of 2011; My Sisters and Brothers All: *Buenos días, y como alegra a ver ustedes!* Good morning and, as one would say in the southern African American church tradition in which I grew up: it's a great "gettin' up" morning!

Yes, it is a great getting up morning because we have gathered to celebrate the accomplishments of this 2011 class of Trinity Washington University.

I want to acknowledge my husband, James Staton, who is having his first visit to this amazing and grace-filled place called Trinity Washington University. I am grateful to my sister-friend, President Pat McGuire and the board for inviting me to offer this commencement address. Sister president Pat, you have been called "the soul of Trinity University." And indeed you are! I also know that you are a powerful force as you continue to lead the transformation of Trinity as a Catholic college into a dynamic and diverse urban university.

Dear sisters of this graduating class and the few but righteous brothers who are among you, before I offer your commencement address, I do want to turn to your families, and ask they join me in expressing profound gratitude to your mothers, brothers, grandmothers, and grandfathers; your aunts and uncles;

your godmothers and godfathers; your spouses, partners, and children. You know, some of these folks have been your human ATM machines. And among your kin are folks who have believed in you when you were not quite sure you believed in yourself. Now to what I want to share with you my dear sisters and all of the "bros" of the class of 2011.

Drawing on some of my own experiences as an African American woman, and lessons I learned when I had the joy of being the president of Spelman and Bennett colleges, I want to say to you what I sincerely and strongly believe is required of you to be the twenty-first-century leaders of our nation and our world that we desperately need.

I grew up in Jacksonville, Florida, in the days of rigid and legal racial segregation. There were two conflicting messages that were routinely delivered to me periodically from most people in the larger white society. I was told that no matter what I did, I would always be inferior to any and all white people. But my family, my church, and indeed my community consistently countered this racist ideology.

My family, extended family, and indeed my teachers, Brownie and Girl Scout leaders, preachers, and librarians all taught me that not only was the notion of African American inferiority simply not true, but that I had the responsibility to help to tear down that profoundly tenacious and harmful untruth.

My folks taught me that education would be a powerful force in helping me to soar to the heights of my possibilities. To this very day, I remained so grateful to two of my teachers who were instrumental in setting the course with my professional and my personal life: Ms. Vance, my first-grade teacher and Ms. Morse, my Latin teacher when I was in middle school.

Because I had pushy southern Black parents, I was sent off to the first grade at age five. On the first day of class in the first grade I was genuinely scared and able to face that experience only because my best friend, first-grader Bebe Ross, was at my side. When Ms. Vance walked into our classroom, everything about her seemed so much larger than her small stature. Her five-foot two-inch stature appeared to be the height of a giant.

"Good morning class," Ms. Vance said with confidence and authority. "I want each of you to stand and tell us your name."

By the time it was my turn I was a bundle of nerves, only calmed to some degree by the mere presence of my best friend Bebe. When it was my turn, I stood, lifted my head slightly and mumbled my name.

Miss Vance shot across the classroom and stood directly in front of me and my friend and she said, "Johnnetta, never again mumble your name. Hold your head up high, speak clearly, and remember, in this classroom, we are preparing leaders."

By the time I reached middle school, I had taken Ms. Vance's instructions to heart, and I had become a young leader.

One day before we went into our Latin class, I called "my girls" together and instructed them on what we would do when Miss Morse walked into our classroom at Boylan Haven, a private Methodist all-girls school where all of the students were Black and Ms. Morse, and all of the teachers, save one, were white.

I instructed "my girls" that when Miss Morse walked into the classroom, and I gave the signal, all of us will say, "Latin, Latin, dead as can be, first it killed the Romans, now it's killing me."

The first day we did this Ms. Morse ignored us, which of course took away half the fun. The next day, again I gave the signal and my girls repeated the phrase, "Latin, Latin, dead as can be, first it killed the Romans, now it's killing me."

This time Ms. Morse said quite strongly, "You girls stop it!"

Seeing that she was becoming annoyed, I called my girls together after class and instructed them that on the following day we would not say the words, but we would just rhythmically suggest the same message.

This time after I gave the signal and we all followed my instructions, Ms. Morse drew up to the fullness of her five-foot, two-inch stature and said this: "You girls stop it! You are not in this Latin class to learn, as you put it, what killed some white men. You are in this Latin class to learn that as Negro girls, you can learn anything."

Years later, when I had the honor and joy of serving as the president of our nation's two historically Black colleges for women, over and over again I witnessed the truth of what I have learned in the classrooms of Ms. Vance and Ms. Morse. Namely, the power of high expectations and the importance of molding women leaders.

Let me share with you words of Dr. Willa B. Player, the first woman president of Bennett College for Women.* She said that her mother repeatedly told her the following: "Willa, we expect nothing of you that is ordinary!" Sophia B. Packard, one of the founders of Spelman College, was fond of saying this: "Spelman women must have a loyal scorn for second best."

At Spelman, Bennett, Trinity, and all of our women's colleges, we are in the business of developing Esthers, that is, as it says in the book of Esther in the Bible, leaders for such a time as this. Let me indicate what I think are the attributes

* Willa Beatrice Player (1909–2003) was president of Bennett College from 1955 to 1966.

of a twenty-first-century leader. To the men in this graduating class, let me assure you that our world will be far better if men folks supported the development of women leaders and, indeed, imitated us on this issue.

First, be bodacious. You must speak up and speak out on what is important to you as a woman and what is important in the world.

One of my sheroes Audre Lorde, once said, "Silence and invisibility go hand in hand with powerlessness" [Lorde 1980].

Another shero, Alice Walker, has said this: "No person is a friend who demands your silence."*

Second, women leaders must be revolutionaries. Let me hasten to say what I mean when I call for women to be revolutionaries. A revolutionary is someone who believes that things can change, and she works to bring about that change. Sojourner Truth was a revolutionary because she believed that slavery was wrong, and she worked diligently to end it. And she also believed that the good Lord made women and men to be equal, so she spoke out and acted as a feminist.

There is so much in our world that needs changing. Hear the words of Spelman alumna, Marian Wright Edelman, the president of the Children's Defense Fund: "If you don't like the way the world is, change it. You just have to do it one step at a time."

Third, women leaders must be of service to others. I grew up hearing repeatedly that doing for others is just the rent you must pay for your room on earth. I know that message is at the heart of the kind of education you have received here at Trinity Washington University. But I am urging you, my sisters and brothers, don't stop now! Whether you are off to do more formal education, or you are doing your best to find a job in this difficult economic climate, you must continue to volunteer in a homeless shelter, do your best to bring comfort to women who have sought protection in the center for the victims of domestic violence, become a Big Sister or Big Brother to a child who needs you.

Doctor Mary McLeod Bethune, who founded Bethune–Cookman College, was fond of saying to gatherings of "high saditty women," "Go on my sisters and climb to the very top, but you must remember to lift others as you climb!"

Elie Wiesel, the great humanitarian who as a boy was put in a concentration camp because he was Jewish, once said this: Our lives no longer belong to us alone; they belong to all those who need us desperately" [Wiesel 1986].

Fourth, and finally, a woman leader for such a time as this must respect and celebrate human diversity. It has always been true but today, as technology

---

* The full quote is "No person is your friend (or kin) who demands your silence, or denies your right to grow and be perceived as fully blossomed as you were intended" (Walker 1983, 36).

transforms our world into a global village, a leader must respect the diversity of humankind and think and act in an inclusive way. I want to share with you the many things that I enjoy in my current job as the director of the Smithsonian's National Museum of African Art. One is that I have the opportunity to continue to learn. Indeed, day in and day out, I am learning more and more about the diverse and dynamic visual arts in Africa.

In my role at the National Museum of African art, I also fully enjoy being surrounded by visual arts that come from the only place on earth from which all human beings have descended. Whether you explain human origin in biblical terms, or by using evolutionary theory, just go back far enough in time and you must see that we are all Africans! Yes, despite our extraordinary diversity, all of us humans are from the same place.

There is a saying among the Sioux Nation, "With all beings, we shall be relatives."

Hear these words from the Quran, "We are made into nations and tribes that we may know and love each other."

I truly believe that God does not have a favorite color for people, a favorite nation, gender, religion, sexual orientation, or language. I believe God does not favor the physically able over those who are differently abled.

And I believe women leaders must understand, and perhaps believe as truth, that we can be for ourselves without being against others. Or to use a favorite expression of the Women's College Coalition: "At a women's college, we are never against men, but oh, are we for women!"

It is time now to bring closure to this commencement address. I want to do so by recounting a story about the great suffragette and feminist, Sojourner Truth.

At a gathering of suffragettes back in the nineteenth century, the agenda once again centered on how women could obtain the right to vote.

A man came into the room of the suffragette tour meeting, and each time a woman stood to make the point he would scream out from the back of the room: "You women cannot have as many rights as men because Christ was a man."

The women tried to ignore him, but he persisted in screaming out those words. Finally, Sojourner Truth could take it no more and she came before the gathering and stood there in the fullness of her tall stature and her midnight dark skin.

This is what she said: "That little man back there says women can't have as many rights as men because Christ was a man. But I want to ask that little man, 'Where did your Christ come from? He came from a God and a woman; man ain't had nothing to do with it. And another thing, if one woman, one day in the garden, could get the world turned upside down, then it seems to me that all the women in here can get it right side up again."

And so, mighty women of the class of 2011 and, yes, the righteous men of this class as well, we are counting on you to be the kind of leaders that will help to get the world right side up again. Peace and blessings to each of you. Congratulations and Godspeed.

Courage, It's What Really Matters

Bennington College, Bennington, VT, May 30, 2014

Sister President Mariko Silver; chair and members of the board of trustees; Bennington faculty and staff; alumnae and alumni; students, families, and friends of this very special college; and, of course, women and men of the class of 2014; My Sisters and Brothers All: Good evening!

And what a very special evening it is as we gather to celebrate the accomplishments of the 2014 class of Bennington College.

When sister President Silver asked that I join you this evening to serve as the speaker at her very first commencement here at Bennington, I felt mighty special, and jumped at the opportunity.

Being here, right here, at this moment is a way that I can express my admiration *and* support of your sister president. What a talented, gifted, and remarkable person you are Mariko Silver. But it certainly does not surprise me that you are all of that and, as the young 'uns would say, and a bag of chips!

I only know of your late father, Tony Silver, an acclaimed documentary director. But I know, respect, and enjoy a sisterly friendship with your mother, Joan Shigekaw, who is currently serving as the acting chairman of the National Endowment for the Arts. And so, when we marvel at who you are, sister president, and the impressive journey you have been on, we can declare with certainty that apple don't fall far from the tree!

Dear graduates, tonight as we celebrate you, let us also celebrate and thank your parents and family members—the folks who have believed in you even during those times when you were not sure you believed in yourself; the folks who have been your human ATMs.

Tonight, we must acknowledge and thank your faculty, the women and men who have been in partnership with you in the challenging yet deeply rewarding process of teaching and learning.

And the Bennington staff? Of course, they too must be recognized and thanked, for it is they who carry out the range of responsibilities that create the kind of environment in which you as students could soar to the height of your possibilities.

As you know, most of my professional career has been in the academy where I have had the privilege and the joy of serving as a professor, administrator, and twice as a college president. And so, I do know a great deal about the mission, the values, and the culture of many colleges and universities. I can honestly say that all that I have read about Bennington College, all that I have heard about Bennington College, all that I sense about your college in the short time that I have been on your campus suggests that this is a special place.

Having served as the president of the only two historically Black colleges for women in America, I feel a close kinship with Bennington because your college began as a women's college when the first class of eighty-seven women arrived on campus in 1932.

While Bennington became fully coeducational in 1969, I hope the principles upon which a women's college rests remain etched into the daily life on your campus. I mean a belief in the fundamental equality of women and men that is captured in a Native American saying: "Women hold up half the sky."

I trust I am correct in assuming that today, at Bennington, women do not stand behind men. For as I would often say to students at Spelman College and Bennett College for Women, the problem with a woman standing behind a man is she can't see where she is going!

The focus on the arts in the curriculum and indeed the very life of the college is another way in which Bennington is a truly special place. I firmly believe that some engagement with the arts is absolutely necessary if one is to not only make a good living, but also live a good life. Eighteenth-century Prussian writer Avigdor Pawsner once said: "If you are looking for Hell, then ask an artist where it is. If you can't find an artist, then you are already in Hell."

I am trained in cultural anthropology, a discipline that draws on knowledge gained from fieldwork in efforts to understand the people and cultures of the world. And so it will not surprise you to hear that I applaud the fact that each academic year Bennington students participate in a seven-week, off-campus winter term called Field Work. In my view, this is one of the reasons your college is such a special place.

Now, dear graduates, what is the message that I want to give to you at your commencement—the beginning of the next leg of your life's journey. It is a basic message, a message that revolves around a single word. And that word is *courage*.

One of my sheroes, Dr. Maya Angelou, who went to glory on Tuesday, used to say, "Courage is the most important of all the virtues because without courage, you cannot practice any other virtue consistently" [cited in Ju 2008].

My charge to you, dear graduates, is you must find and then exercise courage in four very specific ways. First, I urge you to exercise courage as you continue to grow up and to follow your dreams. As e. e. cummings once said: "It takes courage to grow up and become who you really are."

In the process of choosing your first life's work—and your generation is prone to change your careers four to five times in your lifetime—in the process of choosing your first life's work, rather than following your passion it is often easier to become who your parents want you to be; or to choose a profession based on the amount of income it will bring you. Please don't!

How well I remember the day when I had to muster the courage to say to my grandfather that I would not do as he wanted me to do—that is to come into the family insurance business. And when I said to him that I was going to be an anthropologist, and cited Margaret Mead as a model of the profession I would follow, he laughed at me and said: "Baby girl, how in the world are you going to make a living doing something like that?"

As soon as I could break away from my grandfather, I sought comfort from my mother, as I shared with her that Papa had laughed at my ambition and asked me how in the world I thought I would make a living doing what an anthropologist does. I will never forget the counsel my mother gave me. She said, "Your grandfather is right. You must give thought to how you are going to make a living. And this is especially so because you are a woman and must never be dependent on a man for your material well-being."

But she went on to say, "If anthropology is your passion, then you must follow it; if your dream is to become an anthropologist, then you must make that dream come true."

Ellen Johnson Sirleaf, the president of Liberia, and the first woman to serve as the president of any African country, has said this: "If your dreams do not scare you, they are not big enough" [Sirleaf 2011]. And so, I am urging you to design and then to work toward the fulfillment of dreams that truly scare you.

Michael McKee has said, "It may take courage to embrace possibilities of your own potential, but once you have flown past the summit of your fears, nothing will seem impossible."

Second, I urge you, dear graduates, to have the courage to change the path you are on, to let go of the familiar, yes, to take risks.

Steve Jobs once said this: "For the past 33 years, I have looked in the mirror every morning and asked myself: 'If today were the last day of my life, would I want to do what I am about to do today?' And whenever the answer has been 'No' for too many days in a row, I know I need to change something" [Jobs 2005].

There is little in life that is easier than doing the same ole thing in the same ole way. It's called playing it safe; it's like a boat that stays in a harbor. How safe it is when a boat avoids going out into the roughness of the seas, into waters that may be rough and even dangerous. But the problem with a boat remaining in a safe harbor is that it is not going anywhere.

It was five years ago that I had to find the courage to venture into a profession that drew me out of my comfort zone, out of what I knew and had been successful at, and into a world that required me to admit that I did not know it all. In a world where I often did not know what those who would report to me knew far better than I.

After spending most of my professional life in the world of colleges and universities, I dared to enter the world of museums. Believe me, that took more courage than I thought I had. Even though I am an anthropologist, and not an art historian, and even though I had never worked as a curator, I accepted the challenge of serving as the director of the Smithsonian's National Museum of African Art. I made that courageous leap, and I am so very glad that I did.

In the third act of my life—and I do hope the curtain will not come down anytime soon—I took a leap of faith. I will tell you what that kind of faith is. It's like standing on the top of a mountain and deciding you will jump, having faith that when you do so, either the earth will come up and meet your feet, or you will sprout wings.

Over the past five years, it has been incredibly rewarding for me to work in a museum that collects, conserves, exhibits, and educates about the traditional and contemporary visual arts of Africa. The continent that is the very cradle of humanity, the place from which we all descended.

And because I found the courage to change the path I was on, to risk leaving the safety of what I knew and yes, what I was known for, each and every day I encounter the excitement of discovery, the joy of learning.

Third, dear graduates, I ask that you always have the courage to speak up and speak out about what is not right, what is not decent and fair and just.

Perhaps you know the words of Martin Niemöller, a prominent Protestant pastor who became an outspoken public foe of Adolf Hitler and spent the last seven years of Nazi rule in concentration camps. He said: "First they came for the Socialists, and I did not speak out because I was not a Socialist. Then they came for the Trade Unionists, and I did not speak out because I was not a trade unionist. Then they came for the Jews, and I did not speak out because I was not a Jew. Then they came for me and there was no one left to speak for me" [Niemöller n.d.].

It is often fear that keeps us silent when we hear or witness an injustice.

But as another of my sheroes, Eleanor Roosevelt once said, "We gain strength, and courage, and confidence by each experience in which we really stop to look fear in the face . . . we must do that which we think we cannot do."

One of the commitments I have made to myself is that I will not remain silent in the face of bigotry and any and all systems of inequality. To honor that commitment, it sometimes takes more courage than I think I have, but somehow, I find the amount I need to speak up and speak out about racism, sexism, and heterosexism. I muster the courage to call out anyone who expresses in my presence any form of anti-Semitism, and any form of Islamophobia. I challenge bigotry and discrimination based on age, on nationality, and on a person's disability.

Of course, bigotry and discrimination in our own country are not the only injustices that you and I must always have the courage to challenge. As Dr. Martin Luther King said in an open letter written on April 16, 1963, from the Birmingham Jail: "Injustice anywhere is a threat to justice everywhere" [King 1963a].

And hear these words of the great drum major for justice: "We are caught in an inescapable network of mutuality, tied in a single garment of destiny. Whatever affects one directly, affects all indirectly" [King 1963a].

And hear these words of Dr. King, that urges us to have the courage to speak up and speak out: "In the end, we will remember not the words of our enemies, but the silence of our friends" [King 1967b].

Fourth, and finally, dear graduates, I ask of you the courage to be of service to others. When I was growing up in the days of legalized segregation in Jacksonville, Florida, my parents and folks in that community who "grew me" would say in countless ways and, more importantly, they would demonstrate in their behavior, their deep belief that doing for others is the rent you must pay for your room on earth.

Once you say with courage and conviction that you will continuously pay this rent, there is no shortage of ways in which you can be of service to others.

Sometimes, of course, it is in simple acts of kindness to someone in need. But service can also take the form of aligning oneself with an organization or agency that is dedicated to working in the interest of assisting people to change their lives—for the better.

United Way is the organization that I continue to work in that has the chutzpah, the courage to envision a world where all individuals and families achieve their human potential through education, financial stability, and healthy lives.

For years I had worked in local United Ways, and then the day came when I was asked to serve as the chair of the board of United Way of America. It really did take courage for me to step into that top leadership role as the first African American to ever chair the United Way board. I remember seeking and finding courage to do what I had to do by reading about and recalling the lives of champions for positive social change.

I was encouraged by the words of Cesar Chavez, the exemplary Chicano leader who once said: "Our ambitions must be broad enough to include the aspirations and needs of others—for their sakes and for our own" [United Farm Workers n.d.].

I thought about the life and work of the great African American educator, Dr. Mary McLeod Bethune who constantly said to the women she worked with that "It is fine to climb to the top, but you must lift others as you climb."

And throughout my term as the chair of the board of United Way of America, I would find both courage and comfort in the words of the great humanitarian, Elie Wiesel: "Our lives no longer belong to us alone; they belong to all those who need us desperately" [Wiesel 1986].

It is time now for me to move toward closure on this commencement address. I want to do so by telling my version of a well-known story.

A young girl was walking along a beach where thousands of starfish had been washed up during a terrible storm. Indeed, there were starfish on the beach as far as the eye could see.

As she came to each starfish, the young girl would bend down, pick up the starfish and throw it back into the ocean.

An old man who was walking along the beach noticed the young girl and as he approached her, he said: "Good morning! May I ask what it is that you are doing?"

The young girl looked up, and replied: "Good morning sir, I am throwing starfish into the ocean. The tide has washed them up onto the beach and they can't return to the ocean by themselves. When the sun gets high, they will die unless I throw them back into the ocean."

The old man replied: "But there must be tens of thousands of starfish on this beach. You can't save all of these starfish. Can't you see that what you are doing won't make a difference?"

The young girl bent down, picked up another starfish and threw it as far as she could into the ocean. And then she turned to the old man and said: "It made a difference to that one."

Now that little girl had courage. She dreamed of saving starfish and courageously acted in the interest of that dream. When the old man challenged what she was doing, she spoke up and said quite boldly: "But it mattered to this one."

The young girl had the courage to do what she could to change an unfortunate situation. And, yes, she courageously acted in order to be of service to as many starfish as she could.

Courage: it's what really matters!

Congratulations dear Bennington class of 2014! I wish you courage, and Godspeed.

Afterword

THE TRANSCENDENT VOICE OF
DR. JOHNNETTA BETSCH COLE

CELESTE WATKINS-HAYES AND ERICA LORRAINE WILLIAMS

As we conclude this book of speeches, we wanted to reflect on "when and where we enter" in terms of our connection to Johnnetta Betsch Cole and her work. We seek to situate ourselves: who we are, our disciplines of study, and our origin stories for approaching her work and this project. The following sections are revised from a transcript of a recording of a conversation between Celeste Watkins-Hayes and Erica L. Williams.

When and Where We Enter

CELESTE WATKINS-HAYES

When I began Spelman College as a student in 1992, I struggled to find my way. You come into this space with so many amazing Black women, and you're trying to figure out where you fit. When and where do you enter within this community? What's going to be your thing? What interests will you pursue? Because everything seems interesting and everyone's doing such inspiring things. Spelman can be a very exciting, yet intimidating, place. But, even from afar, as I listened to her speeches as a first-year student, Cole was a beacon whose presence assured me that I would find my place.

Spelman professor Mona Phillips introduced me to sociology as a discipline, but it was Cole who made me excited about higher education as a vocation. When I was elected to Spelman's board of trustees as the student trustee, I got to observe her in a board-meeting setting—leading a school. For me, it was just fascinating to think about higher education, not just in terms of what was happening in the classroom, not just in terms of research, but also in terms of what it meant to run an institution dedicated to the education of Black women.

I also got to see Cole as a student. During my senior year, noted anthropologist Mary Catherine Bateson, daughter of Margaret Mead, came to Spelman as a visiting scholar and co-taught a class with Professor Beverly Guy-Sheftall. The class consisted of Spelman students, faculty, staff, and a few friends of the college. Dr. Cole joined our group of about fifteen women, enrolling as a student. There, as we gathered once a week in the Women's Research and Resource Center, we agreed to what is now known as "Vegas rules"—what happens here stays here. We would have discussions about relationships, identity, career, and a host of intellectual ideas. We read the work of Audre Lorde, Toni Cade Bambara, and Beverly Guy-Sheftall. We had incredible discussions that were both scholarly and personal. We shared as women across generations. It was so exciting to sit next to Cole as a student! She would come in carrying her books, her homework done. She would sit at the table and pull out her little notebook and take notes. When we had an assignment, she would ask additional questions, "How many pages should we submit for our papers? What reference style should we use?" She was this awesome student, even though she was running the college. She would come in and say, "I stayed up late to get the reading done." What I appreciated about her in that moment was even though we all knew she was the president, even though we all knew she was Johnnetta Betsch Cole, she showed up in the role of a student. And to be a student is to be vulnerable. So we got to see that. It was just amazing. So, I've seen Cole as a college leader, as a scholar, and as a museum director, but I've also had a chance to see her up close and personal as a student.

We are very aligned in our commitment to social justice, and we both point to our childhoods and our parents as our earliest teachers. My parents grew up in Nashville, and they shared Cole's experience of growing up under the boot of racial segregation yet being deeply nurtured through the pride and love embedded in Black spaces. In fact, my father graduated from Cole's alma mater of Fisk University. My parents moved to Detroit in 1968 after my father was recruited into a bank management trainee program, where he would climb the corporate ranks while my mother entered the teaching profession. My parents instilled in me an understanding that while we were extremely fortunate to have opportunities that allowed my parents to be upwardly mobile, these opportunities were not available to all. Racial inequality and other inequities still shaped life chances and opportunities. This understanding is at the root of my interest in social justice. Cole and my father have something in common besides Fisk University: they racially integrated settings of power, leveraged their authenticity and intelligence to speak truth to power while simultaneously building bridges, and always lifted as they climbed. And my mother and Cole share a critical characteristic: they are both educators at their core.

ERICA LORRAINE WILLIAMS

I'm trying to pinpoint the exact moment when I first encountered Cole, but it seems like she's always been there in a way. If I'm not mistaken, the first time I saw her speak was at a Black Women in the Academy conference at Howard University in 1999. I was participating in a Leadership Alliance summer research program, and I was working with Dr. Michael Blakey and Dr. Mark Mack in the W. Montague Cobb Research Laboratory. They were analyzing the remains of the New York African Burial Ground project. I remember attending this conference where I saw so many Black women who were either pursuing PhDs or who were already professors or administrators. It was transformative because, as a first-generation college student, I had never been in a space like that. I think she spoke at that conference, and that was my very first exposure to her. Later, when I was preparing to pursue a PhD in anthropology, I read *Black Feminist Anthropology* (McClaurin 2001), where she wrote the foreword. From then on, she was just kind of ubiquitous. When I went to my first American Anthropological Association conference as a graduate student, it was big and overwhelming, so I went to the Association of Black Anthropologists and Association for Feminist Anthropology meetings and events. She was always in those spaces. As a graduate student, you're kind of awestruck by these big figures, but she was always so gracious, warm, welcoming, and openhearted. Through that, I had the chance to get to know her a little bit at a time.

In the summer of 2010, I participated in a United Negro College Fund/Mellon Faculty seminar on the archives of Black intellectuals in Atlanta. This seminar offered training in archival research methods and an introduction to the archival collections pertaining to Black intellectual thought and social movements in Atlanta. It was here that I was first introduced to Dr. Cole's Personal and Presidential Papers, housed at the Spelman College Archives. I enjoyed exploring her speeches that brought anthropology into public discourse and seeing traces of her intellectual trajectory. One gem I found in the archives was that she had won an oratorical contest as a college senior. This shows how she was a prodigy who honed her skills as a gifted speaker early on. Years later, my interests culminated in the opportunity to interview her for the Democratizing Knowledge Summer Institute at Spelman College. It was funny because Beverly Guy-Sheftall and Johnnetta Betsch Cole said that I came to the interview prepared because I went back to the archives to gather information so that I could ask thoughtful questions. Then, when I saw Watkins-Hayes speak about her book *Remaking a Life: How Women Living with HIV/AIDS Confront Inequality* in the Spelman Women's Research and Resource Center, and she mentioned this book project, I felt compelled to reach out to express my interest in collaborating on this project. And here we are now.

Now that we have shared our "origin stories" and entry points to this work, we will highlight some of the key themes and takeaways from this collection of Johnnetta Betsch Cole's speeches.

Speechifying, Fluidity, and an Expansive Career

Johnnetta Betsch Cole has occupied many different spaces as a professor, college president, activist, and museum director. She has moved through higher education administration, museum administration, consulting, and civil and women's rights organizational leadership. She has occupied all of these different spaces, even if, at times, she was not fully confident that she could do it. She has been bold about trying new things, even though she sometimes doubted herself. For example, in the interview with Williams, she discusses feeling unqualified to direct a museum. Nonetheless, she stepped out on faith and took on the role. We tend to think that "Dr. Cole" and "confidence" go hand in hand! But she has asked herself, can I really do this? And should I really do this? She demonstrates brave vulnerability, trusting in her skills and ability to learn. This tells us that younger generations of scholars and activists can learn to be bold, take risks, and step outside of their comfort zones.

Cole has also been influential in policy circles, serving as a key resource and thought partner for high-impact leaders. She has served as a moral compass, culminating in her leadership of the historic National Council of Negro Women founded by Mary McLeod Bethune. Like Bethune, Cole has advised presidents and other national figures on how we might best live up to our democratic ideals. Both women served as heads of HBCUs. From Cole's speeches and career trajectory, we note her seat at the table across presidential administrations, with elected and appointed policy officials, and across the political aisle dividing Democrat and Republican. She was the first African American and first woman to be invited to read and reflect upon Lincoln's Gettysburg Address at the Lincoln Memorial; has been appointed to several advisory boards and commissions by presidents, members of the presidential cabinet, governors, and mayors; and has been recognized with some of the highest honors in public and community service. She has experienced firsthand the blows of politics, such as when her activism and research in places like Cuba exposed her to harsh critique during the Clinton cabinet appointment process. We write these reflections at a time in American history when bipartisanship is viewed with extreme skepticism and our cultural landscape increasingly rewards political division. During the writing of this book, Cole was in fact arrested during a voting rights protest at the Capitol.[1] What we see in Cole is a fierce grace, buoyed by her commitment and dedication to the public good, and a willingness to partner widely in order to advance our common humanity and to advocate for the most marginalized among us.

Cole has used speechifying as a tool to discuss the state of the nation, higher education, museums, Black studies, anthropology, and other fields through statistics, formative life stories, reflections, and analysis. Speechifying can reinforce core values, challenge beliefs, and advance calls for social justice. Notably, she does not position herself as someone with all the answers.

She speaks knowledgeably, but with great humility, as she acknowledges that the lessons in her speeches are a two-way street. Her ultimate goal is to instruct and to inspire her audience. Her words move people and motivate them to come together to find solutions to pressing social issues. In her characteristic slow cadence, replete with purposeful pauses and clear articulation, Cole shares multiple lessons in her speeches—some learned from her journey, some learned from historical figures, and even some from her disciplinary training and interdisciplinary exploration. She makes connections between the institutions where she speaks, the people situated therein, and the place where they fit in her life's journey.

Speechifying as Ambassadorship

Many of the speeches collected in this book show how Dr. Cole has long been an ambassador: an ambassador for HBCUs, for women's colleges, for Black studies, for anthropology, and for Black women. Black colleges repeatedly come up in her life and history, long before she became the president of the nation's only two HBCUs for women. Her parents were HBCU graduates from Wilberforce and Knoxville colleges. She went to Fisk University at age fifteen. It is telling that her parents saw Fisk as a nurturing place for her at that young age.

In her 2008 speech to Black graduates at Harvard University Law School (see chapter 5, "Race and Racism"), Cole provides the statistics and context to understand the significance of HBCUs, which are often misunderstood. Some tend to believe the stereotypes that HBCUs are homogeneous spaces, or that they're unnecessary because Black people are now able to attend predominantly white institutions. Nonetheless, she highlights the strengths and accomplishments of HBCUs and HBCU graduates before diverse audiences. For example, in 2019 when Bennett College was experiencing its finance and accreditation crisis, she created a video on social media appealing for pledges and donations to the college.[2]

When we consider Cole's contributions to feminism, feminist studies, and Black women's studies, we can consider her publications like *Gender Talk*, *All American Women*, the foreword to *Black Feminist Anthropology*, and others. Dr. Cole has always been there, contributing to the field and serving as an aspirational model. However, it is also important to emphasize that she has also been an advocate and ambassador in terms of expanding Black feminism and women's studies at Spelman College. While Spelman has always been a women's college, it has not always been a feminist college. It is Dr. Cole who is widely credited with explicitly embedding feminist approaches and frameworks into the highest levels of leadership of Spelman College. She encouraged the idea that students could exist beyond the goal of marriage, and beyond the goal of a very small slice of careers accessible to Black women. She showed up as president as a divorced woman with natural hair. She illustrated that a woman could lead a major institution without having to mimic male leadership. Rather, she could embrace being a woman leader and bring her gendered self into the role. This was radical. We tend to take her feminism for granted, but it was quite radical to be a Black woman in that role at the institution.

Dr. Beverly Guy-Sheftall often tells a story of how Audre Lorde was not well received the first time she visited Spelman College in the 1970s. Apparently, people were not ready for her and her candid discussion of gender and sexuality. She was treated so poorly that she vowed never again to return to Spelman College. However, as president, Cole invited Audre Lorde to return to campus. After all, they were friends. When Audre Lorde returned, it was an entirely different experience, and now Audre Lorde's personal papers are housed in the Spelman College Archives. This is just one of many examples of important interventions that Cole made at Spelman in the areas of feminism and women's studies.

Speechifying as a Unifying Call to Action

In her speeches, Cole translates big ideas to diverse audiences and highlights meaningful elements for thinking about practical things, such as how to diversify institutions of higher education or corporations. As we reflect on this book of speeches as public intellectuals, we want to consider how this book can be a platform. *What are we asking people to do after reading this book?* We encourage scholars to see Cole's speechifying as a model, and to think about what you can do in your own disciplines to reach broader audiences. People often say that when you earn a PhD, your knowledge is specialized. There is often encouragement to stay within one's focal area of knowledge specialization and to only write for academic audiences. Cole's speeches encourage us to contemplate how we can branch out and bring ideas to broader audiences. Moreover, this book is designed to encourage scholars to think about how we can use speechifying and our expertise to effect change and make a meaningful impact on fields and institutions.

In the present moment, it is not only vital for thinkers to expand how they understand their audiences, but also to include high-quality research to contribute to the conversation. Dr. Cole's speeches serve three purposes in this regard. They inform, inspire, and unite people. One aspect of Cole that we honor and admire is her ability to unite people even while discussing complicated topics that could be seen as divisive. That is a very powerful skill that is in short supply. Many people can talk about divisive topics, but not many can do it in a way that unifies people. We see this as a model of public intellectual work that we have tried to follow.

While we must recognize that Cole has a unique talent for speechifying, a facility and a knack for public speaking that she has honed over the decades, she nevertheless offers all of us some useful pointers. She knows how to draw out her pronunciation of a word for heightened impact, how to play with a pregnant pause, and how to share relatable stories, parables, and proverbs that will stay with people forever.

On Mentoring and Her Transcendent Voice

To be sure, one of Dr. Cole's legacies is her ability to really *see* people. The ability to make people feel seen and heard is one of the most powerful gifts that one can give, and Dr. Cole excels at giving that gift. She is relatable and incredibly down-to-earth. Often, when people have racked up accomplishments and accolades, they may seem "on their high horse" or unattainable and unapproachable.

But not Dr. Johnnetta Betsch Cole. She is almost modest about all that she has accomplished.

Cole's speeches reflect her important role as a mentor. Both Watkins-Hayes and Williams have been mentored by her in direct and indirect ways. Cole has guided and mentored countless people who have read her work, heard her speeches, or interacted with her in different ways. In every leadership role she has occupied, she has always taken seriously the idea of mentoring the people coming after her. This is a crucial part of her legacy. We see her mentoring style as unconditional love, very strong support, and very honest feedback. It is also role modeling. Just watching her and paying close attention is a form of mentorship. Just watching how she moves through the world can teach us so much about how to construct impactful lives and who we hope to become.

People sometimes wonder: *Does Dr. Cole talk like that all the time?* We can attest that this is true. Watkins-Hayes recounts a story of when they were in a restaurant ordering lunch, and she looked at the menu and then said in her speechifying voice, "I will have the crab cake sandwich, avocado slices, and an iced tea!" She is absolutely, unapologetically, herself. And it is a pleasure and an honor to be in her presence. Whether our readers have engaged with her hundreds of times or have never engaged with her in person, we hope that through this book of speeches, you will get a slice of the transformative and transcendent voice of Dr. Johnnetta Betsch Cole.

NOTES

1. Williams 2021.

2. See "Watch: Bennett College and Spelman College Are 'United in Sisterhood,'" Bennett College News, January 29, 2019, www.bennett.edu/news/video-bennett -college-and-spelman-college-are-united-in-sisterhood/.

APPENDIX

Dr. Johnnetta Betsch Cole's Service and Honors

Board Service

The Carter Center
Coca-Cola Enterprises
Home Depot
Merck, Inc. (first Black woman to serve
    on the board of directors)
Nations Bank South
Rockefeller Foundation
Wellesley College

Honorary Degrees

Albion College
Barnard College
Bennett College
Berea College
Bethune Cookman University
Brown University
College of New Rochelle
College of Wooster
Columbia University
Dartmouth College
Davidson College
Dennison University

Edward Waters College
Emory University
Fisk University
Gettysburg College
Grinnell College
Hamilton College
Howard University
Hunter College
Kalamazoo College
Lafayette College
Macalester College
Marygrove College
Michigan State University
Mills College
Morehouse College
Morehouse School of Medicine
Mount Holyoke College
New York University
North Carolina A&T University
North Carolina State University
Northeastern University
Northern Michigan University
Northwestern University
Notre Dame University
Oberlin College

Philadelphia University
Pine Manor College
Prairie View A&M University
Princeton University
Queens College
Sarah Lawrence College
Skidmore College
Smith College
South Carolina State University
Southeastern Massachusetts University
Southwestern University
Spelman College
State University of New York at
  Binghamton
Toledo University
Tougaloo College
Trinity College
University of Arkansas
University of Florida

University of Massachusetts at Amherst
University of Massachusetts at
  Dartmouth
University of Michigan
University of North Carolina at Asheville
University of North Carolina at Chapel
  Hill
University of North Carolina at
  Wilmington
University of Pennsylvania
University of Sussex
University of the District of Columbia
University of the Virgin Islands
University of Washington
Washington State University
Wesleyan University
Wheaton College
William Patterson University
Yale University

BIBLIOGRAPHY

Ahmed, Sara. 2017. *Living a Feminist Life*. Durham, NC: Duke University Press.

Angelou, Maya. 2008. Commencement Speech, Cornell University, May 24.

Annie E. Casey Foundation. 2010. *Early Warning! Why Reading by the End of Third Grade Matters: A KIDS COUNT Special Report from the Annie E. Casey Foundation*. Baltimore, MD. https://www.ccf.ny.gov/files/9013/8262/2751/AECF ReporReadingGrade3.pdf.

Baldwin, James. 1962. "As Much Truth as One Can Bear." *New York Times Book Review*, January 14. https://www.nytimes.com/1962/01/14/archives/as-much-truth -as-one-can-bear-to-speak-out-about-the-world-as-it-is.html.

Baldwin, James, and Yran Cazac. *Little Man, Little Man: A Story of Childhood*. Durham, NC: Duke University Press, 2018.

Barnes, Riché J. D. 2018. "Johnnetta Betsch Cole: Eradicating Multiple Systems of Oppression." In *The Second Generation of African American Pioneers in Anthropology*, edited by Ira E. Harrison, Deborah Johnson-Simon, and Erica L. Williams, 84–98. Urbana: University of Illinois Press.

Bateson, Mary Catherine. 1989. *Composing a Life*. New York: Atlantic Monthly Press.

Bernstein, Alison. 1987. "Johnnetta Cole: Serving by Example." *Change: The Magazine of Higher Learning* 19, no. 5: 46–55. https://doi.org/10.1080/00091383.1987 .10570158.

Bethune, Mary McLeod. 1953. "Last Will and Testament." https://www.cookman.edu /history/last-will-testament.html.

BlackPast. 2007. "(1857) Frederick Douglass, 'If There Is No Struggle, There Is No Progress.'" BlackPast, January 25. https://www.blackpast.org/african-american -history/1857-frederick-douglass-if-there-no-struggle-there-no-progress/.

BlackPast. 2012. "(1982) Audre Lorde, 'Learning from the 60s.'" BlackPast, August 12. https://www.blackpast.org/african-american-history/1982-audre-lorde-learning-60s/.

Bolles, A. Lynn. 2001. "Seeking the Ancestors: Forging a Black Feminist Tradition in Anthropology." In *Black Feminist Anthropology: Theory, Politics, Praxis, and Poetics*, edited by Irma McClaurin, 25–48. New Brunswick, NJ: Rutgers University Press.

Brooks, Gwendolyn. 1988. "Agenda." Unpublished poem presented at the inauguration of President Johnnetta Cole at Spelman College, Atlanta, GA.

Burke, Sheila. 2012. "Tennessee Court Decision May Finally End Fisk Art Case." CT Insider, April 24. https://www.ctinsider.com/news/article/Tennessee-court-decision-may-finally-end-Fisk-art-11513089.php.

Burroughs, Margaret. 1963. *What Shall I Tell My Children Who Are Black?* Chicago: M.A.A.H. Press.

Bush, George H. W. 1989. "Remarks to Members of the Institute of International Education." October 25. George H. W. Bush Presidential Library and Museum. https://bush41library.tamu.edu/archives/public-papers/1084.

Center for the Future of Museums. 2015. *Trends Watch 2015*. https://www.aam-us.org/programs/center-for-the-future-of-museums/trendswatch-2015/.

Clark Atlanta University, Tina Maria Dunkley, and Jerry Cullum. 2012. *In the Eye of the Muses: Selections from the Clark Atlanta University Art Collection*. Atlanta: Clark Atlanta University.

Clower, Robert W., George Dalton, Mitchell Harwitz, and A. A. Walters. 1966. *Growth without Development: An Economic Survey of Liberia*. Evanston, IL: Northwestern University Press.

Cole, Johnnetta Betsch. 1986. *All American Women: Lines That Divide, Ties That Bind*. New York: Free Press.

Cole, Johnnetta Betsch. 1988. *Anthropology for the Nineties: Introductory Readings*. New York: Free Press.

Cole, Johnnetta Betsch. 1993. *Conversations: Straight Talk with America's Sister President*. New York: Anchor Books.

Cole, Johnnetta Betsch. 1997. *Dream the Boldest Dreams: And Other Lessons of Life*. Atlanta: Longstreet Press.

Cole, Johnnetta Betsch. 2021. *African Proverbs for All Ages*. Illustrated by Nelda Lateef. New York: Roaring Books Press.

Cole, Johnnetta Betsch, and Beverly Guy-Sheftall, eds. 2003. *Gender Talk: The Struggle for Women's Equality in African American Communities*. New York: Ballantine Books.

Collins, Glenn. 1987. "Spelman College's First 'Sister President.'" *New York Times*, July 20. https://www.nytimes.com/1987/07/20/style/spelman-s-college-s-first-sister-president.html.

Danticat, Edwidge. 1995. *Krik Krak!* New York: Soho Press.

Darling-Hammond, Linda. 2014. "Educational Quality and Equality." In *Divided: The Perils of Our Growing Inequality*, edited by David Cay Johnston, 153–58. New York: New Press.

Delany, Clarissa Scott. n.d. "Interim." https://aaregistry.org/poem/interim-by-cla rissa-scott-delany/. Accessed December 28, 2022.

Dizard, Robin. 1988. "An Appreciation of Sister President." DHG, November 21.

Du Bois, W. E. B. 1903. *The Souls of Black Folk: Essays and Sketches*. Reprint, New York: Johnson Reprint Corp., 1968.

Ehrenfreund, Max. 2015. "Martin Luther King's Warnings on Inequality Were ahead of His Time." *Washington Post*, January 16. https://www.washingtonpost .com/news/wonk/wp/2015/01/16/wonkbook-martin-luther-kings-warnings-on -inequality-were-ahead-of-his-time/.

Equiano, Olaudah. 1789. *The Interesting Narrative of the Life of Olaudah Equiano, or Gustavus Vassa, the African*. Reprint, Boston: Isaac Knapp, 1837. https://nmaahc .si.edu/object/nmaahc_2014.44.

Everett, Edward. 1863. Letter to Abraham Lincoln, November 20, 1863. Edward Everett Papers, vol. 120, letterbook, 23 October 1863 to 28 March 1884, 27. https:// www.masshist.org/database/1780#:~:text=Everett%20had%20been%20the%20 primary,you%20did%20in%20two%20minutes.%22.

Foner, Eric. 2011. *The Fiery Trial: Abraham Lincoln and American Slavery*. New York: Norton.

Gandhi, Mahatma. 1936. Speech at conference, Allahabad, India, April 5. https:// www.mkgandhi.org/articles/cultural_heritage.htm#:~:text=Speaking%20in%20 a%20conference%20at,it%20attempts%20to%20be%20exclusive.

Gates, Henry Louis, Jr. 1989. *Talk That Talk: An Anthology of African-American Storytelling*. New York: Simon and Schuster.

Gelles, David. 2014. "Wooing a New Generation of Museum Patrons." *New York Times*, March 19. https://www.nytimes.com/2014/03/20/arts/artsspecial/wooing-a -new-generation-of-museum-patrons.html.

Giddings, Paula. 1987. "About People. Johnnetta Betsch Cole: Spelman's Sister President." *Essence* 18, no. 7: 34, 125.

Giddings, Paula. 1988. "A Conversation with Johnnetta Betsch Cole." *Sage* 5, no. 2 (Fall): 56–59.

Goldman Sachs. n.d. "Updated Business Principles Codify the Firm's Commitment to Diversity." https://www.goldmansachs.com/our-firm/history/moments/2001 -diversity-language.html.

Goodman, Barak, Pamela Mason Wagner, and Jamila Ephron, dirs. 2013. *Makers: Women Who Make America*. Arlington, VA: PBS Distribution.

Goodwin, Doris Kearns. 2005. *Team of Rivals: The Political Genius of Abraham Lincoln*. New York: Simon and Schuster.

Harrison, Ira E., Deborah Johnson-Simon, and Erica L. Williams, eds. 2018. *The Second Generation of African American Pioneers in Anthropology*. Urbana: University of Illinois Press.

Hart, Betty, and Todd Risley. 2003. "The Early Catastropher: The 30 Million Word Gap by Age 3." *American Educator*, Spring, 4–9.

Hechinger, Fred M. 1981. "About Education." *New York Times*, July 21, C5. https:// www.nytimes.com/1981/07/21/science/about-education.html.

Hepburn, Katharine. 1953. Speech at Bryn Mawr College. https://dp.la/item/b297e64 61c27f50cf929582e53d2ab8d.

Herbes-Sommers, Christine, Llewelyn Smith, and Vincent Brown, dirs. 2009. *Herskovits at the Heart of Blackness*. New York: Films Media Group.

Heyward-Rotimi, Kamela. 1998. "Perspectives of Black Feminist Anthropology: An Interview with Dr. Johnnetta B. Cole." *Voices: A Publication of the Association for Feminist Anthropology* 2, no. 2: 1–5.

Hope, Bob. 1962. Commencement Speech at Georgetown University, Washington, DC, June 4.

Janson, H. W. 1986. *History of Art: A Survey of the Major Visual Arts from the Dawn of History to the Present Day*. 3rd ed. New York: Abrams.

Jobs, Steve. 2005. Commencement address, Stanford University, June 12. https://news.stanford.edu/2005/06/12/youve-got-find-love-jobs-says/.

Jordan, Barbara. 1993. "Op/Art." *Washington Post*, March 21. https://www.washingtonpost.com/archive/lifestyle/style/1993/03/21/opart/d762298d-f38e-4e7d-a14d-08327161b44d/.

Ju, Anne. 2008. "Courage Is the Most Important Virtue, Says Writer and Civil Rights Activist Maya Angelou at Convocation." *Cornell Chronicle*, May 23. https://news.cornell.edu/stories/2008/05/courage-most-important-virtue-maya-angelou-tells-seniors.

Keller, Helen. 1903. *The Story of My Life*. New York: Doubleday, Page & Company.

Kennedy, Randy. 2011. "Brandeis Settles Suit over Proposed Art Sale." *New York Times*, June 30. https://archive.nytimes.com/artsbeat.blogs.nytimes.com/2011/06/30/brandeis-settle-suit-over-proposed-art-sale/.

King, Coretta Scott. 1994. "Remarks on the Introduction of the Employment Non-Discrimination Act of 1994." Press conference, Washington, DC.

King, Coretta Scott. 1998. Remarks at the 25th Anniversary of the Lambda Legal Defense and Education Fund, New York.

King, Martin Luther, Jr. 1957. "Conquering Self-Centeredness." Sermon delivered at Dexter Avenue Baptist Church, Montgomery, AL, August 11. In *The Papers of Martin Luther King, Jr.*, vol. 4, *Symbol of the Movement, January 1957–December 1958*, edited by Clayborne Carson, Susan Carson, Adrienne Clay, Virginia Shadron, and Kieran Taylor. Berkeley: University of California Press, 2000. https://kinginstitute.stanford.edu/king-papers/documents/conquering-self-centeredness-sermon-delivered-dexter-avenue-baptist-church.

King, Martin Luther, Jr. 1963a. "Letter from a Birmingham Jail." In *Why We Can't Wait*, 77–100. New York: Signet Books, 1964.

King, Martin Luther, Jr. 1963b. *Strength to Love*. Boston: Beacon Press.

King, Martin Luther, Jr. 1967a. "The Casualties of War in Vietnam." Speech delivered at the Nation Institute, Los Angeles, February 25. https://www.aavw.org/special_features/speeches_speech_king02.html.

King, Martin Luther, Jr. 1967b. Speech delivered at Victory Baptist Church, Los Angeles, June 25. APM Reports. https://features.apmreports.org/arw/king/b1.html.

King, Martin Luther, Jr. 1967c. "The Three Dimensions of a Complete Life." Speech delivered at New Covenant Baptist Church, Chicago, IL, April 9. https://www .learnoutloud.com/Free-Audio-Video/History/Speeches/The-Three-Dimensions -of-a-Complete-Life/90594.

King, Martin Luther, Jr. 1967d. "Where Do We Go from Here?" Speech delivered at the Eleventh Annual Convention of the Southern Christian Leadership Conference, August 16. http://www-personal.umich.edu/~gmarkus/MLK_WhereDoWeGo.pdf.

King, Martin Luther, Jr. 1967e. "Beyond Vietnam: A Time to Break the Silence." Speech delivered at the Riverside Church in New York City, April 4. https://shec .ashp.cuny.edu/items/show/1261#:~:text=On%20April%204%2C%201967%2C%20 Martin,democratic%2C%20impractical%2C%20and%20unjust.

King, Martin Luther, Jr. 1968. "The Drum Major Instinct." Sermon delivered at Ebenezer Baptist Church, Atlanta, GA, February 4. https://bethlehemfarm.net/wp -content/uploads/2013/02/DrumMajorInstinct.pdf.

The King Center. n.d. "The King Philosophy." https://thekingcenter.org/about-tkc /the-king-philosophy/. Accessed January 30, 2023.

Kluckhohn, Clyde. 1949. *Mirror for Man: The Relation of Anthropology to Modern Life*. New York: Whittlesey House.

Levitan, Monica. 2018. "Dr. Johnnetta B. Cole Appointed Chair and President of the National Council of Negro Women." *Diverse Issues in Higher Education*, November 15. https://diverseeducation.com/article/132085.

Levitt, Peggy. 2015. "Museums Must Attract Diverse Visitors or Risk Irrelevance." *The Atlantic*, November 9. https://www.theatlantic.com/politics/archive/2015/11 /museums-must-attract-diverse-visitors-or-risk-irrelevance/433347/.

Lincoln, Abraham. 1864. "Letter to Albert G. Hodges." In *Collected Works of Abraham Lincoln*, vol. 7, edited by Roy P. Basler, 281–82. New Brunswick, NJ: Rutgers University Press, 1953.

Lorde, Audre. 1980. *The Cancer Journals*. Argyle, NY: Spinsters.

"MaVynee 'Beach Lady' Betsch." n.d. The History Makers. Accessed February 3, 2020. https://www.thehistorymakers.org/biography/mavynee-beach-lady -betsch-39.

McClaurin, Irma. 2001. *Black Feminist Anthropology: Theory, Politics, Praxis, and Poetics*. New Brunswick, NJ: Rutgers University Press.

McHenry, Susan. 1987. "Spelman College Gets Its First Sister President." *Ms.*, October, 98–99.

Niemöller, Martin. n.d. "First They Came for . . ." United States Holocaust Memorial Museum. https://encyclopedia.ushmm.org/content/en/article/martin-niemoeller -first-they-came-for-the-socialists.

NPR. 2023. "Read Martin Luther King Jr.'s 'I Have a Dream' Speech in Its Entirety." January 16. https://www.npr.org/2010/01/18/122701268/i-have-a-dream-speech -in-its-entirety.

Obama, Barack. 2009a. "President Obama's Remarks at a Student Roundtable in Turkey." *New York Times*, April 7. https://www.nytimes.com/2009/04/07/us/pol itics/07obama-turkey-transcript.html.

Obama, Barack. 2009b. "Text: Obama's Speech at the New Economic School." *New York Times*, July 7. https://www.nytimes.com/2009/07/07/world/europe/07prexy.text.html.

Obama, Michelle. 2011. "First Lady Michelle Obama: 'When You Study Abroad, You're Helping to Make America Stronger.'" January 19. https://obamawhitehouse.archives.gov/blog/2011/01/19/first-lady-michelle-obama-when-you-study-abroad-you-re-helping-make-america-stronger.

Powell, Richard J. 1999. "To Conserve a Legacy: American Art from Historically Black Colleges and Universities." In Richard J. Powell and Jock Reynolds, *To Conserve a Legacy: American Art from Historically Black Colleges and Universities*, 103–43. Andover, MA: Addison Gallery of American Art.

The Root Staff. 2014. "Maya Angelou's Words That Spoke to All Our Lives." May 28. https://www.theroot.com/maya-angelou-s-words-that-spoke-to-all-our-lives-1790875890

Rosenbaum, Lee. 2011. "AAMD Issues New Statement Deploring Fisk's $30-Million Crystal Bridges Deal." *CultureGrrl* (blog), December 9. https://www.artsjournal.com/culturegrrl/2011/12/aamds_issues_strong_statement.html.

Rymer, Russ. 2003. "Beach Lady." *Smithsonian Magazine*, June. https://www.smithsonianmag.com/history/beach-lady-84237022/.

Savage, Charles. 2021. "Bill Cosby's Release from Prison, Explained." *New York Times*, July 1. https://www.nytimes.com/2021/07/01/arts/television/bill-cosby-conviction-overturned-why.html.

Schaeffer, Daniel. 2018. *Anna Madgigine Jai Kingsley: African Princess, Florida Slave, Plantation Slaveowner*. Gainesville: University Press of Florida.

Schmelzer, Elise. 2015. "Why Are All of the Kids on My Study Abroad Trip White?" *USA Today*, March 11. https://www.usatoday.com/story/college/2015/03/11/why-are-all-of-the-kids-on-my-study-abroad-trip-white/37401183/.

Shriver, Maria. 2010. "Art Is Fundamental—and Fundamental to Support." *Huffpost*, June 25. https://www.huffpost.com/entry/art-is-fundamental-and_b_626294.

Sirleaf, Ellen Johnson. 2011. Commencement Speech, Harvard University, May 26. https://news.harvard.edu/gazette/story/2011/05/text-of-ellen-johnson-sirleafs-speech/.

Sweeney, Karyn. 2013. "Inclusive Excellence and Underrepresentation of Students of Color in Study Abroad." *Frontiers: The Interdisciplinary Journal of Study Abroad* 23, no. 1 (Fall). https://frontiersjournal.org/index.php/Frontiers/article/view/326.

Truth, Sojourner. 1851. "Ain't I a Woman?" In *Civil Rights and Conflict in the United States: Selected Speeches*. Lit2Go Edition. https://etc.usf.edu/lit2go/185/civil-rights-and-conflict-in-the-united-states-selected-speeches/3089/aint-i-a-woman/.

Truth, Sojourner. 1867. Speech to the American Equal Rights Association, Church of the Puritans, New York, May 9. https://www.newframe.com/from-the-archive-speech-to-the-american-equal-rights-association%EF%BB%BF/.

United Farm Workers. n.d. "Education of the Heart: Cesar Chavez in His Own Words." https://ufw.org/research/history/education-heart-cesar-chavez-words/.

Walker, Alice. 1983. "A Talk: Convocation 1972." In *In Search of Our Mother's Gardens: Womanist Prose*, 33–41. San Diego: Harcourt Brace Jovanovich.

Watson, Krista. 2016. "Why Richer Areas Get More School Funding than Poorer Ones." Global Citizen, August 3. https://www.globalcitizen.org/en/content/cost-of-education-in-us/.

West, Cornel. 1993. *Race Matters*. Boston: Beacon Press.

Wiesel, Elie. 1986. Nobel Peace Prize Acceptance Speech, Oslo, December 10. https://www.nobelprize.org/prizes/peace/1986/wiesel/acceptance-speech/.

Williams, Vanessa. 2021. "Rep. Sheila Jackson Lee Arrested at Voting Rights Protest on Capitol Hill." *Washington Post*, July 29. https://www.washingtonpost.com/politics/2021/07/29/rep-sheila-jackson-lee-arrested-voting-rights-protests-capitol-hill/.

Wilson, William Julius. 1987. *The Truly Disadvantaged: The Inner City, the Underclass, and Public Policy*. Chicago: University of Chicago Press.

Yelvington, K. A. 2003. "An Interview with Johnnetta Betsch Cole." *Current Anthropology* 44, no. 2: 275–88.

INDEX

art: African, 43, 55, 186–89, 203 (*see also* Cole, Johnnetta Betsch, career); African diaspora, 82, 191–92, 199–206; education, 181–82, 252; and museums, 177–79, 190–98; ownership of, 200–206

"Art of Negro" murals, Clark Atlanta University, 199

Asa G. Hilliard Model of Excellence Award, 114

Asian community museum experience, 193–94

Association for Feminist Anthropology, 261

Association of Black Anthropologists, 261

Atlanta Art Conservation Center, 205

AU (African Union), 131

Baldwin, James, 110, 117, 176, 215

Baltimore, MD, 46

Barnes, Albert, 201–2

Barnes Foundation, 201–2

Bateson, Mary Catherine, 12, 260

Belafonte, Harry, 169

Beloved Community (King), 218–19

Bennett College for Women: and community service, 58; first art gallery, 200; recruiting students, 129; and study abroad programs, 227–28. *See also* Cole, Johnnetta Betsch, career

Berhel, Martha, 92

Bethune, Mary McLeod: doing for others, 75, 82; education, 118, 141, 142; founding Bethune–Cookman College, 92–93; leadership of, 124, 129, 138, 262; life of, 141–42; "lift others as you climb" quote, 47, 105, 160–61, 248, 256

Bethune–Cookman College/University, 47, 141

Bible, references to, 48, 80, 161, 240, 247

Big Brothers and Big Sisters, 58

Biggers, John, 205

bigotry, unlearning, 105, 113, 117, 164, 215, 220, 242

Black churches (US), 3, 25–26, 47, 62, 80, 136–39

Black communities (US): building bridges, 47, 72–73, 138; gender dynamics in, 27–28, 186–88; museum experiences of, 193–94; poverty and Martin Luther King Jr., 169; selling heritage of, 203; spectrum of economic classes within, 118. *See also* young Black people

Black education (US): Asa G. Hilliard, 114; requirements for successful, 115–17; student's realities, 117, 128; white America's stake in, 90

Black feminism, 7–10, 20–21, 188–89, 248, 264

Black Feminist Anthropology (McLaurin), 20, 261

Black Heritage Month, 219

Black intellectuals in Atlanta, archives of, 261–62

Black Lives Matter, 11, 46

Black men (US): in Civil War (US), 64; as gendered beings, 188; as nurturers, 122–23

Black Panthers, 11–12

Black studies: conceptions and misconceptions about, 98–101; history of discipline, 95–98; and representation of Black women, 9, 224; at Washington State University, 8, 11, 115. *See also* Cole, Johnnetta Betsch, career

Black Studies committee, Washington State University, 98

Black women (US): childbirth complications, 127, 149–50; Clarissa Scott Delany, 70–71; on corporate boards, 49–50; and education, 126–29; false images of, 121–25; histories portrayed, 187–89; and museums, 194; and pay gap, 127, 150, 158, 194; perspectives of, 90; and poverty, 127, 159; violence against, 159, 188; working harder to advance, 184. *See also* Christian Black women (US)

Black Women in the Academy conference, Howard University, 261

Black women's studies, 67, 72, 90, 119, 128, 224

Blakey, Michael, 261

structured into higher education, 58, 72–73, 87; and women leaders, 161, 248; and women's colleges, 58, 104–5

Composing a Life (Bateson), 12

Congressional Black Caucus, 174–76

Cook Ross, 17, 34, 38

Cosby, Bill and Camille, 39, 72

courage, 16, 253–57

Crenshaw, Kimberle, 112

Crystal Bridges Museum, 202

cultural anthropology, 47–48, 52–54

cultural biases, 229, 235, 241

cultural retention, African diasporic, 53, 87, 175

curricula, inclusive: African-centered, 114; call for relevant curricula, 83, 99, 218; central to excellence in education, 109, 214; commitment to at Williams College, 108; integrating Black (US) art collections, 97, 200, 203–4; in liberal arts, 71–72; studying Black women in international contexts, 128; studying race and gender as intersectional, 154

curricula, noninclusive, 109–10

Dagit, Deb, 224

Darling-Hammond, Linda, 158

data, 32–33. *See also* statistics

Davis, W. Allison and John Aubrey, 106–8

Declaration of Independence, 63, 175

Delany, Clarissa Scott, "Interim," 70–71

Delany, Martin, 95, 103

Delta Sigma Theta Sorority, 126–29

democracy, 64, 241

Democratizing Knowledge Summer Institute, Spelman College, 7, 262

demonstrations: anti-war, 12, 168–69; Poor People's March, 170–71; Reagan budget cutbacks, 152; voting rights, 263

descendants of Africa, everyone as, 131, 140, 213, 249, 254

desegregation, 86, 153–55, 158, 169

diaspora studies, African, 53, 55

differences, human, 18, 45, 214, 222, 241

disability, people who experience, 195, 217

discrimination: Black women experiencing, 127–29; calling out, 155, 223; call to own histories of, 176; and criminal justice system (US), 159, 223; and inclusion in workplace, 210; structural, 11; struggle against, 20, 83, 134–35, 166, 220–22, 240–44, 255; in study abroad programs, 232. *See also isms*; oppression, experiencing; *racism entries*; segregation; sexism

Diversity Abroad Conference, 226

diversity, equity, and inclusion: editors' introduction, 207–8; broad statistics (US), 112; business case for, 111, 192–95, 210–11, 216–17; on campuses, 105, 110, 213–18; Cook Ross, 17; and educational excellence, 109, 214; imperative to teach values early, 191; moral imperative for, 111, 144, 207, 210, 216; moving beyond tolerance, 210; in museums (US), 190–98; as necessity for success of nation (US), 240–43; pedagogical case for, 216–17; respect for, 184; in study abroad programs, 226–35; in volunteer sector, 59; and women leaders, 248–49; in workplace, 49–50, 207, 209–12, 241

Diversity, Race, and Learning, National Conference on, 213–18

doing for others, 47, 57, 72, 129, 138, 185. *See also* community service

Douglass, Frederick, 175, 187, 189, 216

dreaming, 90, 182–85, 253

Du Bois, W. E. B., 45–46, 114, 139, 158, 160, 214

Duke Ellington School of the Arts, 180–85

Duncan, Arne, 117

Early Warning! Why Reading by the End of Third Grade Matters (Annie E. Casey Foundation), 143

economic justice (US), 31–32, 169–171

Glanton, Richard, 202
golden rule, Christianity, 132, 184
Goldman Sachs, 209–12
Goodwin, Bob, 57
Goodwin, Doris Kearns, 64–65
Greater Harvest Missionary Baptist
  Church, 53
*Growth without Development: An
  Economic Survey of Liberia* (Clower
  et al.), 54
Guy-Sheftall, Beverly, 8–10, 13, 109,
  191, 260, 262, 264

Hamer, Fannie Lou, 35, 124, 172, 197,
  206, 211–12, 244
Hampton University, 201
Hansberry, Lorraine, 145, 156
Hansen, Erik, 226
Harding, Vincent, 168–69
Harjo, Joy, 28, 110
Harvard Black Law Students Association, 156–61
Harvard University Law School,
  232, 264
HBCUs (historically Black colleges
  and universities): art collections,
  199–206; famous graduates, 75, 81;
  financial management of, 76–78,
  204; impacts and successes, 75–76,
  82, 159; Nelson Mandela honorary
  degrees, 162–63; ongoing existence
  of, 111; partnerships with, 77–78,
  205–6; and social responsibility,
  57, 75, 81–82. *See also* historically
  Black colleges for women; *individual
  universities*
HBCU Symposium (2008), 76
healthcare disparities, 127, 134, 137,
  149–50, 153, 158, 170, 175
Height, Dorothy, 138
Height, Irene, 176
Hepburn, Katharine, 103
heroes: defined, 4; from HBCUs, 75;
  James Baldwin, 147; Martin Luther
  King Jr., 147, 176. *See also* sheroes
Herskovits, Melville J., 52–54
Herskovits at the Heart of Blackness
  (film), 53

heterosexism, 115, 187, 223
*Hide/Seek: Difference and Desire in
  American Portraiture* (exhibition),
  Smithsonian Institution's National
  Portrait Gallery, 195
High Museum, 205
Hilliard, Asa G., 114
Hirschel, Tony, 193
Hispanic serving institutions, ongoing
  existence of, 111
historically Black colleges for women
  (HBCUs): Celeste Watkins-Hayes
  on leadership of, 260; climate
  of acceptance for Black women,
  91–92, 115, 117; producing science
  graduates, 81; women and com-
  munity service at, 58. *See also* Cole,
  Johnnetta Betsch, career; HBCUs
histories: of Black (US) communities
  as intersectional, 187–89; of slavery,
  60–63, 174–76, 240, 248
History of Art (Janson), 194
HIV and AIDS, 158, 195
Holland, Bob, 39
homophobia, 151–54, 221–22
hope, 134, 157, 200
Hope, Bob, 240
house divided (US), 240–44
housing disparities (US), 158
Howard University, 79–83, 126, 167–69,
  203–4, 261
Hunter College, 48–49, 54, 115, 224
Hurston, Zora Neale, 184–85

identities, multiple, 48–49, 112–13, 214,
  217, 222, 223
incarceration, 11–12, 159, 175, 223
inclusiveness: on campuses, 230,
  233–34; in marketing, 234, 241
injustice. *See* discrimination
insufficiently resourced schools, 117,
  158
"Interim" (Delany), 70–71
intersectionality, 112, 154, 187–89
*In the Eye of the Muses: Selections from
  the Clark Atlanta University Art Collection* (Dunkley and Cullum), 199
Iraq War, 167

violence against women, 90, 159, 188
volunteerism. *See* community service
Voting Rights Act (1964), 175

Walker, Alice, 248
Walker, Rev. Robert, 25–26
Walton, Alice, 202
war, links to poverty and racism, 166–73
Wardlaw, Alvia, 205
Washington State University, 11, 54, 97–101, 115
W. E. B. Du Bois Department of Afro-American Studies, University of Massachusetts, 115
Wells, Ida B., 89, 93, 124
"What Shall I Tell My Children Who Are Black?" (Burroughs), 46
white people: and Black history, 86; and cultural institutions, 191, 203; dominating curricula, 97; and stereotype of Black inferiority, 46, 52, 57, 64, 84, 107, 246; and structural racism, 158–60, 171, 175, 214; Western, white, womanless, 10, 109, 218; white America's stake in Black education (US), 90; white faculty and students of color, 110, 118, 215; white men, 50, 247; white skin privilege, 112, 216, 220, 224; white students, 100–101, 229, 230; white supremacy, 117–18; white women, 48, 109, 127, 187–88, 217, 222. *See also* descendants of Africa, everyone as
Wiesel, Elie, 138, 185, 248, 256
Wilberforce College, 47

Williams, Erica Lorraine, 261–62
Williams College, 106–13
women: false images of, 122–24; as orators, 28–29; and philanthropic clout, 194–95; in politics, 132–34, 187; rights of, 130–35, 137, 241
Women in Philanthropy, United Way, 140–42
women of color writers (US), 110
Women's College Coalition, 102, 104, 249
women's colleges, 104, 111, 263–64
Women's Empowerment Conference, 136–39
women's studies, 9, 67, 72, 224. *See also* Black women's studies
Woodruff murals, Talladega College, 205
workforce diversity: Africa, 133; business case for, 207, 209–12, 241; museums, 193
worldliness, 20, 89–90
Wright, Marian Edelman, 28, 170

Yale University, 165–73
young Black people: access to education, 158; benefit of HBCU presence, 82; and criminal injustice, 171; educators and students' life realities, 118; teaching Black culture to, 128; teaching Black feminist culture to, 189
young people: and Barack Obama, 157, 182; and community service, 57; and the global economy, 228; imperative to teach diversity to early, 191; millennials and museums, 195–96

Printed in the USA
CPSIA information can be obtained
at www.ICGtesting.com
LVHW091952141023
760419LV00003B/15